GOVERNMENT GONE WILD

How D.C. Politicians Are Taking You for a Ride—and What You Can Do About It

KRISTIN TATE

CENTER
STREET

New York Boston Nashville

Copyright © 2016 by Kristin Tate

Cover design by Janet Perr
Cover copyright © 2016 by Hachette Book Group, Inc.

Center Street
Hachette Book Group
1290 Avenue of the Americas
New York, NY 10104
centerstreet.com
twitter.com/centerstreet

Originally published in hardcover by Center Street, 2016
First Trade Paperback Edition: April 2017

Center Street is a division of Hachette Book Group, Inc.
The Center Street name and logo are trademarks of Hachette Book Group, Inc.

The publisher is not responsible for websites (or their content) that are not owned by the publisher.

The Hachette Speakers Bureau provides a wide range of authors for speaking events. To find out more, go to www.HachetteSpeakersBureau.com or call (866) 376-6591.

Library of Congress Cataloging-in-Publication Data has been applied for.

ISBNs: 978-1-4555-6623-5 (paperback), 978-1-4555-6622-8 (ebook)

Printed in the United States of America

LSC-C

10 9 8 7 6 5 4 3 2 1

Dedicated to my late grandmother Linda Viveiros. You were everything I want to be: fearless, hilarious, and entrepreneurial—yet loving, passionate, and caring. You were the biggest badass I've ever met, even at age sixty-seven. You never let anything stop you from living life to the fullest, and I promised you I would do the same. Your spirit lives in me.

Contents

Acknowledgments

I would like to first express my gratitude to my family: To my mom, Dawn, for providing me with unconditional love and encouragement. Whenever I have a hard day, you're the first person I call; your advice and encouragement means everything to me. To my dad, Steve, for taking an interest in everything I pursue and always pushing me to do better. My entire life, you've inspired me to follow my passions. And to my brother, Austin. I wouldn't be the person I am today without any of you.

To my best friend Andrew Spalding, for not killing me during the book-writing process (seriously). Even during my worst moods, you've continued to be the most loyal and patient friend I could ever ask for.

To Ronald Goldfarb, for your unflagging support and advocacy. Your feedback, critiques, and thoughts were invaluable to me as I organized the book and brought my ideas to life.

And finally, to the team at Hachette Book Group for giving me the opportunity to publish my first book. I couldn't have asked for a better experience with better people. An extra special thank-you to my editor, Kate Hartson, for believing in me from the beginning of this process.

INTRODUCTION

We're Screwed...But We Can Get Un-Screwed

"Dude, this is pretty f*cked up right here."
~ Stan Marsh ~

America, we have a weight problem. As our government grows faster than Kanye West's ego and Kim Kardashian's luscious badonkadonk, the freedoms that our once-great nation was built upon are being suffocated.

It sucks, right? And maybe you've felt some of the pressure. But that's what we get for electing entrenched, out-of-touch blowhards who look out only for their own interests. They ship our friends and families overseas to fight wars we shouldn't be fighting. They send police to break down our doors and haul us away to overcrowded prisons packed with people who never committed a single crime against anyone but themselves. They spend our hard-earned cash on things no disciplined family or company would buy, and manage to rack up millions—no, billions, no, *trillions*—of dollars in debt. They take lavish jaunts around the world, staying in five-star hotels and eating in Michelin-starred restaurants—and it comes straight out of our paychecks.

And how do they thank us? They spy on us by monitoring

our e-mails, recording our phone calls, and peering into our bank statements. They tell us how to run our businesses, whom we're allowed to marry, and what we can put in our own bodies, even if none of this has any impact on other people.

That, my friends, is no way to live. And it certainly isn't the way to run a country.

The liberties established by our Founding Fathers have been defended, time and again, in war and peace, through protest and conflict. These are the paramount values in our society, and they shouldn't be messed with. Our freedoms are sacred—yes, sacred, dammit—and must be above and beyond the reach of any intrusive government, even if that happens to be our own.

Freedom means the ability to live your life as you please, as long as you aren't hurting anyone. Your life is your own damn business! Do whatever you want with it. Make that massive fortune and build a yacht so big that it's visible from space, or live in your parents' basement doing bong hits and watching *South Park* until your mom and dad are sent off to retirement homes.

"Wait, dude. Did she just mention *bong hits*?"

Yup, I did. And try to keep up, Smokey. Joints, spliffs, and bongs should be completely legal. If you're over twenty-one and want to smoke up until your eyes roll into the back of your empty skull, who am I to tell you no? And it's certainly not the government's place to tell you that, either. Sure, that wouldn't be the smartest path to take in life. But your path is yours to choose or to ruin if you wish. That's the joy of freedom—sink or swim on your own terms.

Think of the millions of Americans who have drunk themselves to a slow death, and those who are busy doing it right now, at bars and in La-Z-Boys across America. Who cares if it's a case of beer while watching the perils of Prohibition on *Boardwalk Empire* or a bottle of rotgut tequila in a dive bar or glass after glass of pricey Chardonnay on a Fifth Avenue terrace? We're exercising our right to indulge to our heart's content.

The big game changer here is if you then think you can drive or handle heavy machinery while you're all liquored up. Do that, and I am all for sending your sorry ass to prison, because you've violated someone else's freedom. You can ruin your life however you wish, but mess with others, infringe on their rights and liberties, endanger or harm them, and there will be consequences. Our society should be an open one for sure—but not anarchical.

Consider cigarettes. We all know they're bad as hell for you. The nicotine, the carcinogens—they're killers. But we still sell them, right? And the government rakes in all that dough from the taxes. This is how we should approach the issue of illegal drugs. It's better to have them distributed safely in the open than via some trembling, strung-out, sleaze-ball dealer who might be selling you Drano instead of heroin (and who is probably armed and could just as easily rob or kill you instead). We're starting to move in that direction when it comes to marijuana, with Colorado and Washington State leading the way.

But the issue is so much more than pot. The illegal narcotics industry as a whole—coke, heroin, meth, you name it—is one of the biggest on earth. The only ones that are bigger are petroleum and porn. And what does it produce? Hmm, let's see: mafias, guerrillas, cartels, thieves, corrupt cops and soldiers, and billions of dollars a year in waste trying to fight them. It's been proven time and again: the War on Drugs doesn't work. As long as people want to get stoned, buzzed, or baked—as long as they seek that needle in the vein and the thrill of the high—nothing will stop other people from growing, harvesting, producing, smuggling, and selling the stuff. It's simple supply and demand, and no amount of policing or lawmaking will change that dynamic.

Got your attention, huh? Good. I've got more about the futile War on Drugs later on (see chapter 1). Just don't get too stoned and miss it.

Hey, you need to open your eyes! You need a wake-up call! Think big picture. You're not anywhere near as free as you think you are—*but you can be*. We're not as prosperous as we once were—*but we can be prosperous again*.

Both the Democrats and the Republicans have shown over and over, year in and year out, no matter who controls Congress or the White House, they're not interested in us as individuals or in protecting our rights and freedoms. They prefer to call all the shots in Washington, D.C. They claim to know what's best for us. But for them, it's not about us. Instead it's all about *their* power, *their* privilege, and doing just enough to make sure that they're elected to another term. And another, and another...

You'd be amazed at how many of our "representatives" are way over the age the government tells us we can retire and collect Social Security. A congressman's term is two years, and most have been in office for four, five, or even six terms. John Conyers (D, Michigan) is currently serving his twenty-seventh term as congressman. At least John Dingell (D, Michigan—is there something in the water there?) announced that he would not seek reelection—for what would be his thirtieth term. Thirty terms! That's sixty years! And let's not forget old Strom Thurmond. He was in office until he was one hundred years old. These people are so entrenched that they care more about their status on various committees, about climbing the greasy pole of power, than doing what's right for the people they were elected to *serve*.

That's right: They are there to serve us—or at least they're supposed to, if the Constitution is to be taken seriously. I can't emphasize that enough. Don't ever forget this, ever! Politicians are there because *we* send them there. Without our votes they are nothing. Nada. Big fat zeroes. Send them out to pasture if they don't do what *we* ask.

Sadly, most of us are apathetic. A pathetic 57 percent of eligible voters turned out in 2012. We shrug our shoulders, crack open a beer, and, frankly, don't care as much as we should. We pay more attention to the comings and goings of big-boobed airheads on reality TV, the dramas of *Duck Dynasty*, and Charlie Sheen's nighttime antics than we do about the stuff that really matters. I should know. I'm a sucker for *Bridalplasty*. It's a reality show about bridezillas fighting over nose jobs and boob lifts. (I know, I know, I should be reading a good book...)

So we put up our feet up at the end of the day, then every four years we wish away our problems with the false hope that some candidate—maybe Donald Trump, maybe Hillary Clinton—will turn it all around *this time*. "Sure," we think, "it's bad right now. But it could be worse."

The scariest thing about this—and it *is* scary—is that we are *less* free because of our apathy. A lot less free. And every day that passes under this status quo makes it worse. We can do better than this, guys. We've got to.

The fact is, our freedoms in the past twenty years have been squeezed harder than a stress ball on Wall Street. After the September 11 attacks, that lovable idiot who ran our country for eight years pushed through some of the most ineffective and expensive legislation since the New Deal, all under the guise of "homeland security." Please. We all know the reasons behind that power grab and the two wars that followed, which, by the way, were colossal failures and are still costing us $10.5 million every hour.

This is nothing new. The big boys in Washington have long been getting away with blowing what you earned on things that don't work. And they're blowing money they don't even have! Right now our federal government is operating with a near-$20 *trillion* debt. That's twelve zeroes. And if you really want to blow your mind, punch up http://www .usdebtclock.org. See what I mean? Their rampant spending has resulted in well over $150,000 of debt per U.S. taxpayer, and most of it is from programs and entire departments that we don't even need.

I often wonder what Thomas Jefferson might think if he came back and saw the state of our Union. My guess is he'd be horrified and sick to his stomach. A lot of it makes me sick, too, and as you read on, you may start feeling ill yourself.

And angry. Remember, we're the dumbasses who are going to pay for it in the end if we keep rolling over and playing dead, wallowing in our own apathy. We already are paying for it to a degree, thanks to all the tax dollars we send to D.C. But I mean "pay for it" in a much bigger way—and I'll show you why you should be upset and confused and maybe a little paranoid at what they've been up to.

But there is hope! The first step toward recovery and renewal is recognizing that things are bad and that change is still possible. There are ideas we can live by and things we can do to reverse this collapse and to reclaim our civil liberties, as individuals and as a nation. And by "things we can do," I'm not talking about following any party platforms. I'll show you why both the Democrats and the Republicans are screwing us.

I'm here to shake you from your way-too-relaxed slacker slumber so we can all face the music together and actually fix our government. Don't worry, though—I won't lecture you or pile facts on you until your eyes glaze over. If you're like me, with the attention span of a circus monkey, you wouldn't sit through anything too boring anyway. The journey within these pages will be easy to digest, though it may be difficult to stomach at times.

Wait—have I lost you already? Come on. Put down that iPhone. Get off Instagram for a few minutes. Stay with me. You won't regret it, even though you won't like a lot of what I have to tell you.

In the words of Bender from *Futurama*, "We're boned." But it's not too late to get ourselves out of this mess. We may have short attention spans, but we're innovative as hell—and we're tired of getting kicked around by those in power. It's just a matter of recognizing the problem and then using our strengths to take action and fix them. The time is now to step in, step up, and win our freedoms and our nation back.

You ready? Buckle up, bitches.

CHAPTER 1

Don't Tell Us How to Live Our Lives

"Ain't nothing wrong with being gay; everyone's a
little gay."
~ Honey Boo Boo ~

I guess you could say that socially, I was a late bloomer. It didn't help that I grew up in the sticks of New Hampshire, a forty-minute drive to the nearest grocery store or the closest Walmart. We were so isolated that the latest trends and pop culture didn't reach us until about two years after they'd expired everywhere else in the world. My town was too small to have its own high school, so I attended a large regional public school slightly farther away than Walmart. As a student there, I was stuck in that tragic phase of possessing both acne and the social skills of a young adult still watching Nick Jr. I certainly wasn't a loser—most people knew who I was and didn't retch at the sight of me. But my general awkwardness never allowed me to make it anywhere near the top of the social ladder. So for four years, I was basically a dorky rat, scurrying through the halls, trying to avoid situations where I might be forced to interact with members of "the Pit."

The Pit was a coed, off-brand version of the Queen Bees

from *Mean Girls*. Think Regina George but with flannel, less hair product, and the noxious reek of patchouli. So basically the opposite of Regina George—but nonetheless these stoner kids ruled our school.

Our high school had an indoor atrium full of tables where students could hang out, socialize, and (not really) study. It was the place where our status hierarchy was most evident and would have made a great subject for an anthropology dissertation.

The table where the cool kids sat was in an area that was sunk about two feet into the floor. The group was known as the Pit, and it was understood that no one else was allowed at their table. Woe unto the miserable worm who crossed into that forbidden territory! When we B-listers walked by the Pit, we usually followed standard protocol: Look down at your feet like they hold the secrets of life everlasting, avoid all eye contact, and pray they don't notice your brown-bagged egg salad lunch, packed by your mommy.

I avoided speaking at length to any members of the Pit for the first few years of high school. Sure, I had an occasional class with some of them, but there was never much interaction. They mostly left me alone, and I knew to stay out of their way. Senior year, though, I got to know one of them—we'll call him Greg—when we were paired as partners for a project in a history class.

I discovered Greg was pretty funny, and we became friends. A few weeks in, we met up to work on the project during a period when students were allowed to leave campus. We worked for thirty minutes or so at his house and then took a break. It was a sunny day, and Greg led me to his deck. He brought this huge, red bong out with us and fired it right up. I had seen people smoking before, and I knew Greg was a stoner, so I wasn't exactly shocked.

After letting loose a cloud the size of a beach ball, he leaned his head toward me and croaked like the big, snack-happy toad from *Pan's Labyrinth*, "Wanna take a hit from Big Red?"

In that moment I decided that I wanted to be a badass. Maybe it was because I'd been in a fight with my mom that week, and I knew she wouldn't have approved. Maybe it was seeing Greg, sitting on the deck, wearing aviators and clearly taking this bud like a champ. Maybe it was the allure of doing something illegal. Regardless, I decided to go for it.

After I finished coughing, it was time to drive back to school for my physics class (nothing like weed to prime you for some velocity and vector talk). Greg and I parted ways, and as I walked through the hallway I couldn't help but feel smug; I, Kristin Tate, had just smoked weed with a member of the Pit. Did this make me an official Pit girl? Probably not, but at least it was a start.

I had almost made it to physics when I began feeling uneasy. My mind started racing and I couldn't get it to stop. I couldn't go to class—not now—so I dipped into the closest bathroom. That was when the paranoia set in. What if my mom found out? I would be grounded for months. What if my physics teacher smelled the weed and reported me? I'd get suspended or worse—they'd call the cops and haul me off to jail. Why was I freaking out? This couldn't be normal. The weed must have been laced with something. Maybe Greg did it when I wasn't looking. Maybe it was all an elaborate joke because I wasn't cool enough to be in the Pit and now I was about to die from a heart attack in a high school bathroom before I had the chance to grow up, graduate, and marry Johnny Depp (which seemed more feasible than ever in my stoner's haze).

Everything started spinning. I felt like I couldn't even stand up. There was only one thing I could do.

I hobbled to the school nurse and blurted out what I had done: I had smoked weed, and I was really, really sorry. It was a veritable gold medal performance in the Apology Olympics. I begged her to check everything: my blood pressure, my temperature, and anything else she had an instrument for. After she concluded that I was not, in fact, dying, I felt a wave of relief. Nobody would have to come up with an epitaph for my tombstone yet. (*Kristin—too exquisite for this world...but couldn't say no to drugs.*) But then it hit me that I had just turned myself in. Was she going to call the police?

Long story short: The cops were not called, but my parents were. I was grounded, and the school punished me by not allowing me to leave campus for a few months. I had disappointed everyone: my mom, the nurse, the principal, and even myself, a little. But at least I hadn't died or been arrested.

I haven't smoked weed since. But looking back, I realize that I probably never would have smoked that day if marijuana had been legal. Hell, maybe the Pit kids wouldn't have either! The fact that it was forbidden gave it this elite, hardcore status. You had to rebel in this manner to be a member of the Pit—to be cool.

Weed was so mysterious to me. I didn't know how it was

supposed to make me feel, who Greg bought it from, or why it was so bad. I just knew I wasn't allowed to do it, which made rebellious, teenaged me (and so many others) want to do it. I'd entered some august company when it came to succumbing to the allure of the forbidden: Eve with the apple, Abelard and Heloise, Oscar Wilde and the "Love that dare not speak its name," Winnie the Pooh and that tantalizingly out-of-reach honey pot.

Once I got to college, I became friends with lots of people who smoked weed—it wasn't just the Pit kids anymore. It quickly became obvious that marijuana didn't have a drastically negative effect on my college friends the way alcohol did. After a late night at the bar, my roommates and I would come home sick as hell—we pretty much got our degrees in "pulling trigger" (putting your finger down your throat) when facing a severe hangover, or, the ultimate, actual alcohol poisoning. Suffice it to say, vomiting is no fun, but it is a surefire means of learning your limit.

Our nights of college drinking resulted in plenty of awkward situations, but we always made it home safely. Tragically, I knew other people who died in drunk-driving accidents.

But weed was different. I never saw any of my stoner friends have sloppy nights full of regret. More often than not, they'd end up sleepy and hungry, which was awesome for me because I'm almost *always* sleepy and hungry (and I'll never turn down a friend who wants to eat Fritos and watch *Adventure Time*).

While marijuana may have been a contributing factor in some deaths, there is no documented death caused solely by overdosing on pot.[1] Weed has triggered underlying heart conditions in a small handful of cases, but the drug itself was not the cause of death. In other incidents, people have done stupid things while under the influence of marijuana; in one case, a man jumped off a balcony and died after eating several pot cookies.[2] So, yes, marijuana—like alcohol—can impair judgment and cause users to do dumb things they normally wouldn't. But there's no proof that "overdosing" on the drug can, by itself, cause death.

A marijuana smoker would have to consume 20,000 to 40,000 times the amount of THC in a joint in order to be at risk.[3] And study after study has shown that marijuana does not lead to lung cancer.[4]

But how harmful—or harmless—weed is should be a moot point. An adult should have every right to do whatever they please in the privacy of their own home, so long as nobody else is affected. Eating too much junk food can make you morbidly obese, which we all know leads to heart disease, diabetes, and often death. But if you want to sit on the couch and stuff deep-fried nachos into your face until your heart seizes up, that's your prerogative! No one is going to stop you, and no one should stop you—it's your body. And since you're allowed to contaminate your body with fatty foods, alcohol, or cigarettes, why not with weed? Why not with cocaine or even heroin?

After all, legalizing drugs would allow them to be regulated and sold out in the open. This would make the entire industry safer; consumers would know exactly what they were putting in their bodies. This would eliminate the risk of injecting cleaning fluid or smoking pencil shavings and hence would save many lives.

For many of us, this issue is more than just theoretical.

Almost everyone has heard of families who have lost a loved one to laced drugs. I know more than just one: Over the last couple of years, there have been dozens of accidental overdoses near my hometown caused by batches of tainted heroin. Some of those overdoses even ended in death.

Chardonnay Colonese died of an overdose on October 13, 2014. Everyone in the area called her Nay. I was lounging on my couch, spending another quality evening on Facebook (yes, I have quite the exciting social life), and was up to the usual: stalking old boyfriends and creeping on pictures of my frenemies, when I suddenly noticed a flood of "R.I.P." messages in my newsfeed. I remember thinking, "Oh no, not again." There had already been a string of untimely deaths in my hometown that year, mostly drug related and involving kids still attending my old high school in my younger brother's class. I was scared to see who the latest victim was. This time it was Nay. My heart dropped. She was only eighteen years old. I didn't know Nay well, but lots of my friends did. It was clear that they were completely shattered by her death. One of my friends posted a status that night that read, "Seriously, Nay? I'm so hurt by you right now. The last thing you said to me was, 'If we lose another person, I'm going to wake them up and kill them again.' And here we are, you left me. We had plans and you left before we could do them. I'm so heartbroken right now."

The saddest thing about this story? Nay didn't have to die. It's one thing to kill yourself willingly, but it's another thing entirely to kill yourself accidentally. Nay trusted the drug dealer who sold her heroin—he didn't tell her that it was laced with fentanyl, an opioid used as a painkiller in hospitals. She had no clue that it would end her life.

As kids, we all make dumb decisions. But we shouldn't die because of them. Think about this for a second: If heroin had been legal, Nay probably wouldn't be dead today. She could have bought clean heroin produced in a sterilized lab instead of turning to the black market. When people want to take drugs, they're going to find a way to take drugs regardless of whether or not they're illegal. We may as well bring the industry out of the shadows and allow it to operate in a safer and regulated manner.

I know, I know, the thought of hard drugs such as heroin being openly sold on the market doesn't sit well with a lot of people. I get it. But if you don't like something, then you can choose not to associate with it. (You'll notice this theme recurring throughout the book.)

Still not with me? OK. Imagine for a moment what would happen if the feds decided to ban Pepsi. People would find other ways to get the soda, and a black market would be born. Pepsi would be produced in filthy basements and then handed off to dealers who would distribute it to thousands of soda addicts looking to get their fix. It would all work pretty well until someone decided to bulk up their Pepsi supply with a bit of, say, cleaning fluid to make a larger profit. Then some unknowing customers would drop dead the following week, just like that, all because they wanted to get a caffeine buzz and a sugar rush. The people who created this toxic batch would most likely get away with mass murder, since their operation would hardly be out in the open.

Sound familiar?

People who disagree with me say that drug use would hit harder than the latest iPhone if drugs were legalized. I don't buy that argument. Prohibition rarely works. Back in 1920, alcohol was made illegal to reduce crime, solve social issues, and improve citizens' health. Prohibition was dubbed the "noble experiment." However noble the intentions of this experiment may have been, it was an epic flop. Immediately following the ban, alcohol consumption did drop a small amount, given that it was harder to find—at first. But as Launcelot said in *The Merchant of Venice*, "in the end truth will out." Two years later, consumption actually increased sharply and then remained higher than it was prior to the ban.[5]

As a result, the feds funneled immense resources into enforcing Prohibition. Not counting the increased spending of local and state governments, the federal Bureau of Prohibition increased its annual budget from $4.4 million to $13.4 million during the ban.[6] Despite this, people kept guzzling booze. A thriving underground industry was created, with production and distribution carried out by an army of entrepreneurs operating in the black market. And just like those laced drugs, alcohol also became more dangerous to consume.

The Iron Law of Prohibition, coined by activist Richard Cowan, states that illegal substances become increasingly potent as law enforcement increases. Rather than producing lighter alcohols like beer, producers operating in the shadows are incentivized to create more concentrated spirits like whiskey and wines. The reasons are simple: More potent alcoholic beverages take up less space in storage, are lighter to transport, and sell at a higher price. Go big or go home! Nobody would risk jail time for crafting the bootleg equivalent of Bud Light.

But it wasn't just the potency of the alcohol that made it

more dangerous to drink. Lots of amateurs started producing moonshine during Prohibition, and some of it contained lethal ingredients. The annual death rate from spiked liquor almost quadrupled between 1920 and 1925.[7]

Crime (and tough guys talking out of the corners of their mouths) also increased during Prohibition. Prisons became overcrowded and filled to capacity with bootleggers. So funds weren't being spent only in an effort to enforce the ban but also to keep thousands of people in prison for violating it. Federal spending on prisons increased almost 1,000 percent during Prohibition![8]

Put simply: Prohibition was a bigger failure than Britney Spears's marriage to Kevin Federline. It resulted in a bloated government, astronomical spending, and gangsters in fedoras running speakeasies. If you've ever seen an episode of *Boardwalk Empire*, you know what I'm talking about.

The War on Drugs hasn't been any more successful. Just like the thousands of patrons getting drunk in speakeasies during Prohibition, Americans are getting high in basements, in parked cars, and on the decks of their classmates' homes in this country each and every day—and what's so much worse is that many are sitting in jail for it, their lives sustained by tax dollars that would be better put to use elsewhere.

Every year hundreds of thousands of Americans are arrested for "offenses" related to pot. A guy I knew in high school named Tyler (not a member of the Pit, as it happens) is serving time for a marijuana-related offense. Tyler got an especially long sentence, because he had one prior nonviolent marijuana conviction. I remember sitting next to him in a computer lit class during freshman year; we spent most of the class sneakily photographing the teacher when she wasn't looking, then Photoshopping her butt. (We both became proficient in Adobe's Creative Suite products that semester.) Tyler was a funny kid with a good sense of humor. Sure, he wasn't the "sharpest blunt," but he wouldn't hurt a fly. He doesn't deserve to be sitting in jail right now—and we taxpayers don't deserve to be footing the bill.

Unfortunately, Tyler isn't the only one behind bars for victimless, pot-related offenses. Almost 650,000 people were arrested in 2015 alone for marijuana law violations. Eighty-nine percent of those arrests were for possession only.[9] Why the hell are we paying for these people to be sitting in jail? Every year we spend $51 *billion* on the War on Drugs.[10] Yet in spite of all the spending, 1.5 million people are still arrested every year on nonviolent drug charges.[11] Did our lawmakers fail math? Let the pot smokers out of jail already and reserve that space for actual criminals who have harmed other people instead of just their own brain cells.

Here's an idea: instead of wasting billions on initiatives that simply don't work, why don't we allow people to smoke their doobies out in the open, since they're doing it anyway? We could regulate and tax the sale of weed; if all fifty states legalized marijuana today, more than $3 *billion* would be collected in taxes annually.[12] We could actually start making money off the marijuana business and putting it toward the national debt (although knowing the buffoons we have in Washington, they'd probably just blow it on unnecessary crap like overpriced office chairs and monogrammed pens they'll lose faster than our hard-earned dollars).

Don't get me wrong—we still need rules in place when

it comes to drugs. Do whatever you want in the privacy of your home. But if you show up at a public playground high on meth then you absolutely deserve to go to jail, because you're putting the safety of others at risk. All drugs, if legalized, could be regulated just like alcohol; driving under the influence and public intoxication would result in swift punishment. In this newfangled, drug-tolerant society, private businesses should also have the right to ban drugs on their premises. The law shouldn't be able to force a restaurant owner to allow smoking in his or her restaurant, just as it can't force a restaurant owner to serve alcohol in their place of business. The business owner should be able to decide on these issues and we, the consumers, can decide whether or not we wish to do business with them on these terms.

A few states have led the charge to end this War on Drugs by decriminalizing marijuana. In Colorado residents can grow up to six cannabis plants and possess one ounce of weed while traveling.[13] Weed is basically treated the same way as alcohol, and Colorado's citizens are basically treated as adults. Colorado Amendment 64, which outlines the state's marijuana policies, was passed in 2012. Three years have passed since then, and here's what hasn't happened: The state hasn't been destroyed and hospitals aren't overflowing with "marijuana overdose" cases. But what *has* happened? Arrests, crime rates, the unemployment rate, and traffic fatalities have all gone down, while tax revenue has gone up.[14] As of October 2014, less than one year after marijuana was decriminalized, the state had already raked in more than $40 million in marijuana taxes.[15]

As may happen with any decriminalization effort, the

state has faced some challenges since Amendment 64 passed. Over the last few years, a small handful of children have been admitted to hospitals after accidentally ingesting marijuana products. Of course this is a major concern. But it's unclear if the decriminalization was directly responsible for these incidents, and thousands of children are treated at hospitals each year for consuming household cleaners and other products.[16] Colorado has also seen a "fourfold increase" in household pets, primarily dogs, accidentally ingesting marijuana-laced brownies since the decriminalization.[17] Again, this is a serious concern, but there are plenty of other foods such as chocolate and raisins that are dangerous (even fatal) for dogs to consume. Owners should be aware of any risks associated with their pets ingesting marijuana, and they are responsible for keeping these substances out of the reach of their furry friends. If a pet owner is unable to follow simple procedures to keep their pet safe, perhaps he or she shouldn't own a pet in the first place.

If Colorado carefully treats and regulates marijuana like it does alcohol, the industry will likely continue to benefit the economy and bring a once-dangerous industry out of the shadows. Sounds like the rest of the nation should start paying attention and follow Colorado's lead.

I'm Feeling Like a Bitch Today

As insulting as it can be to have some Big Brother overseer telling us what we can and can't put into our bodies, it's downright creepy when that oversight extends to our bedrooms. Folks, it's 2017. We all have friends or family members who are openly gay, and many of them are brave enough to be out and proud. It's an issue affecting many of our loved ones, and it's time for politicians to stop pushing their own ideas of whomever their god wants us to love. Our elected officials are supposed to be serving and representing us—not lamenting the depravity of our sex lives.

It was my first day at Emerson College in Boston. After settling into my eleventh-floor room in the dorm building, I got in the elevator to go outside and explore the city. A slim, dapper guy wearing Sperry shoes got into the elevator with me. The doors began to close when a girl in the hall started running toward us. She shouted, "Hey, hold the door!"

Sperry Guy and I glanced at each other—he was closest to the elevator buttons. While watching that girl pant and run, he reached down and hit Door Close. As the doors shut and we began our descent to the lobby, Sperry Guy looked at me and said, "I'm feeling like a bitch today."

I knew at that moment that he and I would be friends.

Sperry Guy's name was Todd. He and I remain close to this day. Todd is gay, flamboyantly so, and the life of every party. He's also so much more than the token gay guy who pulls out the world's great one-liners. I can honestly say that he is one of the best friends I have ever had. Whenever I'm sad or need a pick-me-up, I call Todd.

My friendship with him forced me to see life through rainbow-tinted lenses; it was clear that Todd was proud to be gay but that he faced challenges because of his sexuality. I never saw him harassed outright for his homosexuality, but when we went out together, I noticed a subtle categorization occurring more often than not. It was painfully obvious that everyone around us immediately labeled him as the Gay Guy, as if that was all he was. Yes, Todd is gay, but he's also a person with his own strengths, weaknesses, and quirks. After graduation Todd moved to Los Angeles, where he now lives with his boyfriend, Michael, and their dog.

The 2015 Supreme Court ruling *Obergefell v. Hodges* gave Todd and Michael the right to marry in any state. The ruling was a big win for liberty, but it disturbs me that it took us so long to get to this point. Denying two people basic rights simply because they have matching genitals is some seriously outdated, bigoted stuff. For too long the government has behaved like a bouncer at the marriage club, only letting in groups it approved of. I never understood why two (or more) consenting adults shouldn't be allowed to enter into private unions and contracts without first garnering permission from Uncle Sam.

Oh, you don't like gay marriage? Lucky you—you're completely free to attend a church that doesn't recognize or practice it. You're also free to not marry someone of the same sex. But why on earth do we want politicians dictating the private lives of peaceful people based on their own beliefs? That's a Pandora's box you don't want to open. Because eventually one of those politicians will come along with a moral compass that doesn't align with your own, and when that day comes, do you want your personal liberties stomped on because some gray-haired bureaucrat in D.C. thinks you're a pervert?

The scary thing is that there are lots of politicians in D.C. right now actively (if largely with astonishing ineptitude) trying to strip Todd and Michael of their ability to get married. Ted

Cruz (R, Texas), for example, went out of his way to instruct states to ignore the SCOTUS ruling if they weren't specifically mentioned in it.[18] *Obergefell* only considered Ohio, Tennessee, Michigan, and Kentucky. That means that Todd and Michael would be denied this basic right in states like good ol' Texas. Wisconsin governor Scott Walker went even further, calling for an amendment to reverse the decision altogether.[19]

Walker said, "I believe this Supreme Court decision is a grave mistake. Five unelected judges have taken it upon themselves to redefine the institution of marriage, an institution that the author of this decision acknowledges has been with us for millennia." The governor demanded that the ability to define marriage be given back to the states, and along with it, the ability to ban gays from participating in matrimony. If you ask me, the real perverts are the ones who can't keep anti-LGBT issues off their minds and out of their mouths.

Perhaps that's the root of the problem: Why is government—federal or state—defining marriage in the first place? Whatever happened to separation of church and state? No one should be in the all-powerful position of defining what marriage should mean for every single American.

Maybe my church decides to form unions between gay couples, and calls that marriage, but your church only considers unions between one man and one woman marriage. And hell, maybe a church down the street considers unions between one man and *three* women marriages. Don't like it? Then don't associate with that church. It's none of our damn business what they're doing at the church down the street anyway. Marriage is a personal matter—not a political one. We don't need the government to wave its magic wand and make our opinions legitimate. Ideally, the only time the state would get involved is when someone's rights are being violated, like when a person enters a marriage by force or when children are involved.

One thing I hear from Republicans over and over is that they don't want gay marriage because they don't believe same-sex couples should be recognized for federal tax purposes. I agree with that—gay married couples shouldn't get tax breaks. But neither should *any* married couple! Big whoop, you partnered up. You already get a financial break in the sense that now there's someone around to split the rent with you. Again, it all boils down to getting the government out of the marriage business. By giving tax benefits to married couples, the government is penalizing those who choose not to get married (or who can't find a partner), as well as those who enter into nontraditional unions. The same set of rules should apply to every individual who files taxes, married or not. Anything else would be prejudicial.

Critics of nontraditional marriage often say, "Well what's next? Allowing people to marry their dogs?" Sorry, but that is one of the dumbest questions I've ever heard. Animals and children can't consent to marriage or sex, so no, people will not be permitted to marry their dogs. There's a huge difference between forcing a person or an animal to marry you and marrying the person (or persons) you love. The scenarios aren't in any way comparable, and to suggest otherwise makes us look like a country of crusty old pervs.

The Right to Discriminate

We've all read the horror stories circulated on social media about Christian-run bakeries refusing wedding cakes to gay couples. One of these incidents occurred in the liberal mecca of Portland, Oregon. Aaron and Melissa Klein, owners of Sweet Cakes by Melissa, are devout Christians. In 2013, a lesbian couple, Laurel and Rachel Bowman-Cryer, visited Sweet Cakes hoping to buy a cake for their commitment ceremony.[20] The women walked out of the shop after Aaron Klein denied service to them, citing his religious beliefs. The couple claimed Aaron also recited Leviticus 20:13 at them (which, interestingly enough, doesn't even mention women lieth-ing together). It says only that, "If a man also lie with mankind, as he lieth with a woman, both of them have committed an abomination: they shall surely be put to death; their blood shall be upon them."[21]

A few weeks later the bakers received a surprise in the mail: a notice that they were facing a civil complaint because they didn't provide equal service to the lesbian couple in a place of public accommodation. The couple said in their lawsuit that they had suffered "emotional damages," listing eighty-eight symptoms of distress.[22] They even asserted that they had been "mentally raped" by the Kleins.[23] Oregon labor commissioner Brad Avakian wanted to make an example of the bakery and ordered the Kleins to pay $135,000 to Laurel and Rachel to help them deal with the effects of Aaron Klein's actions.[24]

Sweet Cakes was a mom-and-pop business; the Kleins didn't exactly have $135,000 just lying around. They weren't able to cough up the dough by the deadline, and the publicity of the incident prompted large activist groups to launch boycotts against any wedding vendor that associated or did business with Sweet Cakes.[25] The Kleins ended up losing their bakery (but have since landed on their feet after raising $109,000 on GoFundMe and $352,000 via ContinueToGive, two online crowd-funding websites).[26]

After forcing them to pay up, Avakian went the extra mile and ordered the Kleins to "cease and desist" from openly stating that they won't serve gay couples because of their religious beliefs.[27]

Crowd-funding miracle aside, even those of us who aren't cuckoo-evangelical-social right wingers should be alarmed by the outcome of this situation. The state stripped the Kleins of their First Amendment rights, and told them they must remain quiet about their faith. Mr. Klein said in an interview, "You're looking at a government agency telling a private citizen what they can and cannot say. This should scare every American."

And it should.

I've had the gay marriage debate hundreds of times with my socially conservative friends, and I usually get the same response over and over again, no matter what argument I try to present: "Gay marriage goes against my religious beliefs!" I totally get that. And this is where things get kind of complicated. The government certainly shouldn't be able to ban gay couples from getting married, but should it be able to force individuals to preside over or cater a gay wedding? *No.* Individuals and businesses should never be forced to provide services to *anyone*, gay or straight, black or white. In a free country, we should have the right to discriminate as long as that discrimination isn't government-sponsored.

After the SCOTUS ruling on gay marriage, a huge group

of homophobic leaders gathered in Dallas. Spewing hate-
ful, disgusting rhetoric, the group of scowling gargoyles
attempted to organize marches and protests against gay
marriage. Dr. Steven Hotze, president of the Conservative
Republicans of Texas, said at the meeting, "Homosexual marriage isn't really a marriage. It's a counterfeit. It's a lie."[28]

I sure as hell don't agree with Hotze and his bigoted,
outdated group. But you know what? They have every
right to be bigots, just like Todd and Michael have every
right to marry each other. Just because you find something
distasteful—whether it's gay marriage, hurtful speech, or the
hairstyles on *Sister Wives*—you do not have the right to ban
or censor it. By all means, decline that wedding invitation,
block that spewing of hate on social media, or change the
channel on your TV. There's an important distinction to be
made between what Hotze and his friends were doing, and
what Cruz was trying to do following the gay marriage ruling. Voicing your disgust with someone's actions, or even dis-
criminating because of them, as a private citizen or business,
is a lot different from attempting to use the heavy hand of
government to flat-out ban that action.

Citizens in a free country have the right to be bigots, and
that right extends far beyond free speech alone. If you own
a photography business but don't want to take pictures at a
gay wedding, you should have every right to decline. It's *your*
business. You invested your own money to open its doors. But
as government continues to mandate "inclusion," Uncle Sam
will make you pay up if you deny service to anyone for any
reason.

Brad Avakian's initial efforts to eliminate prejudice

against gay couples by awarding that lesbian couple $135,000 for their "mental rape" ironically resulted in even more prejudice—in this case, prejudice against Christians. Some attorneys have even come forward and suggested that the Kleins could file a civil rights case against Avakian. The ruling was used as a means to intimidate other Christians. The message was more obvious than my acne in middle school: Make your Christian beliefs known, especially in your place of business, and you will be swiftly and harshly punished.

Narrow-minded, all-powerful government officials have continued to single out Christian business owners again and again over the years. Apparently, Christians aren't a protected class. In 2014, another baker, Jack Phillips, the owner of Masterpiece Cakeshop in Colorado, was also ordered to cease and desist from expressing his Christian beliefs in the workplace.[29] Phillips's story should sound familiar at this point.

In 2012, the baker refused service to a gay couple, stating that he couldn't make them a cake because of his faith. After the gay couple filed a complaint, the state ruled that Phillips must either serve gay couples or face hefty fines.[30] The Orwellian ruling additionally forces Phillips to submit quarterly reports to Colorado's Civil Rights Commission to prove that he hasn't turned away any gay or lesbian couples. Fox News's Todd Stearnes called it "reverse conversion therapy (or straight man's rehab)."[31] And just like that gay conversion therapy, this one also won't result in "straightening" out anybody.

In another case of apparent Christian persecution, the prior fire chief of Atlanta, Kelvin Cochran, was suspended from his job in November 2014 after he wrote a book for a bible study group at his Baptist church.[32] One of the book's passages focused on homosexuality and was titled, "Who Told You That You Were Naked?" Cochran was supposed to return to work after the thirty-day suspension, but was officially fired in 2015.[33] Even though I disagree with Cochran's views, I can't help but feel bad for the guy. He was punished for practicing his fundamental right to free speech, and within his church, of all places. This wasn't an opinion he forced on his coworkers or neighbors.

Are you starting to see a trend here? These cases aren't just about religious freedom—they're also about the freedom of speech. The First Amendment guarantees both the freedom of religion and the freedom of expression. It says, "Congress shall make no law respecting an establishment of religion, or prohibiting the free exercise thereof."[34]

As clear as that language is, our elected officials continue to impinge on our First Amendment rights. What makes this all even more unsettling is that many Americans don't seem to care about the erosion of these fundamental rights. Immediately following the same-sex marriage ruling, a survey conducted by the Barna Group found that one in five Americans thinks that "religious institutions or clergy should be required to perform same-sex marriages."[35]

Seriously? Wake up, people! If that isn't a violation of religious freedom, then I don't know what is.

Thankfully, some individuals in the LGBT community are starting to sound the alarm on the violation of free expression in the name of "equality." Jesse Bartholomew is a gay baker and chef who made a viral YouTube video expressing his frustration with gay and lesbian couples who filed complaints against Christian bakers.[36] "I cannot tell you how disgusted I am with my fellow gay and lesbian community—that they would stoop so low as to force someone to bake a cake for them who simply doesn't agree with them," Bartholomew said. He continued, "It's plain and simple: you are bullying someone, you are forcing someone, you are being a Nazi and forcing someone to bake a damn wedding cake for you when there are hundreds of other gays and lesbians that would gladly have your business. Shame on you."

Here's the bottom line: It's scary when a person can't express his or her beliefs without fearing punishment. If you're Christian or Muslim, Arab or Jew, Hindu or Buddhist, Scientologist or pagan, you should be allowed to worship as you wish without fear. As long as you aren't harming others, you should be able to follow your faith.

In fact, I believe that you should have the freedom to practice what you believe even if you aren't religious. If you start a business, you ought to be able to make your own rules. Maybe you want to serve only atheists and Satanists. If you're especially bigoted, the public will most likely find your practices distasteful and the free market will punish you. Do you really think patrons would buy food from a deli that refuses to serve black people? Get real. Groups would boycott that business and launch massive protests. The deli would make little money and would likely shut down in a matter of weeks.

Government interventions to ensure equal rights were needed in the past—but such steps were necessary to right the wrongs of negative *government-imposed* discriminatory laws. Antiblack Jim Crow laws, for example, operated until the mid-1960s. These laws were a form of government-backed racism that rendered black Americans second-class citizens. Under Jim Crow laws, African-Americans and Caucasians weren't allowed to eat together; a black male couldn't even offer to shake hands with a white male because it implied that they were equals.[37] What's more, African Americans were prohibited from publicly showing affection toward one another.[38] It should be obvious why government action was needed to reverse the crippling effects of this state-enforced racism. But the bigoted actions of private citizens, businesses, and groups are completely different.

We allow hate groups to spew putrid language and hold rallies every day across the nation in the name of the First Amendment. During the summer of 2015, the Ku Klux Klan and the New Black Panthers faced off outside of the South Carolina Capitol.[39] They clashed over the Confederate flag, which many believe is a symbol of hate. The confrontation between the two groups resulted in a bigger clusterf*ck than Courtney Love's bachelorette pad ever featured, with shouts of hatred on both sides. In this incident, the government had the right response: Police were present to protect both groups. And I couldn't help but chuckle when I saw this tweet from Columbia mayor Steve Benjamin: "If a tree falls in the forest & there's no one there to hear it, does it make a sound? If the KKK marches and there's no one there...#ignorethem."[40]

Don't like what the KKK or what the New Black Panthers have to say? Turn off your TV. It's simple. I think the stuff Al Sharpton says on his TV show every day is destructive and offensive, but I still believe he should have every right to speak his mind. So I simply don't tune in (and based on his cable ratings I'm not the only one).[41] Christian bakers and the like should also enjoy these First Amendment rights.

For all of you who were drifting off, playing Snapchat, and Facebooking during the last several pages, here's my point in a nutshell: A nation that allows its people to live as they choose grants them the freedom of expression. Sometimes that expression is beautiful and full of love. But often, that expression is distasteful and discriminatory. And that's OK, because this is America where you can have your cake and eat it, too—even if you have to bake it yourself.

Finding Common Sense on Common Ground

So when your nerdy cousin Flynn says...

> "We should crack down on marijuana, because it's destructive to our communities."

You say: "Weed dumbs people down and makes them lazy— too lazy to venture out for more than a bag of powdered donuts, let alone commit crimes. Sure, your pothead neighbor might take a while to mow his yard, but destroy a community? Nah, bro, nah."

> "Marijuana is a gateway drug!"

You say: "Cigarettes, pipes, and alcohol are also gateway drugs to far worse things. Should we outlaw them, too? Why not? It worked so well in the 1920s!"

> "Gays are fundamentally ruining the institution of marriage!"

You say: "Wrong. The government is ruining the institution of marriage. There was no controversy about marriage for thousands of years, until the government stepped in to enforce new rules and regulations. And if you're going to punish gays for wrecking 'the sanctity of marriage' (which I'd love to hear you define), maybe it's time to force divorcees to remain single as well."

"I don't think gays should be allowed to marry."

You say: "If you hate gays so much, wouldn't you want them to have the same right to be miserable, too?"

"I'm offended by that baker who won't serve gay couples."

You say: "Are you also offended by the Jewish baker who won't bake an ISIS cake? Does the black baker who doesn't want to bake a Ku Klux Klan cake offend you? Are you offended by the liberal baker who won't bake a Confederate flag cake? My goodness! Isn't it exhausting being offended by so many things? You'd better check your Facebook feed— you don't want to run out of the personal beliefs of other people to be offended by!"

CHAPTER 2

...And Don't Tell Us How to Spend Our Money

"I got my mind on my money, and my money on
my mind."

~ Snoop Dogg ~

I've never taken a finance class. During high school and college, in order to fulfill various bullshit graduation requirements, I took classes like Deconstructing Twentieth-Century Art and Music, Gender in a Global Perspective, The Culture of Hip Hop, and Love and Eroticism in Western Culture. But something actually useful, like a finance or accounting course? Nope. I don't even remember those even being offered at my college, and if they were, the school clearly didn't think those were skills we'd need to be functioning adults. Is it any wonder that new college grads struggle so much these days?

I saw this problem firsthand. After four years of high school and a few more years at a decent private university, I still had no clue how to manage money. During my senior year, I received a credit card in the mail. You always remember your first, am I right, ladies? Mine was a sleek, shiny, and blue MasterCard. I'd been preapproved as someone the company just *knew* was qualified to spend wisely and pay her bills on time.

I rolled my eyes when the card showed up in the mail and my mom said, "Be careful with that thing! It's so easy to get into trouble."

How complicated could it be? Moms are such worrywarts.

I started using my credit card for everything. It was great to be able to buy things and not have the money taken right out of my checking account. During the first month or so, I paid off the balance every couple of days. I practically treated it like a debit card. But then I made a few expensive but necessary purchases: a mattress, dining room table, and couch for my new apartment. I logged into my online account that night and saw that I owed over $2,000. *Wow, that's a lot,* I thought. *I'd better pay part of it now and cover the rest after my next paycheck.*

Bad idea.

I'm sure you can see where this is going. By the time I got that month's paycheck, I had made more purchases, and my balance had swollen to over $3,500. I couldn't pay the bill in full, so I just took care of what I could and ate the interest charge.

For months, I kicked the can down the road and let the balance grow. I had lost any sense of urgency to pay the bill. This credit card thing was awesome! I could basically buy whatever I wanted and then pay it off when I either got a promotion or married a millionaire (my back-up plan at the time). Using the MasterCard I bought Dre headphones, a Michael Kors bag, a Mia Clarisonic face cleaning brush,

Louis Vuitton pumps, tons of overpriced Sephora makeup, and a two-story yacht.

JK about the yacht. But I did buy all that other crap, and it was all stuff that I didn't need. Well, actually, in my defense, you couldn't really ride the New York City subway train with dignity in 2012 unless you were listening to your music with a pair of Beats by Dre, so we'll call that one an "essential" purchase.

The balance on my MasterCard kept getting higher and higher, and I had no money to pay it off. But I didn't care. No one was beating down my door, threatening to break my kneecaps if I didn't pay, and I sure was enjoying the luxury of owning things I could never have afforded in the past.

Then I moved to a new city and got a rude wake-up call when I tried to buy a car. I was shocked to learn that due to my less-than-perfect credit score, I couldn't get approved for a loan. I was forced to go crawling back to Mommy for help, and she swooped in as a cosigner. It was the only way they'd let me have the loan. Smugness oozed out of my mom's pores; she reminded me that just a few months ago, she had tried to warn me of the dangers of credit card debt. With a bailout from my parents I managed to pay off the balance. And to the delight of my mom, I've since learned my lesson and am now extra careful with my MasterCard. I (almost) never buy anything I can't afford these days.

It's important for all of us to be fiscally responsible. If you keep putting off your bills, the consequences get nastier as time goes on. You can face steep late fees, delinquency, collections, and even judgment.[1] Yes, you can actually get in legal trouble for failing to pay off your debts.

Why, then, is our own government not held to those same standards? You won't see any judgments against the administration of President Barack Obama for spending our money like a crackhead on payday and then defaulting on its bills. Our government is worse than that proverbial twenty-year-old with her first credit card. They've been at it for centuries—literally—wasting tax dollars on things we don't need and can't afford. They just don't seem to get it. And the feds haven't just racked up a measly three or four thousand bucks in debt. They've gotten us over $20 *trillion* in the hole. Let's take a look at that figure:

$20,000,000,000,000.00.

Holy crap.

At the time of this writing, if federal spending came to an abrupt halt (which we all know will never happen), each man, woman, and child in the United States would need to shell out $61,000 to repay our debt.[2] That's more than the average working adult makes *in a year*, and that figure is getting larger by the second. But the reality is even grimmer, since children, the disabled, and the poor don't pay taxes. Adjusted for that, the debt per U.S. taxpayer balloons to more than $166,000.[3] I don't know about you, but I certainly don't have that kind of money lying around to bail out Uncle Sam. And even if we were able to put a dent in the debt, the feds would just keep on spending, like a seventy-year-old billionaire at an overpriced strip club.

If you've ever visited New York City, you've probably seen the National Debt Clock near Times Square. When real estate mogul Seymour Durst first put the clock up in 1989, the federal debt was a shocking, unbelievable, insurmountable...$2.7 trillion.[4]

The clock was turned off for a few years in the 1990s when we didn't have a deficit (thanks, Bill!), but other than that, it's been blowing up faster than Kylie Jenner's lips. I took a photo of it back in February 2008; at that time, the federal debt was right around $9,200,000,000,000. By October, the clock had run out of digits when the debt surpassed $10 trillion. It had to be replaced with a new clock, which is apparently able to track debt up to a quadrillion dollars (yeah, apparently that's a real number). Just seven years later, the debt has doubled. If that continues, we'll be over $36 trillion deep in 2022.

Our government spends more than $10 billion per day.[5] Bonkers, right? For those of us who are trying to scrape together $1 for a big 'n' cheesy, this will help you wrap your mind around just how large one billion is:

- One billion seconds ago, it was 1959.
- One billion minutes ago, Jesus was alive.
- One billion hours ago, our ancestors were living in the Stone Age.[6]

Yet the government can spend $1 billion several times a day!

What really freaks me out is that most people don't seem to give a flying you-know-what about this catastrophic mess. When I talk to my friends about the implications of budget sequestration, or the coming entitlement tsunami that will bankrupt the nation, more often than not I get a blank stare and a cannabis-induced grin. I know, I know, it's a lot of numbers to deal with, but I promise you, *this matters*. Even though the national debt seems kind of abstract, it actually does affect all of us. More debt means fewer jobs, less economic progress, and lower salaries. The stifled growth is especially hard on young Americans, who are barely making ends meet as it is (assuming they can even find a job). Of course, D.C. sees fit to lean on them with steep tax burdens to fund the latest federal spending spree.

With all this continuing unchecked, the United States is on the fast track to becoming the next Greece, or even a larger-scale Detroit.

What happened in Detroit is the stuff of an epic movie plot. The once-bustling metropolis with the nation's highest per capita income has since faded into a virtual ghost town.[7] America's manufacturing decline in the 1970s hit the city hard, but rather than implementing sound economic policies and bolstering a diversified private sector, Detroit's leaders chose to funnel money into the public sector and jack up taxes. Because when folks are strapped for cash, they can *totally* afford to feed more of it to the government.

As 60 percent of the population fled, the hulking city government continued to swell. Today, 35 percent of Detroit's remaining citizens are on food stamps, and 40 percent are stuck in poverty.[8] The city today looks like a horror movie set. Abandoned homes with broken windows, many of which were once ornate Victorian mansions, line the streets. Former luxury car factories have been stripped of their copper wire and now house squatting criminals and junkies. If you've never taken a virtual tour of Detroit on Google Maps' Street View, do it. Now. It's seriously creepy.

In 2013, Detroit finally filed for bankruptcy—at $18

billion in debt, half of which came from unrealistic promises to city government workers: $3 billion in pension payments and $6 billion in postemployment benefits for retirees.[9] Although the Obama Administration initially said it would avoid a Detroit bailout, it inevitably caved and gave the city $100 million in taxpayer cash, most of which got funneled into city employee pension funds.[10]

Let's just put that in perspective for a second: hardworking people in financially responsible cities—like Madison, Wisconsin, and Sioux City, Iowa—are stuck handing over their hard-earned tax dollars to fund the pensions of Detroit bureaucrats. Chief White House economic adviser Gene Sperling said the situation in Detroit was "the largest city bankruptcy in the history of our country, on our watch, and we've got to do something."[11]

But why couldn't Detroit solve its own problems? It seems we've given up on responsible city management and proven economic policies. But then again, why bother doing things the right way when you can just get a giant wad of cash from Uncle Sam when you screw up? What kind of message is Washington sending?

Detroit set a scary precedent. Now, whenever a state or city government gets itself in financial trouble, it's expected that the feds will come to the rescue. At the time of this writing, Puerto Rico is over $113 billion in debt that's supposedly "not payable." Not surprisingly, many are demanding that the federal government bail them out, too. It's the same old story: liberal policies have created generations of dependent Puerto Rican families stuck in poverty. Thanks to welfare that often pays better than jobs, Puerto Rico's workforce participation rate is a paltry 40 percent.[12]

With our snowballing federal debt, we are well on our way to becoming the next Detroit or Puerto Rico, but on a *way* bigger scale. Imagine that for a second. If the federal government found itself in such a grim economic situation, who would come to the rescue with a bailout? It's scary to think about. Almost as scary as what the feds are getting away with right now.

Dear IRS, Suck It

My second year out of college, I was doing relatively well for myself. Working as an independent contractor for several companies, I busted my ass and was able to earn about $125,000. No taxes had been taken out of that income, so I knew I was in for a doozy of a surprise once April rolled around. Early in the month, my tax guy tallied up how much I owed Uncle Sam. Even though I was expecting a high number, when he told me what it was, I may have died inside a little. At twenty-two years old, fresh out of college, I owed the IRS over $26,000. I was told that I didn't qualify for any of the usual postgrad exemptions because I'd earned too much. My blood was boiling while I wrote that check. Twenty-six Gs. To the IRS.

Excuse my French, but that's bullshit. We all know how bad the job market is for recent grads—nearly 14 percent are unemployed, in fact.[13] An even higher percentage is "underemployed," or working menial, part-time jobs because they're unable to find a real career. I was one of the lucky ones, capitalizing on every opportunity and quickly excelling in a well-paying field. It's puzzling that amid the awful job market, the government goes out of its way to *punish* success—$26,000 isn't chump change, especially not to a new graduate who is trying to get her life started.

Currently, the top marginal tax rate is 39.6 percent for individuals making over $400,000. Thirty-nine point six percent seems high as is, but those on the left want to increase that. Some have even called for tax rates as high as 90 percent for the superwealthy.[14]

Good grief. Shouldn't success be encouraged and rewarded? Not if you ask our government. The more money you make, the higher percentage of your income you fork over to the IRS. The system makes absolutely no sense when you really think about it.

Remember Herman Cain from the 2012 election? Yeah, I know, the guy was a total loon who didn't know Libya from Lady Liberty, but he did have one idea worth exploring. Cain was always yapping about his "999 Plan," the idea that all current taxes could be replaced with a 9 percent business transaction tax, a 9 percent personal income tax, and a 9 percent federal sales tax. This kind of plan makes a lot more sense than the overcomplicated and unfair system we're burdened with today. With a flat tax, everyone would pay the same rate, so people making $200,000 per year would still be paying a lot more than those making just $30,000 per year, but the higher earner wouldn't be punished for his success by being forced to pay a steeper percentage. It's similar to a fair tax, which would replace all income taxes, payroll taxes, gift taxes, and estate taxes with a single consumption tax on retail goods.

Many on the left complain that the fair tax system would hurt the poor most, but that simply isn't true. Low-income households would receive a monthly prebate on their purchases, which would offset their sales tax purchases. The amount of the prebate would increase for larger families.

Imagine a system with no income taxes, payroll taxes—we'd see a nice boost in economic and job growth from international businesses actually moving here for a change. Businesses would prosper and unemployment would go down. Everyone wins. Granted, the fair tax system isn't perfect—opponents of both it and the flat tax have valid arguments—but they're a lot better than the hot mess we have now.

Taxing income in the first place doesn't make a lot of sense, when you really think about it. Ronald Reagan once said, "If you want more of something, subsidize it; if you want less of something, tax it."[15] It's common sense. We want to discourage people from smoking, so we put a hefty tax on cigarettes. So wouldn't it be logical that a hefty tax on working would discourage people from working? Especially when the alternative is to stay at home and collect government benefits for doing nothing, and maybe retire in Puerto Rico.

But with all the flaws in our overzealous tax system, at least we can all sleep well at night, knowing that our money is going to a good cause, right?

LOL.

Yes, some of our tax dollars go toward things that are necessary for our society to function, like building roads and all of that stuff. But you'd be sick to your stomach if you knew what a lot of your money was getting blown on, mostly thanks to irresponsible politicians who are more concerned about their own political careers than solving the problems they were elected to address.

Congressmen and congresswomen are supposed to hold the executive branch accountable and make sure the country is being run in your best interest. The key words there are "supposed to." But in reality, they often do the exact opposite just to ensure they get reelected. In 2014, the USDA proposed closing a sheep station near Dubois, Idaho, because it was unnecessary and cost federal taxpayers $2 million each year.[16] Well, you see where this is going, folks. In stepped local lawmakers who fought for the facility to remain open, no matter how expensive or redundant it was. They didn't care as long as it would win them votes from the area come election season.

Not all of our politicians are bad, though. There are a few people in Washington who have actually made an effort to end some of the frivolous funding of silly projects and programs. Former Oklahoma senator Tom Coburn practically made his career out of it, and when he retired in 2014, I cried. Really, I did. My boyfriend came over that evening, and when I answered the door, he thought my kitten had died. Each year, Coburn would release a "Wastebook" chock-full of absurd ways our federal tax dollars are spent. Here are a few of my personal favorites from his most recent edition:[17]

- **$387,000 was spent on Swedish massages for rabbits.** The National Institutes of Health decided it would be smart to give six figures to the National Center for Complementary and Alternative Medicine (whatever the hell *that* means) to find out if Swedish massages help rabbits recover from sicknesses.

We literally paid for a group of rabbits to receive rub-downs from a machine that simulates the strokes used during Swedish massages.

- **$371,026 was spent to figure out if moms love dogs as much as kids.** The scientists who conducted this expensive study described their work as "the first report of a comparison of MRI-related brain activation patterns in women when they view images of their child and dog." Ummm...OK. I think there's a reason why that's never been done before.

- **$15,000 was spent to conduct a "stoner symphony."** That was the price tag for the Colorado Symphony Orchestra to host a show called, "Classically Cannabis: The High Note Series," a weed-themed series of musical performances. What were they smoking when they passed this one?

- **$307,524 was spent on synchronized swimming for sea monkeys.** For all of you who don't know, sea monkeys are tiny brine shrimp that kids often keep as pets. The government took it upon itself to figure out if sea monkeys were able to follow a beam of light in a group. Turns out, it proved to be "more difficult than it sounds," according to one of the study's scientists. Drat! If only we could harness the power of sea monkeys, we could control...children's aquariums around the world. Or at least within the reach of this flashlight.

- **$80 million to build a real-life "Iron Man" suit.** No joke. The Department of Defense decided it'd be a good idea to build a suit powered by futuristic energy sources that's able to withstand bullets. This is what you get when you give overgrown man-children the latest technology and a blank check. The Tactical Assault Light Operator Suit (TALOS) employed not only defense contractors but also Hollywood costume designers (because that shit *has* to look cool, or there's no point, right?) After $80 million and no results, one industry professional said that the suit will "need about a billion dollars" to be completed successfully. Because the DoD doesn't mess around about going a *little* over budget.

I just want to take a moment to remind you that these are all real things that happened. I mean, who the hell is signing off on these projects? I could go on and on, but we have other fish to fry, and you can read Coburn's Wastebooks online. Just keep a barf bag handy.

The waste parade extends far beyond this government-sponsored science fair. Exorbitant spending goes all the way down to the basic practices of large government agencies, and few departments are exempt from this. In fact, one of the worst offenders when it comes to wasting our tax dollars is the IRS.

Wait. What?!?

Yup, the very same agency that bends us over and shoves its hand deep into our pocketbooks every April is turning around and spending our cash on dumb shit. Ironic, isn't it? During recent years, the IRS spent $4 million on office furniture (OMG, spinny chairs!), $8,000 on a "fitness equipment stair climber," and thousands more on trinkets like stuffed animals and rubber Thomas the Tank Engine wristbands.[18] They also spent $60,000 to produce two videos of its employees parodying *Star Trek* and *Gilligan's Island*.[19] Another video, which cost the agency $1,600, showed their employees dancing in a line.

If you haven't seen these videos, you've gotta Google them. You'll laugh your ass off (until you remember that it's our cash that's gone to fund Washington's Funniest Home Videos). As if spending as much as a new BMW costs on parodies isn't bad enough, the actual quality of the video is about that of Hulk Hogan's sex tape (don't act like you don't know what I'm talking about—we've all seen it).

During April 2015, amid the spending sprees, the IRS claimed that devastating budget cuts forced it to ignore calls from the majority of taxpayers seeking help. But of course, they were still able to come up with the money to audit your ass despite your poverty-level income and flawless accounting. Never mind that numerous congressmen and senators have tried to bring some accountability to the agency's spending habits, IRS Commissioner John Koskinen had the *cojones* to ask Congress for a larger budget.[20]

A few years back, the Department of Justice managed to spend almost $500,000 on food and beverages at only ten conferences.[21] That's the kind of menu I'd love to see at my next conference…except it didn't turn out to be anything special. It was just wasteful. At one conference, they bought muffins at $16 a piece. $16 for a damn muffin! You've been to Dunkin' Donuts or Starbucks. Ever seen a muffin that costs $16? Exactly. Even if you did, would you buy it? But guess what? We did. And we bought the DOJ $8 cups of coffee to wash them down. Must have been some overpriced hotel ripping off the ripe target of a government agency that collects money!

But at least we can assume that they were working at those conferences. It's not like we're paying for our government to kick back and sip mai tais, right?

BZZZT! Wrong! Each year, taxpayers shell out around $19 million just for politicians' vacations.[22] And sometimes these vacations go to the least deserving representatives. At normal companies, if you do something wrong, you get fired. In Washington, however, federal employees are often "punished" for misconduct, underperformance, or illegal activity with paid vacations. Yes, you read that correctly. This is the norm at many federal agencies, including the Department of Veterans Affairs (VA).

For example, VA officials were found guilty of manipulating data to get pay raises at the expense of dying veterans. How were they punished? With paid leave, of course! Other VA employees who enjoyed paid leave in 2014 include one who sexually abused a patient, and another who caused a fatal accident while driving drunk. These aren't isolated incidents; these irresponsible practices happen time and time again on Capitol Hill. In a single year, the Social Security Administration spent $40 million to pay 10,000 employees not to work, while the Department of Homeland Security spent $4.3 million to pay 237 employees not to work, and the U.S. Postal Service spent $3 million to pay 1,500 employees not to work.[23] Noticing a trend here?

Milton Friedman, an economist and one of the smartest, most awesome dudes to ever grace the earth with his presence, once said, "Very few people spend other people's money as carefully as they spend their own." If you've ever had the pleasure of using someone else's credit card, you get what Friedman was talking about.

Back when I was living with my parents, I would go to the mall for school shopping and buy tons of expensive, brand-name outfits—there was no such thing as too much Abercrombie. I didn't even look at the prices. Why bother when Mommy was picking up the bill? That all changed when I started earning money and paying my own way.

Suddenly, I began buying clothes only if I truly needed them and looking for good value rather than brand names. The government is operating just like a young me with her mom's credit card, not giving a second thought to cost or value.

Even though Washington's waste is blatantly obvious, politicians will do everything in their power to make it seem like they need more and more and more funding. Mention the words "budget cut" around any entrenched bureaucrat, and they'll swear up and down that none of us can survive without millions of dollars being pumped into the D.C. machine every minute.

Remember when the government shut down in 2013? The sixteen-day shutdown began after the Republican-led House voted to keep the government funded through December 15 of that year, so long as the president agreed to defund a major new burden on the federal budget—Obamacare. Not surprisingly, the Democratic-led Senate rejected all proposals from the House that cut Obamacare's funding. Commence the federal shutdown! OMG!

In an epic anticlimax that we haven't seen since Y2K or

perhaps the end of the Mayan calendar, all services and payments necessary to ensure national and public safety...continued as normal, without interruption. Huh? All that really happened during this national disaster was that "nonessential" employees and departments were furloughed.[24]

Ignoring the fact that we're all apparently paying for nonessential services, it's rather pathetic that the Obama Administration stooped to closing down services that were most likely to offend the public to make the government shutdown appear to be devastating. The national parks were closed; the World War II Memorial was shut down and barricaded, even though it's a 24/7 open-air memorial that isn't regularly staffed; over 100 privately run parks were closed, despite requiring no federal funds to operate; the Amber Alert website was taken down.[25] The government even halted the program that offers last-chance cancer treatments to dying children.[26] Seriously.

Funny, though, that while the White House was punishing as many people as possible to make a political point, Obama's personal employees and facilities appeared to be largely untouched.[27] The White House chefs weren't furloughed, and the president's Camp David and military golf course both remained open. Because, ya know, Obama's chefs are totally essential. But Amber Alerts? Nah.

It's clear that there's no such thing as fiscal responsibility in Washington. Heck, even humanity can be hard to come by in our nation's capital. But in a painfully ironic twist, that waste and disregard become even more obvious when you look at some of D.C.'s most bloated, ineffective programs that are touted as being necessary to the well-being of all American citizens.

Social (In)Security

Meet my grandmother, Lucy: She is seventy-eight years old and lives a fabulous life in the New York City area. She studied chemistry at a prestigious university in the northeast but never worked a day in her life after meeting my grandfather, a chemist at a large pharmaceutical company. The two got married and lived a cushy life in New Jersey, where they had two kids, lots of friends and a lovely house. When my grandfather died, all of his money was left to my grandmother. Now, let's just say my grandfather did pretty well in his day, and Nana Lucy has been living large ever since. I'm not talking Diddy-level wealth here, but enough to live a comfy life in a huge apartment overlooking the NYC skyline. My nana spends her time attending beauty appointments, applying various salves, and making appearances at lavish New York soirees. She's living it up—and more power to her!

Now I want you to meet my old college roommate and one of my closest friends, Rachel: She is twenty-five years old and struggles to make ends meet in Boston. Rachel graduated with a BA in liberal arts and was finally able to land a job as a travel agent after a year of seeking work. Her $34,000 annual salary allows her to squeak by every month—let's just say she eats lots of ramen noodles. She spends her weekdays slaving away at the office and her weekends getting herself involved in drunken shenanigans that might give Snooki pause. But that's what we're supposed to do when we're young, isn't it? It's not easy out there for young adults right now, and most twenty-somethings like Rachel consider themselves lucky to have even found a job.

Now here's the crazy thing: Rachel, who can barely get by, is paying my well-to-do grandmother every month. Yup, you read that right. Of course, I don't mean that Rachel's making the trek to New York and physically handing her the money with flowers and a tin of shortbread, but a significant portion of Rachel's paycheck is taken from her every month and put toward Social Security, which is then paid out to old people, including my grandmother. FYI, the government considers "old" (the age at which you can collect these entitlements) to be a mere sixty-two, which might have made sense when the program started back in 1935, but now that we have things like statin drugs, bypass surgeries, and other life-saving technologies, sixty-two is starting to look a lot more like forty-two.

Now, of course I understand that the cases of Rachel and my grandmother are purely anecdotal. There are plenty of old people out there who really need a hand, and plenty of us spring chickens are doing just fine financially. But the point is this: Why the *hell* are rich old farts (sorry, Nana) entitled to money from those us of who are breaking our backs to pay for our crappy, rat-ridden apartments or, if we're lucky, fixer-upper first homes?

Here's a list of a few old-timers receiving checks every month that we're paying for: Donald Trump, Warren Buffett, Hillary Clinton, Rupert Murdoch, and Hugh Hefner. About 53 percent of all entitlement spending is going to the elderly, which may seem reasonable until you find out that they're also the wealthiest age group in America. Then it just makes no sense. Moreover, about 15 percent of every dollar we earn is going to Social Security. There should, of course, be a safety net for the elderly who are struggling, but there is no reason why Trump or Hefner (or definitely Clinton) should be taking what I worked for.

Add my seventy-year-old great-aunt to that list. I love her to pieces, but as the wife of a retired surgeon, she's not exactly spending her days clipping grocery store coupons and waiting for that next check from the government. In fact, there's this great thing she does at Thanksgiving—you'll love it: She tells these hilarious stories about giving her Social Security checks to her son, the pot-smoking "artist" who lives a life of leisure in New York City.

You're paying for this, folks. You're literally funding the lifestyle of my freeloading second cousin, who grew up in his parents' New Jersey mansion and never really worked a day in his life.

According to D.C., this is how we should handle retirement. You should pay taxes into a government account, and when you reach your golden years, that same money should come back to you, regardless of how well off you might be.

Sorry to break it to you, but that money isn't going into an account—it's being spent by the feds the same year they get it, and at an alarming rate.[28] "But don't worry," they tell us, "you'll get the same benefits when your time comes." I believe that about as much as I believed my roommate when she swore she never drank my Maker's Mark while I was out.

So how do we know the government will keep its promise to us? Simply put, we don't. And it doesn't look good. By the time we hit our midsixties, we're each projected to have paid almost $400,000 in Social Security taxes, but we'll only receive about $335,000 in benefits, not factoring in inflation. The program has run cash deficits for years (translation: The taxes collected aren't covering the released benefits). And as soon as the Social Security trust fund dries up, the feds are expected to start borrowing to dole out the payments (and we all know that when the fed borrows cash, it's rarely paid back).

Even though it's clear that Social Security is *not* sustainable, many politicians are actually pushing to *expand* the program. Genius, right? Bernie Sanders, the self-described "socialist" from Vermont and a failed 2016 presidential contender, recently said, "We should not be talking about cutting Social Security benefits. We should be talking about expanding benefits to make sure that every American can retire with dignity."[29] His proposed bill would increase Social Security benefits by $65 per month. *Yay! We all deserve free stuff!* Of course, Sanders made no mention of how we would finance any of this. The same voters who cheer Sanders's feel-good rhetoric rarely stop to think about the fact that all of that money would come from their paychecks (assuming they have jobs).

When it comes to Social Security, the situation boils down to this: Not only is the system we have in place ineffective and horribly managed, it is a ticking time bomb. Serious reform is necessary to ensure that future generations are taken care of in old age. One solution is to means-test the program (i.e., allow only the elderly with limited resources to collect the benefits). This would potentially solve the problem of cutting checks to high-income seniors who simply don't need help. Another option is to allow young people to invest their Social Security taxes through individual accounts. Opponents of this idea insist that private investment is "too risky." Nonsense. The Cato Institute found that "if workers who retired in 2011 had been allowed to invest the employee half of the Social Security payroll tax over their working life-time, they would retire with more income than if they relied on Social Security."[30]

Meanwhile, that time bomb? It's set for a $21 trillion shortfall.[31] Eventually, it will be impossible to dole out the promised cash. Still think private investment sounds riskier?

But folks, we haven't even gotten started. You'd think the feds would have learned their lesson with this colossal fail-ure, right? Guess again!

Paying an Arm and a Leg

Speaking of unsustainable programs that hit us squarely in the pocketbook, I have a real whopper for you: Obamacare. There's no doubt that Barack Insane Obama was an old school, Great Society, tax-and-spend liberal, just like most Demo-crats out there. Got a problem? Throw more money at it. Obamacare—sorry, the Affordable Health Care Act, which is anything but affordable—is already causing real harm to people in need of health care.

Democrats continue to complain that Republican poli-ticians are out to control their personal lives, yet in the same breath, they insist that Obamacare is the best solution for the U.S. health-care system. It really is laughable—what could be more personal than your medical care? And they've turned it into a government mandate! According to many liberals, it's barbaric for gray-haired politicians in D.C. to tell a woman that she can't have an abortion, but it's totally OK for them to force everyone to pay for health-care services they might not want, need, or even agree with morally. Let me know if you can fig-ure out the sense behind that logic, because I definitely can't.

And not only is it invasive, it comes as a serious financial drain on our income at a time when we really can't afford it. Obamacare will cost taxpayers about $1.5 trillion (more than 5 percent of the national debt), and so far it has been nothing short of a disaster.[32] Under Obamacare, we're all forced to either obtain insurance directly through the government or through a private insurance company that offers federally approved plans. Besides being mandated to provide specific services and coverage plans, insurance companies selling through Obamacare must get their premiums approved by regulators.[33] Wait a second, this totally reminds me of something...oh, right. Socialism!

Tens of thousands of Americans have received letters in the mail, informing them that they are required to get rid of their "sub-par" insurance plans and must purchase more "comprehensive" (government-speak for "more expensive") plans even if there's nothing wrong with the care they've been receiving.

My own mother was one of the unlucky souls who received a cancellation notice for her individual health insurance policy (which she'd been perfectly happy with for many years). The government told her that she had to get a more expensive plan that included—get this—maternity coverage. Now, keep in mind that, with me being a millennial, my mother is in her early fifties (sorry for disclosing that, Mom...you don't look a day over forty!), I won't be getting a new sibling in this lifetime. But unfortunately the politicians behind this program aren't bothering to consult doctors (or common sense). So at the end of the day, my mother is stuck paying for coverage she'll never use.

Now, let's say that you're a healthy twenty-nine-year-old

with no insurance. You don't want insurance because you rarely get sick and can't even remember the last time you went to the doctor. So naturally, you decide not to comply with Obamacare's mandates. What happens next? You pay up, with a $695 fine.[34] That's a bit too much like extortion for my taste.

Adding insult to injury, we can fully expect the feds to waste all this money once they get it in their grubby little paws. Take a look at the Post Office, for example. In 2013 the USPS was $5 billion in the red despite revenue growth.[35] That was its seventh consecutive year operating with a net loss. If any private business produced those results, it would close its doors in a heartbeat. Compared to private-sector options (think UPS and DHL), the USPS is also incredibly inefficient—because they simply don't care. And they don't have to. After all, they live off the government teat just like any other welfare case. They're in no danger of closing because they'll just keep getting (involuntary) support from us taxpayers. But if you look at the private businesses that live and die by the free market, it's a different matter entirely. UPS continuously operates at a profit while delivering a superhuman three hundred packages per minute. Private companies like UPS are forced to meet the needs of consumers in a cost-efficient manner or risk going out of business. But in the world of government institutions, profits, efficiency, and productivity don't matter.

What makes us think it'll be any different with our health care? Heck, within minutes of Obamacare being launched the feds proved too incompetent to even successfully run the system's website. Despite spending $840 million for the development of the Obamacare website (I know a pimply guy who lives with his parents who would have created the site for a measly hundred grand), HealthCare.gov was not working properly for *more than a year* after its rollout.[36] The site was even hacked in July 2014, potentially putting personal health information at risk.

Despite then-President Obama insisting that the health-care act had been a roaring success, strong evidence shows that it has been nothing short of a disaster. Despite Obama insisting that the average American family would save $2,500 on premiums each year, the opposite happened: Most families saw increases on premiums after the bill passed. How surprised are you?

The problems were even evident inside doctors' offices. Many health-care professionals complained that the one-size-fits-all nature of Obamacare jeopardized the doctor-patient relationship. What incentive did doctors have to nurture personal relationships with their patients when they get paid for quantity, not quality? They're better off scheduling as many patients in a day as possible, even if that won't allow them to give adequate time to care for each person. The result could easily be sloppy and rushed medical work. Just how is this supposed to make us all healthier?

President Donald Trump has said that he wants to repeal Obamacare and move toward a more privatized system. If he sticks to his word, this would be a remarkable first step toward making our health-care system considerably more efficient and affordable.

Our Money, Our Interests

I don't think anyone has embodied "mo' money, mo' problems" better than the federal government. So remind me again why we trust an entrenched group of career politicians to know how to spend our hard-earned cash in our best interest. Wouldn't you think we'd be able to do that ourselves, buying what we need directly instead of being forced into wasteful, bloated, government programs? We're going to have to if we want to defuse that ticking time bomb of federal deficit spending. Perhaps the time has come to stand up and adopt a new slogan, "Keep Washington out of our wallets!"

Finding Common Sense on Common Ground

So when Willie, the D.C.-loving wonk, says...

> "We're in debt because of George W. Bush and the
> War on Terror! He's to blame for the debt,
> not Obama."

You say: "Both of them ran up the debt faster than a teenager with Daddy's AmEx card. Bush went on a spending spree defending us against the 'bogeyman' and Obama dropped a ton on an out-of-control health-care plan."

> "We should tax the rich more! They're greedy."

You say: "Greedy? More like motivated to succeed! Without the rich creating companies, technology and innovations, we'd be without jobs or the things we love most—our computers, phones, and Xboxes."

> "Your grandma may be rich but Social Security helps
> tons of poor old people who have no money."

You say: "Agreed. All I'm saying is the rich old farts don't need a payout. Stop paying the Donald Trumps of the world who don't need it."

"Why are you hating on Obamacare? It gave people access to affordable health care who can't get it otherwise."

You say: "That's a generalization that just isn't true for the majority of Americans who were doing just fine with their own health insurance."

"Aren't you exaggerating about all the crazy government subsidies, I mean come *on*!"

You Say: "You think I'm cherry picking? Google Senator Coburn's 'Wastebook.' Or for this year's information check out Sen. Rand Paul's 'Waste Report,' which keeps Coburn's tradition alive by outlining many (many, many) ways the federal government continues to waste our money. You'll see there are enough insane subsidies being handed out by the Fed to fill a book!"

CHAPTER 3

The Department of Duh-fense

"War sucks."
~ Chris Kyle ~

I grew up firmly believing that I was a Republican; I knew that I wanted to belong to the "Party of Small Government," the party of Thomas Jefferson. Well, that all changed pretty quickly when I attended my first (and last) College Republicans meeting.

It began well. Surrounded by nicely dressed—albeit very pimply—political nerds, I thought I had found my sanctuary in the otherwise liberal dystopia known as "campus." The group spoke about cutting welfare spending (I liked that), downsizing the federal government (I *loved* that), and the "need" to deploy more military forces abroad (I...wait, huh?). The roomful of adolescent elephants then proceeded to discuss why it was "absolutely necessary" to "lead with force" in other countries—specifically those in the Middle East, where the local ideology certainly didn't match up with that of the guy next to me—a pasty twenty-year-old from New Hampshire named after the bank from which his wealth flowed.

As a passionate journalism student, I wanted to get to

the bottom of this, but the more I talked with them and the deeper I dug, the more adamant they became about wanting the United States to act like an annoying helicopter mom, with all the nations in the world playing the roles of errant children.

For those of you who don't know what a helicopter mom is, consider yourselves lucky. You may have actually been able to retain some shred of dignity during your teen years. In short, a helicopter mom is one who can't seem to accept that her kidlets are their own people and need to grow and learn by themselves every once in a while. Instead, she sees it as her life's mission to protect her children from themselves, constantly asking about, spying on, and generally hovering over little future therapy patients. The second she senses any kind of screw-up, *BOOM*—you're grounded for life. Or, in the case of a country like Libya, you get a bomb dropped on you. *It's OK. You'll welcome us as liberators. And if not, you'll thank us when you're older.* Right.

It was at this College Republicans meeting that I realized Republicans aren't the Party of Small Government at all, and that this kind of thinking is now expected among its members. Many establishment Republicans, like John McCain, push hard to *increase* spending each fiscal year in the name of national security. Our hawkish tendencies cost billions each year and continue to be funded by the military-industrial complex.

What's the military-industrial complex, you ask? Don't worry; it's not as wonkish as it sounds (well, it kind of is, but I'll make it simple). Basically it's a big circle jerk of balding old men ensuring that big money is pumped into the arms industry every year. Politicians, the armed forces, and the arms industry all work together to pass exorbitant military spending. Together these three form a collaborative "iron triangle" (yes, that's really what it's called), and as long as all three sides of the triangle are getting what they want, well then, screw the American people.

Former president Dwight Eisenhower warned about the military-industrial complex well more than half a century ago during his farewell address. Ike was a five-star general who was instrumental in winning World War II, so he knew exactly the kind of insatiable beast the American war machine could become and just how much it could sap our economy and our freedoms. Unfortunately, we didn't take his warning seriously. True to form, the politicians in D.C. chose to ignore facts and experience in favor of shiny new things that blow up other things...and also line the pockets of their manufacturer friends.

For those of you who like numbers (and aren't distracted by shiny things), a single base-model F-35A fighter plane costs us taxpayers $148 million.[1] And if you want the F-35C with the leather seats, moon roof, and Beats by Dre stereo system, you're looking at $337 million. For a single airplane. That's up from the $273 million the same plane cost a year ago, and we're only in year fifteen of what's expected to be a fifty-five-year plan for the F-35. Not to mention the fact that it's a bad product that continues to be plagued by technical problems. And what does the Pentagon do about it? In their infinite wisdom, they order 2,400 of them. And that's only one of countless military products we're (over)paying for.

Folks, we don't need that kind of firepower. In 2011 alone,

the U.S. government spent almost $720 billion on "defense and international security assistance."[2] That's more than we spent on Medicare! C'mon guys, it doesn't take a genius to see how ridiculous this is. And as long as we're pumping our hard-earned tax dollars into the M-I complex, you can bet that our politicians will keep finding reasons to get involved in other nations' business, policing the world, and starting unnecessary wars. *OMG, those people who are different! They must be up to something. Let's bomb them and then leave soldiers there for the rest of forever. It's the only way we'll be safe.*

The Forever Wars

Some of the younger voters may not remember September 11, 2001, all that well, and consequently they may also not remember a time when we weren't at war. I'm right there with you. When the twin towers fell, I was still in elementary school, a happy, naïve little kid who was into Barbies and hunting zombies. But even then, watching my parents and teachers, angry, shocked, and above all sad for that senseless loss of innocent lives, I knew something had changed forever.

Now, I'm all for going after those who have threatened our liberties. We declared war on Imperial Japan because they attacked us at Pearl Harbor—and it's why we declared war on the Taliban, Osama bin Laden, and al Qaeda—because they attacked us on 9/11. But something that we often forget is that as soon as we declared war on Japan, Adolf Hitler and his Nazi nightmare regime turned around and declared war on us.

We now know that President Franklin D. Roosevelt

wanted to help in the fight against Nazi Germany, but he was also dealing with a very divided United States and a powerful movement known as America First. While not strict isolationists, the America First movement was determined that America stay out of the world's messes. At the time, thanks to the Great Depression, we had enough problems of our own. (Kind of like now, don't you think? What's been dubbed the Great Recession, which hit in 2008, is still lingering, and we've got a lot to deal with here at home.) FDR definitely did not have the public support to get us involved in what was fast becoming World War II. The Japanese attack changed all of that, kind of like 9/11 changed our world.

Make no mistake, when you're attacked—when your way of life is threatened and your values and freedoms are challenged—you should fight back. There are wars of choice, guys, and wars of necessity. Every nation must be prepared and willing to fight the latter. If not, then all the liberties we take for granted, all the rights that were won in war against the British, could be lost. Not on my watch.

Unfortunately, the Pentagon seems to have lost that focus, and it highlights a big issue I have with the Republicans—and a lot of Dems, too—about the role of America in the world. Yes, we need to protect our homeland, and we absolutely must have a military that can ensure our safety and freedom. But that does not mean we should give them a blank check so they can grossly overspend, establish a large U.S. military presence all over the globe, send billions in military aid to other countries, and blunder into a years-long war we didn't need to fight in the first place. How's the search for WMDs in Iraq going, Dick Cheney? And have we all forgotten that our then commander in chief said, "One of the hardest parts of my job is to connect Iraq to the war on terror?"

Wars of choice are inherently dangerous. The Democrats started two big ones: Korea back in 1950 and Vietnam in 1964. Neither was a war we absolutely had to fight, where our land or our liberties were at stake—and in the case of Korea, we're still paying for it. Nearly thirty thousand U.S. troops remain on the border between North and South Korea to keep the peace.[3] And let's just say our efforts there haven't been cheap. In addition to the cost of providing food, shelter, and care for a small football stadium's worth of people (while not being able to do the same at home when Hurricane Katrina hit), the Senate Armed Services Committee reported that our nonpersonnel military costs in South Korea totaled $1.1 billion in 2012 alone.[4]

And it's not just our own financial impact that is being felt because we just *had* to stick our big what-have-you into Korea. You know that crazy little man named Kim Jong-un? That walking Napoleon complex with little more to do than cancel Seth Rogen films, lob missiles into the ocean, and starve and oppress his own people so he can live it up in an enormous mansion? Well, he's just the latest in a dynasty of tyrants that has ruled Korea, stretching back more than sixty years. Remind me again what we've gained from Korea, Vietnam, and yes, Iraq—wars that cost us dearly. Pin two squarely on the Democrats' door and one on the Republicans'.

Yes, though most of our catastrophic debt can be traced back to tax-and-spend liberal policies, we must remember that it was the Republicans who got us into the quagmire of Iraq. Like Korea and Vietnam, it opened us up to charges of being an aggressor nation with imperial ambitions. It weakened our case when we point the self-righteous finger at other countries, like Russia interfering in Ukraine or Israel in Gaza. And our invasion and occupation of Iraq has also cost us—you and me—upward of $5 trillion.[5] That's almost one-third of our national debt. Thanks, Dubya! And at the time of this writing, a bunch of jihadist lunatics have taken over the northern city of Mosul and declared a medieval caliphate. If it's been a while for you since Carmen Sandiego, Mosul is near where a lot of that Iraqi oil flows—the same oil that Dick Cheney and his pals, who really ran our country for eight years, promised would actually pay for the war and wipe away our $5 trillion tab. We know how that worked out. And now ISIS is in control of that oil and using it to fund their reign of terror.

The $5 trillion figure doesn't take into account the thousands of formerly able-bodied young men and women who have been treated for crippling physical and mental ailments that will be with them the rest of their lives. And they are the lucky ones. To date, over three thousand Americans have returned home from Iraq in flag-covered pine boxes. A medal and a hero's funeral are nice gestures, but their families would rather have their brothers and sisters back. Yes, and there's the kicker, folks. It's not like the rich old men in D.C. are sending their kids to walk into Fallujah and take an IED for the team.

We have become a nation of acceptance. We accept that there will be "collateral damage" with each war, that loss of life is just part of the cost. We accept that all of the cost is a necessity. We are spoon-fed the idea that unless we spend trillions we can't win the War on Terror, and if you don't support the war than you must not be a patriot. At what point does enough become enough? Is it 25,000 lives and $25 trillion more, or 50,000 more lives and $50 trillion more?

There is a cycle to this madness that has been played out time and time again since World War II. You know the drill: We foot the bill for the war with taxpayer dollars and American lives, then we foot the bill to rebuild the countries that we were at war with or at war in. And guess who wins those big contracts? Why, the same cronies in the iron triangle, of course. At the start of the Iraq war, then vice president Dick Cheney's old company, Halliburton, got the call for that job—a job no other company was allowed to bid for. This is the same company that has been plagued by scandal, bribery, and millions of dollars in overbilling.

We have been rebuilding Iraq and Afghanistan—"winning hearts and minds"—to the tune of maybe $100 billion, maybe $10 trillion…it all depends on whom you ask. Can you imagine what we could do with that money right here at home? As we send troops to toil away in the Middle East and help rebuild all the things we blew up, they are spit at, cursed at, shot at, and bombed. They have the honor of training the Iraqi army and Afghani nationals who then turn around and shoot them. These kinds of incidents are rarely reported, but the Associated Press did a short story about three years ago on "green on green" war casualties (friendlies killing friendlies), including an incident in Iraq when two American soldiers were after a trainee who smuggled live ammo into a training session:

Both officials spoke on condition of anonymity because they were not authorized to release the information. A U.S. statement confirmed that two soldiers were killed and a third was wounded by small-arms fire by what the military described as "an individual wearing an Iraqi army uniform."

"This incident occurred during a training event being conducted by U.S. forces as part of their advise and assist mission with Iraqi security forces," the U.S. military said in a statement.

The Americans were not identified pending notification of next of kin, and the statement provided few other details. The U.S. troops were from the 4th Brigade, 1st Cavalry Division, based at Ft. Hood, Texas.[6]

If this story weren't so sad, it would be laughable. Let's recap:

1. We invade a country.
2. Bomb the country and kill the citizens.
3. Depose their leader.
4. Give their angry men weapons and say, "This is how you use these, but don't use them against your enemies...only ours."

Call me crazy, but I think it makes sense that if you blow up someone's country, they might get a little irritated. Even if a handful think, "Wow, that was awesome. Thanks for blowing up my neighbor; I hated that asshole," there will still be others who think, "You blew up my neighbor, whom I liked, and who still had my Tupperware, and now you want to train us to fight your enemies? OK, sure. Give me the gun"...*BANG!*

How did the greatest country in the world get itself into such a crazy position? More important, how are we allowing this to continue? I don't know about you, but I am definitely *not* cool with this situation.

According to Washington, we've won some of these battles in the War on Terror, right? Iraq...Afghanistan... "Mission Accomplished." But what exactly did we win? Iraq is a worse mess than ever and a breeding ground for ISIS terrorists. The Taliban is making a comeback in Afghanistan. Sure, we found bin Laden, but couldn't that have happened without spending trillions?

The list of modern conflicts in the Middle East goes back to before World War I, and most memorably for Americans of a certain age includes the attack on our embassy in the Iranian crisis of 1970. The first war in Iraq was in 1990, when Saddam Hussein invaded our friend Kuwait and George Bush Sr. declared that this aggression "will not stand." Eleven years later, some in the administration of George W. Bush were still smarting from the decision not to take out Saddam during that war, so Iraq became a target after 9/11.

There's a lot of bad blood between the United States and the nations of the Middle East. And like the relationship between Angelina Jolie and Jennifer Aniston, we too will probably never see perfectly eye to eye. So why keep looking for a reason to pick a fight?

Our military is spread across the Middle East: Syria, Iraq, Kuwait, Afghanistan, and Pakistan—at least at the time of this writing. We have boots on the ground in all of these countries either training rebels, "keeping the peace," hunting suspected terrorists, or fighting insurgents. We have assumed the role of invaders in these countries, just with our presence.

The War on Terror is a lot like the old War on Communism and far too much like the sci-fi novel and movie *The Forever War*. Unfortunately, unlike in the fictional Forever War, Channing Tatum will not be stepping in to save us all. We're locked in a battle and suffering from a great deal of confusion as to who are our enemies and how best to defeat them. Yet we continue to flex American muscle in hopes of keeping the wolves at bay.

The worst part of it all? The Department of Defense heavily relies on this mess continuing, without an end in sight. Both parties say things like, "No one wants a war." Except guess what? There are a lot of people who *do* want a war. Have you heard the old saying that when the economy is bad what we need is a war? War siphons off workers to go fight, which means that more jobs become available. War opens up possibilities for industry—and profit. World War II taught us the value of war to the economy—it opened up manufacturing opportunities, and gave people jobs as soldiers and in industry that were sorely lacking in the depths of the Great Depression. During World War II, priorities shifted from producing goods for consumption to producing goods in support of the war effort. Manufacturers of materiel recognized that war is profitable and, ideally, can be permanent, even if it is "cold."

We have become numb to the numbers: the cost, the lives, and news of the wounded quickly flash across the news crawls that we click by in pursuit of the latest episode of our favorite TV series.

This kind of apathy is dangerous, because the powers that be on both sides of the aisle are taking advantage of it. They are filling their friends' wallets with large defense contracts, keeping lobbyists employed, and spending money—our money—recklessly. But does that mean we don't need a DoD? Does it mean that just because war is profitable for some industries we never need to go to war? The answer is no on both counts. We do need the DoD, and there are times when war is a necessity, but there has to be a better standard for deciding how the DoD is used.

The Color of Money

Tracking down where all the money is going is a task that even the D.C. bean counters can't seem to handle. There are so many conflicting reports on the amount of money that the DoD is spending that it really is unclear exactly how much our "freedom" is costing. The DoD, like other government agencies, uses a "color of money" system that is at best confusing.[7] The "colors" of money are categories, and the categories can be things like Research and Development, Procurement, MILPERS (Military Personnel), and MILCON (Military Construction). One color can borrow from another in a time of crisis, so things get pretty murky pretty quickly.

The problem with this color system is you have to know where to look to get a true(ish) picture of what the DoD is spending. Transparency is conveniently not their strong suit, and all they need to do to hide funding is to label something "classified." Then it falls under the "black budget," which is supposedly used for covert operations that are in line with national security. Most people have no idea this budget even exists, and when the *Washington Post* recently tried to get some information on it, they were effectively given the runaround:

> There is no specific entry for the CIA's fleet of armed drones in the budget summary, but a broad line item hints at the dimensions of the agency's expanded paramilitary role, providing more than $2.6 billion for "covert action programs" that would include drone operations in Pakistan and Yemen, payments to militias in Afghanistan and Africa, and attempts to sabotage Iran's nuclear program.[8]

Even under FOIA rules, black budget information is typically redacted in the interest of national security. What does this mean? It means that we will likely never know how much these wars are really costing. Government accountability at its best.

And all this cash isn't just for military spending. Our government also attempts to buy peace through aid. In 2013, *Time* named Afghanistan the "winner" in snagging humanitarian aid from the United States to the tune of $12.9 billion.[9] That seems to be an extremely low-ball figure, considering the interesting findings by Brown University's Watson Institute:

> As of September 30, 2014, the US had appropriated $104.1 billion for the relief and reconstruction of Afghanistan, with the FY2015 budget request raising that total to $109.9 billion. The majority of these funds ($66 billion) have been administered by the Department of Defense, with other amounts funneled through USAID ($18 billion), and, less significantly,

through the State Department and other or multiple agencies. An additional $10.1 billion has been paid out to Afghanistan through two international trust funds to which the US is the primary donor. A total of $7.7 billion has been paid by the US directly to Afghan government agencies or through these trust funds. These amounts far exceed the $61 billion reconstruction dollars spent in Iraq from 2003–2012.[10]

Two billion dollars alone was spent on building roads from the north to the south in Afghanistan to help improve the Afghanis' ability to trade—and to make it easier for them to set IEDs (OK, I threw in that last part).[11] This at a time when one of every nine bridges in the United States is deemed structurally unsound and potentially dangerous.

But wait, it gets worse!

The United States Agency for International Development, in conjunction with the DoD, decided that the young Afghanis could be persuaded to not become jihadists if they had some training and help. The majority of the population in Afghanistan is under thirty years old. The average life expectancy is forty-nine years. One of the big selling points on the training-and-help program was that members of the Taliban and al Qaeda were portrayed basically as just bored kids, and if they had something else to occupy their time they wouldn't be building bombs.[12]

A three-year program was set up to help educate the population and provide other opportunities to the youth of Afghanistan. The budget was set at $50 million.[13]

About two years into the program, it was determined that

things were not working out. The progress was summed up by the Inspector General of the United States in charge of Afghanistan affairs, who said that there is "little evidence that the project has made progress toward" its goals.[14] Perhaps dropping $50 million on an "Arts and Crafts for Terrorists" program is not the answer. The program was cut, but the $50 million was still spent. Just an idea: Maybe we could have taken that $50 million and invested it in American youth.

Of course the DoD is fond of slapping acronyms on all these programs and producing reports showing us how great everything is working out (that's me being sarcastic). But they can't completely hide the results.

Afghani trainees killed four soldiers outside the gate of Bagram AFB, and another trainee used what he learned to shoot an American general—the highest-ranking American serviceman killed in a war zone since Vietnam.[15] This general was in charge of overseeing all such training in Afghanistan, and the man who pulled the trigger had been vetted by the U.S. armed forces. The killer simply walked into the compound, having been invited as a trusted friend, went to the meeting, and shot the general in front of his armed staff.

Hmm. These training programs can really make you scratch your head. Remember those wackjobs who flew into the towers on 9/11? They were all trained to fly right here in the good ol' US of A, at private flight schools, admittedly.[16] Although there was no way of knowing beforehand that the training would be used against us—we do know it now. Knowing this history, the question begs to be asked: Who thought this Afghani training program was a good idea? Who thought we should use soldiers and DoD resources to make it happen? Are we not learning anything at all, or is the DoD simply manufacturing the evidence that we need to hear and see to support an ongoing war effort?

Even the Afghanis think we are nuts and wasting money on ineffective programs. Masood Farivar, an Afghani journalist who has written for the *New York Times*, was asked what all of this spending has accomplished. "The short answer is not much," Farivar said.[17] Or, as the International Crisis Group wrote in a report, "Despite billions of dollars in aid, state institutions remain fragile and unable to provide good governance, deliver basic services to the majority of the population or guarantee human security."[18] Of course, the former commander in Afghanistan, Karl Eikenberry, who is very much a part of the DoD machine, begs to differ. According to him, "There have been impressive gains in education and health," and "Transportation in Afghanistan is better than at any time in history."[19] This is no doubt true, since Afghanistan was a country with living standards that harked back to the Middle Ages when Americans arrived to fight the Taliban. It wouldn't have taken much to improve things.

Of course, Afghanistan is not the only place we are funneling billions of dollars into. You'd think that one of the questions we are all entitled to ask as American citizens would be: How much money have we spent on training the Iraqi army so that they can take over and police their own country? Unfortunately, this simple question elicits a number of vague responses. You have to follow the trail and do the math, and even then it's a little fuzzy. The DoD gets very creative when it uses that color of money coding system. As of 2013, here are the best estimates:[20]

- $1.32 billion spent on training exercises
- $2.6 billion spent on providing training gear, mainte-
  nance support, and logistical support
- $4.1 billion spent on building Iraqi military bases
- $237 million spent on helping Iraq build a counterter-
  rorism team

And it's not like the Iraqis are thrilled about all of this. According to the Special Investigator General for Iraq Reconstruction (SIGIR) there is a 3–8 percent AWOL rate every month, so their military is dwindling rather quickly.[21] A new campaign to recruit fresh members has been in the works for two years but has yet to be deployed. Those AWOL individuals could easily take the knowledge that they gained, turn around, and share it with insurgents. And they probably are doing just that. Good job, DoD. We train Iraqis in the fine art of warfare; the trainees jump ship, join the insurgents, and then share their knowledge and give us a reason to stay and fight.

Oh, and don't forget, we are also paying for humanitarian efforts in Iraq. Just like the $50 million "Arts and Crafts for Terrorists" fiasco in Afghanistan, we have a Sons of Iraq program (which is its official name, BTW). The goal of this program is the same—to give the citizens something to do beside train at the terrorist camps. This program, however, dwarfs the Afghani one, costing us taxpayers a whopping $370 million.[22] And of course there is no evidence at all that participants are not still training in terrorist camps or that there has been a decline in terrorist group membership. Three hundred and seventy million dollars to train Iraqis to do something other than be terrorists...Let that sink in for a minute.

We also spent hundreds of millions on unused facilities in Iraq: a $40 million prison just north of Baghdad and a $165 million children's hospital in the south both sit empty.[23] And that isn't even getting into the number of expensive facilities we've abandoned midconstruction.

Sorry, I digressed from the question: How much have we spent to train the Iraqi army? The short answer is that no one really knows. But our wallet is still open, and the funds are still flowing.

After all of this training and taxpayer money, Iraq apparently *still* isn't able to police itself. In July 2015, another batch of Eighty-Second Airborne Division troopers went to Iraq to support the Iraqi Army with training, logistics, and fire support.[24]

For all our commander in chief's talk of not tolerating terrorism, we sure are fond of giving money to countries that host terrorists. Countries that we know have and welcome a high population of ISIS members regularly get a bagful of money from us.

Who are these countries?[25]

Country	Total Aid in 2013
Afghanistan	$7.2 Billion
Syria	$795 Million
Pakistan	$980 Million
Iran	$1 Million

Why are we sending money to countries that are home to terrorist camps? Just like any parental figure who wants control, we will give you what you need until you end up depending on us. Then, if you misbehave, we cut that lifeline. We treat it as leverage. And then, when the DoD wants a little action, they can say, *Sure, no one wants a war, but they left us no choice. We tried to be nice. We gave them money, and they still didn't choose democracy. Now we have to send more troops and spend more money.* Of course it is not quite as simple as that, but that's what it all really boils down to.

Even if you're fond of that kind of strategy, you have to wonder why we're doing it on our own. Why are our allies not helping foot the bill? What about Saudi Arabia and the United Arab Emirates? These are filthy-rich countries within the immediate striking distance of those terrorists, and they're not chipping in their fair share. Why would they if they knew they didn't have to? America is so full of itself that it won't give up the idea of being *that* country that will forever pick up the tab. We've become the all-too-eager friend at the bar who always grabs the check when it's time to settle up. Even when you know he's broke, he'll still reach across the table and fight you for it until you eventually give in and let him pay.

It's simple: Other countries put the well-being of their own citizens first. Most other countries do not feel compelled to be the world's helicopter mom. Maybe if we stopped policing the world, we'd have more resources to help out our veterans who risked life and limb in these overseas efforts. Disabled veterans' benefits max out at a paltry $2,000 per month,[26] and the Veterans Health Administration is an inefficient joke. Trust me, I know firsthand: My grandfather died in a VA hospital. I'll never forget walking to his hospital room and hearing him moan in pain from down the hall. It was clear he was in pain, but there wasn't a nurse to be found anywhere. I had to physically track one down and walk her back to his room in order for my grandfather to receive the attention he needed. The VA health-care system is infamous for being ridden with malpractice, lack of care, and poor management. Systematic problems affecting VA hospitals may have killed more than a thousand veterans over the last decade, according to a 2014 report by Sen. Tom Coburn.[27]

We're picking up the tabs for endless, manufactured wars, but apparently we can't afford to give our disabled veterans the care they need.

The Business of War

The NFL is a great organization. Few things can make you feel as uniquely American as tuning in on Sunday in front of a big screen with a beer in one hand (and let's be honest, a beer in the other hand, too), and for good reason. The flag, the national anthem, the tributes to the troops worn on uniforms and acted out during halftime—this is a very patriotic game. You should watch those displays with a sense of pride, because you paid for them. Fourteen NFL teams were given $5.4 million by the DoD to include patriotic displays in their games.[28] How depressing is that? Is nothing off-limits to these insidious bureaucrats? They even have to pollute our love of football by turning it into something that is used to brainwash us? It should make you wonder what other tricks they are using to get you blindly dedicated to their wars.

It is a double slap, because up until recently the NFL was a nonprofit, meaning it didn't even pay taxes, *and still* it took that money from the DoD.[29] Your money. All in the name of making you feel more American and more dedicated to their warmongering.

The "Department of Defense" isn't even the best description for what they do. They should really be called the Department of Offense. Without a war, would we need all this bureaucracy? The war machine is always moving, and there are many jobs that depend upon it, down to the mailroom employees in the Pentagon. Of course no one is more dependent on the machine than the fat-cat contractors, except maybe the lobbyists that they hire.

Sometimes we're able to force spending cutbacks on the DoD, but it doesn't quite work out how you'd think it would. When the belt tightens on defense spending it is not the contractors, suppliers, or upper echelon that feel the cuts but the folks down in the trenches (literally, down in the trenches) that are pinched hardest of all: soldiers, sailors, airmen, marines—those who are actually risking their lives in the name of freedom. Even in government institutions, shit rolls straight downhill every time.

At outposts in Afghanistan's most dangerous areas, meals were cut back from three per day to one, supplemented with one MRE (basically preserved, vacuum-packed human chow) because it was deemed too costly to get food to these places.[30] All the while, Afghani nationals stayed gainfully employed preparing meals at Bagram AFB and other hub locations. We aren't about to lay them off, because we don't want to cause a rift with their local tribes. Dallas-based Kellogg, Brown, &

Root is the Army contracting company that "hires locals to cook." You may have heard of KBR as well as Fluor and Dyn-Corp, all card-carrying members of the military-industrial complex.

No one wanted to lay off the Afghanis, but it's apparently just fine to starve our soldiers. What kind of messed-up priorities do we have when our own Department of Defense respects the rights of those who want to see us dead and allows our soldiers to go hungry simply because it ups their bottom line?

The DoD isn't trying to cover this up, either. No, they have something much more sinister in mind. Instead they're advertising that the soldiers do not have enough supplies and are using them as poster children for convincing us to pump more money into the defense budget. At the time of this writing, the DoD website has a section dedicated entirely to freaking us out over budget cuts.[31] A big banner across the page says, "Sequestration: Across-the-board cuts could threaten national security." We all know that strong supply chains win wars. Hungry soldiers cannot fight. Unfortunately, the DoD neglects to mention that big defense contractors continue to make millions during these times of "financial crisis" and are in no risk of losing their hold on the government teat.

Still having a hard time wrapping your brain around the military-industrial complex? The military's use of MRAP (Mine Resistant Ambush Protected) vehicles is another good example of the iron triangle in action. When the never-ending war in Iraq first started, young men and women were regularly being blown up by IEDs (Improvised Explosive Devices) as they drove along the nation's roadways. The Humvees that they drove were not reinforced and could not withstand the impact of the explosions.

Enter the MRAP vehicles. These monstrous troop carriers could withstand a direct hit from an IED and easily protect the passengers, or so the story goes. Under pressure from then defense secretary Robert Gates, the Pentagon pushed for the funding to get these vehicles in 2004. They went from inception, to testing, to production very quickly, and today there are almost twenty-eight thousand MRAPs in existence.[32]

The DoD spent $373 million on the MRAP initiative using three different government contractors employing thirty thousand employees each to manufacture the vehicles.[33] They were fraught with problems from the beginning but largely self-regulated by the companies manufacturing them. Sort of like an honors system, because, ya know, people are usually very honest when it comes to making money off the government. (Right!) One of the manufacturing partners in the MRAP fiasco was General Dynamics, which was sued by the feds a few years later for using "faulty parts" and defrauding the government.[34] Surprise, surprise!

There was no government standard, just a wink and a nod from the contractors that everything was OK. In 2014, when the drawdown began in Afghanistan, it was decided that MRAPs were too costly to return to the states, and it just so happens that production came to a halt because, according to Deputy Secretary of Defense Ashton Carter, "a new strategic era is dawning."[35] The Pentagon now predicts that there will be a need for a faster, lighter ground vehicle. Really? Have the insurgents stopped making IEDs?

Let's get real: MRAPs were simply another folly of the military-industrial machine. They often rolled over during operations, trapping the occupants who were under enemy fire, so when the opportunity came to retire them, everyone got on board with the idea of the vehicles being "too expensive" to ship back. Because that was much easier than telling the defense contractors who built them, "Hey, you guys ripped us off, and we want our money back."

No longer wanted by the military, brand new MRAPs, still covered in plastic, were chopped up by contractors from DynCorp and Fluor, then thrown in ditches, covered with jet fuel, and burned throughout Afghanistan.[36] Some of these vehicles, along with other military surplus, will be sold off to allies, which always works out sooooo well for us. Not too long ago, who was our ally, but Afghanistan, in the fight against Russia. And that general I mentioned earlier shot by an Afghan? He was killed by a NATO-issued weapon.[37] And then there's the disturbing fact that we accidentally armed ISIS. At least 74,000 machine guns, 2,300 Humvees, and 40 M1A battle tanks left behind by the U.S.-backed Iraqi army in Mosul were taken by ISIS militants in 2014, and are now being used against us.[38] Maybe during the next go-round, our new enemies who were once allies will run us over with our old MRAPs.

Of course, the DoD refuses to admit what an utter failure the MRAP initiative was. Information about the program is full of propaganda that includes wild estimates of all the lives they saved (which has never been documented officially).

If they worked so well, why get rid of them—especially since hundreds of millions of dollars was spent to manufacture them? Does somebody else need a job; is that why a change has been announced? Is there a defense contractor waiting in the wings to fulfill a large order that was promised for some new vehicle that will also be decommissioned ten years down the road?

This is only one example of how once the war machine gets chugging, it's hard to stop and hard to figure out. We do know that at least $373 million was spent on vehicles that will now be destroyed or sold or given away to allies.[39] And according to the secretary of defense, we are still at war.

There are only two items in the federal budget ahead of the DoD in spending. "Federal pensions" and "federal health insurance" are numbers one and two on Uncle Sam's list of bills, with defense as number three. I am not certain if it's sad, or just so ironic that it's funny, that the only two things that beat out spending for wars are benefits for the same government officials who benefit from the war machine.

We Must Protect This House

Yes, the DoD is a necessity. It helps to keep our country safe, but the key word is *defense*, and in many instances we are not on the defense; we are on the offense. When people refer to the government as "they," it distorts reality. We are "they." We cannot blame "them" if we are not proactive. We are a citizen government, and we can set the agenda. Here is a piece of advice we should all follow: Don't try to clean anyone else's house until yours is spotless. We have so many domestic issues that need to be addressed that, frankly, we cannot afford to fix any other country's problems right now. They, them, us, we need to take a good hard look at what is happening right here in our own backyard and put some money back where it belongs. It's time that the DoD is paid attention to and held accountable.

The balance is off, and it is time for it to be restored. We can be safe without spending trillions of dollars and losing thousands of young lives. It can happen; we just need to break old habits. If "No one wants a war," let's take that to heart and focus on our problems at home.

Finding Common Sense on Common Ground

So when Sam, your flag-waving cousin, says...

> "If 'Murica doesn't protect the world from tyranny,
> who the hell will?"

You say: "Why should it be our job to protect the whole world? We should focus on helping our own citizens, and taking care of the problems right here at home, before trying to save the entire globe."

> "Isn't giving disability to soldiers a handout that will
> just balloon the welfare state?"

You say: "You throw yourself in front of a bullet for my freedom and you get my support any day."

> "Wouldn't we be living on Planet Nazi if we had
> 'kept out of it' during the Second World War?"

You say: "There are wars of choice and wars of necessity. The Second World War was a war of necessity—but not Korea or Vietnam and definitely not Iraq. Nuff said."

"C'mon, we're not imperialists! We're the greatest,
most prosperous democracy in the world. Why
shouldn't we help other countries be like us?"

You say: "Stop living in the past. We're not so 'star-spangled awesome' anymore. Like that Jeff Daniels character in *The Newsroom* said, we lead the world in only three categories: number of incarcerated citizens per capita, number of adults who believe angels are real, and defense spending—more than the next twenty-six countries *combined*—twenty-five of whom are our *allies*. Besides, it's none of our damn business how other countries decide to govern themselves."

"You got a problem with the Department of Defense
paying NFL teams to wave the flag? That just ain't
American!"

You say: "I love the red, white, and blue pregame as much as anyone but not the $337 million F-35C fighter jet flybys. I can't afford leather seats in my own car, why should I pay for theirs?"

"How can you blame the defense spending
free-for-all on the elephants when two of the three
most unnecessary wars were started by donkeys?"

You say: "Republicans almost had me at hello, but it's both parties who are at fault. Power corrupts any animal in the big chair. No one's innocent in D.C."

CHAPTER 4

How Do You Spell "Educashun"?

"Can I be excused for the rest of my life?"
~ SpongeBob Squarepants ~

When I was a little girl, I used to fantasize about having a pen pal. The idea of sending a letter to some other kid in a far-off place and having her respond was strangely enticing. For those of you who remember, the late nineties was a simpler time. If you wanted to learn about a foreign place, you had to either read an encyclopedia (a cumbersome chore) or get a pen pal.

Through the grapevine, my mom found out about a service that would provide you with the name and address of a kid who lived in a faraway city. I was ecstatic when I found out that my new pen pal, a kid named Sasha, lived in Los Angeles. I knew that Hollywood is in LA, and I immediately imagined Sasha having lunch with Britney Spears and Mariah Carey. I fantasized that she wore glamorous designer brands and partied with celebrities. I was sure her life was way better than my simple life in rural New Hampshire.

In my first letter to Sasha, I included some photos of me, my friends, my family, my house, and my dog, Scruffles. I told her how excited I was to have a real pen pal from Hollywood.

Two weeks later, I received a response—straight from LA! I tore open the envelope in which she had stuffed in lots of pictures of her own.

My mouth dropped open at what I saw.

Sasha, a pretty young black girl, had also sent me pictures of her with family and friends. But Britney Spears and Mariah Carey weren't in them. There were no pictures of Hollywood movie sets or glamorous beaches.

I still have the photos Sasha sent me. One was of her with her mother and three brothers. They stood in front of a small house with peeling paint. There were also several snapshots of Sasha with her friends at school. Her school, which looked more like a prison, complete with bars on the windows, exposed me to something I had never seen in my short life: inner-city public facilities.

There appeared to be forty or more small, sticky-looking desks stuffed into the dingy classroom. The kids looked so much older—and tougher—than the ones I went to school with. There was no teacher in sight.

I couldn't believe it. My public elementary school had bright, welcoming decorations, new computers, spacious desks, and nice teachers who were always there when we needed help.

I continued to write to Sasha for a couple of years— eventually the iPod was invented, and we got bored with each other. But by getting a glimpse of her world, I learned that our country is an unfair place. Not every kid here gets an equal shot.

I just accepted that fact as I grew older: Some places were poor and simply couldn't afford good teachers or new equipment. It sucked, but that was just the way things were, I thought.

But then, the teachers' strike happened in Chicago—a city with one of the worst public school districts in the nation—and my eyes were opened. Teachers, many of whom complained about how thankless their jobs were, walked out on students for *weeks* because they thought they deserved a pay raise. Around the same time, cell phone video started to emerge of truly awful, lazy teachers in those same Chicago schools, letting their classroom become a circus while they sat back and ignored their students.

Turns out, these teachers weren't making peanuts, either. In Chicago, the "bad" teachers were making $75,000 per year—which was significantly more than teachers at Chicago's private schools (where the "rich" kids are sent).[1] Not only that, but public school teachers work an average of only thirty-six hours per week, for a portion of the year. If you break down their salary per hour, they're making more money than nurses, accountants, and architects. But still not as much as NFL players or Hilton sisters. Unfair! Better strike!

If these public school teachers are making so much money, why do so many of their schools suck?

I have two words for you, my friends: teachers' unions.

Plain and simple, the Chicago Teachers Union doesn't care about the city's students. While 93 percent of the teachers are rated superior or excellent,[2] kids are graduating from high school with little more than a fifth-grade education, and 80 percent of eighth graders in the city are not proficient in mathematics.[3]

Yeah, these teachers sound *really* superior. Give me a break.

And many left-wing politicians are no better than these union stooges. Former President Obama, Hillary Clinton, and Al Gore—all who call themselves pro-union—sent their own children to private schools.

It's not that hard to figure out what's really going on. In the private sector, ineffective employees are fired. Those who work hard are rewarded with raises and promotions. The same thing should be happening in our public schools: Fire all the lazy teachers and reward those who are making an effort. After all, there are still teachers who work hard and inspire our youth to succeed (thanks again, Mrs. Johnson!).

Teachers' unions put the kids at risk by taking the focus away from the students and attempt to protect the teacher above all else. It doesn't matter if some children get left behind. It doesn't matter that the United States doesn't even make it into the top ten in education ranking anymore.[4] None of it matters, because these are government workers who are unionized, and their rights apparently come before a child's right to learn. And according to them, union rights include things like huge pay raises and million-dollar pensions.[5] Must be nice. In many states, the unions have become so powerful that teachers are actually forced to join them. In Illinois, for example, state workers *must* pay "fair share" fees to unions for collective bargaining.[6] For years, Illinois Republican governor Bruce Rauner has been fighting to allow state workers to opt out of union fees.[7]

It's such a simple solution, and not without precedent. Some states have right-to-work laws, which let state employees decide for themselves whether or not they want to join or give money to a union. There's no reason why every state shouldn't have these laws in place. Union fees are often used to negotiate directly with the government, so the dues you pay are essentially funding political activity. No one should be forced to fund a political effort they don't support, period. But of course, the mighty unions continue to fight right-to-work laws tooth and nail, since they spell less revenue and less political sway for the unions. And without all that power, ineffective state workers would be at risk of (gasp) being fired.

In all industries—except, of course, those run by the federal government—if you don't perform up to standard, you get booted out the door and replaced by someone who will. That's how free markets become strong—by eliminating their weakest links. In order to get rid of the teachers who just don't make the grade, the teachers' union juggernaut would need to be dismantled. Unfortunately, though, this has become nearly impossible.

These unions have been lining the pockets of public servants for decades. Obama received $400 million from unions during his 2008 presidential campaign, and another huge lump sum in 2012.[8] Teachers' unions contributed $16 million to support Democrats leading up to the 2014 midterm election—you know, the one when almost nobody votes?[9] It isn't hard to see why Obama and his buddies on the left will do everything possible not to piss off union leaders or decrease their pay. These politicians keep the unions in business and are rewarded for it each election with fat campaign contributions. And ultimately, no one really is looking after the interests of the kids.

Want to Teach Your Own Kids?

Back when I was a college student, I met Becky in a Boston café, where we were both working on our laptops. When I first glanced over at her, all I saw was hair—a black, unbrushed mane that cascaded down her back. We started chatting after she noticed my screen saver, a picture of my dad's obese bulldog, Buster (her family had a bulldog, too—bulldog owners are obsessed with bulldogs; it's kind of a cult thing).

Becky and I spent the rest of the afternoon talking and not working. She was a graduate student in the music department of an elite university in Boston. She had two pet ferrets in her apartment. She knew everything about every Woody Allen movie. She had backpacked all around South America. This chick was *awesome*.

Later on, I found out that Becky had been homeschooled growing up. Instead of sending her to a public high school, her dad taught her himself, on a sailboat; they traveled around the world while Becky explored and read about subjects that fascinated her. Oftentimes, she told me, she and her dad would sail to the locations that she was learning about in her history books. How supercool is that?

As I've gotten older, I've noticed that whenever I meet someone especially interesting, 95 percent of the time it turns out they were homeschooled. Many U.S. parents are so disgusted with the state of public education they have decided to take matters into their own hands. Some homeschool for religious reasons, and others, like Becky's father, simply believe in a different approach to education. Currently, over 1.7 million

U.S. students are homeschooled—that's roughly 3.4 percent of the school-aged population.[10] Statistically speaking, these students fare better than their publicly educated counterparts, typically scoring 15–30 percent higher on standardized tests.[11]

Right now, there are no federal laws that apply to homeschoolers, but there have been many attempts to pass legislation that would affect homeschoolers. Teachers' unions have been the biggest critics of homeschooling (surprise, surprise). The California Teachers Association once claimed in a court brief that allowing parents to educate their children from home would result in "educational anarchy."[12]

But the attack against homeschooling doesn't stop with the unions. In 2008, a judge in Los Angeles's Second District Court of Appeals essentially ruled that homeschooling was illegal in California. All children aged six to eighteen must be taught by credentialed teachers in public or private schools, the ruling stated. If parents wanted to teach their kids from home, they had to obtain a teaching degree. And if they didn't comply, they'd be subject to criminal action.[13] That's right—people trying to educate their own children without the proper government credentials were criminals, according to California. Those terrible, terrible people, thinking they have the right to teach their children anything. How dare they!

Can you imagine going to jail for teaching your kid second-grade math? Just don't tell the judge you also packed little Johnny's lunch without first getting a culinary arts degree and then drove him to the library without a commercial driver's license for transporting schoolchildren.

The controversial California ruling was made after a couple, Philip and Mary Long, tried to homeschool their children for religious reasons. At first, this particular case wasn't so much about homeschooling as it was about "child safety." There were allegations of abuse by one of the Long's seven children. The abuse charges were later deemed unfounded, but the battle for the right to homeschool wound up taking precedence in the matter. Eventually, after a long battle, the Home School Legal Defense Association was able to get the judges to recant their earlier opinion.[14] Still, the fact that some smug, all-powerful judge thought he could strip parents of the right to control their own children's education is seriously scary stuff.

Homeschooling is a great thing, but it's not an option for many households, especially if both parents have full-time jobs. Thankfully, there's another option for these families if the local public school isn't up to par: charter schools.

Kids in poor inner-city neighborhoods usually get the short end of the stick when it comes to education. Because parents of these children can't afford private school tuition costing tens of thousands of dollars a year, the children often wind up in public schools that are falling apart and run by ineffective, unionized teachers. That's why charter schools are so critical for these kids.

Charter schools receive public funding but are operated privately—the local school district has zero jurisdiction over them. Students are allowed to attend free of charge. There are over 6,500 charter schools in the United States with millions of children enrolled.[15] The beauty of these schools is their autonomy and their freedom to teach and experiment with different methods. Yes, I just wrote *freedom* and *teach* in the same sentence! Crazy, right?

Even though charter schools have only been around since 1992, many have already achieved phenomenal success. Underprivileged kids in New York City have been given the chance to succeed through the city's thirty-two Success Academy Charter Schools. Free from government one-size-fits-all curricula, Success inspires its students with activities like art, dance, theater, and chess.

The schools set a high bar for students. Discipline and high academic performance are not simply sought after, they're expected. Students' test scores are often posted in the hallway for all to see—those who are in the "red zone," at the bottom of the list, are given aggressive help until they get back on track.[16]

Students, who all wear uniforms, must sit in class with their backs straight and their feet on the floor. They walk to and from class in orderly, single-file lines. Success doesn't tolerate doped out kids wandering through the halls, arrogant Justin Bieber wannabes talking back to teachers, and girls parading around with butt cheeks hanging out of miniskirts. The school does everything possible to make sure their students are engaged and learning.

And it helps to have good teachers. Bucking teachers' unions, the effective educators at Success Academy are promoted quickly; some of the New York charter schools even have principals who are in their twenties.[17] And the teachers who don't produce results are demoted or fired.

Success's students are primarily poor minority kids who would otherwise be at some of the nation's worst public schools. Yet Success continues to outperform not just the surrounding public schools but also those in many of New York's wealthiest suburbs. Get this: During 2014 in New York City, 29 percent of students at public schools passed the state reading tests, while 64 percent of students at Success passed the same tests. When it came to state math tests, only 35 percent of students at public schools passed compared to 94 percent of the students at Success.[18]

Translation: Success has been a big effing success.

And here's the real kicker: they're achieving better results with fewer taxpayer dollars. On average, charter schools receive $3,814 less in federal funding *per student* than public schools.[19]

Despite this astounding success and cost-efficiency, government officials have gone out of their way to make it as hard as possible for charter schools to exist. In February 2014, New York City mayor Bill de Blasio attempted to punish the city's charter schools by reversing a former policy that allowed them to operate in public buildings for free. De Blasio actually evicted three of the Success schools from the spaces in which they were operating. Thankfully, the state's governor, Andrew Cuomo, stepped in and found other space for those three schools to use.[20]

Charter schools are a threat to the status quo. The success of these schools cannot be denied, and that makes the people in power nervous. Some states are more charter-friendly than others. Louisiana recently stepped up to the plate for their kids, developing the first charter school district in New Orleans. Since this initiative, 91 percent of New Orleans's students now attend charter schools. The result? A rise from a pathetic high school graduation rate of 54 percent to an encouraging 78 percent.[21] And that figure is expected to climb over the next few years.

Implementing a charter school district was a bold move. The local government realized that its public school system simply wasn't getting the job done, and they actually did something productive about it.

It's not just Louisiana that's putting its kids first. Tennessee is also proactively improving education in the inner city. In the state's lowest-performing public schools, just one in six kids can read on their grade level. The worst of these schools—those in the bottom 5 percent—are being transformed into charters. Tennessee has set a goal of moving these schools into the top 25 percent over the next five years.

While that may sound very ambitious, it's evidently possible. It's already happening at the Hanley Elementary School in Memphis. Initially, just 3 percent of Hanley's students were reading at grade level. But after it was taken over by Aspire Public Schools, a California-based charter organization, that figure jumped to 25 percent.[22] The proof is in the scores. Charter schools are offering better opportunities for the students most in need.

Tennessee and Louisiana should be applauded for putting their kids above political BS. What are other states waiting for? Charters have clearly built the proverbial better mousetrap. Perhaps it is time for big government to step out of the way of education reform.

Why Do We Need the Department of Education?

Let's look at the money pit called the Department of Education (DoE) and all of the wonderful, noble, amazing things it has done to shape our education system.

(Crickets.)

OK, bear with me. The DoE began in 1980 as the result of combining several education-related agencies. Think of it as a bunch of agencies rolled into one big government burrito. Currently the DoE has over 4,400 employees with a budget of $69 billion.[23] What are we getting for our $69 billion?

Reality Check: The federal government has *no* business in education. Zero. The Tenth Amendment states: "The powers not delegated to the United States by the Constitution, nor prohibited by it to the States, are reserved to the States respectively, or to the people." Education is not one of the powers granted to the federal government by the Constitution and therefore belongs in the capable hands of the individual states or the people.

Aside from all of this Tenth Amendment business, the DoE is just plain redundant. We're being forced to foot the bill for 4,400 DoE employees at the federal level when we already have state departments of education in place. Go look at virtually any state's education department website, and you'll find a description of services that is very similar to the one given by the DoE on its website. Wait...what? That means we taxpayers are being charged twice for what appear to be the same services (which we clearly are not getting from either group, if you consider the state of education in the United States).

And the question still begs to be answered: What, exactly, has the DoE done for us in the last forty years? The answer is—drumroll, please—nothing. Since the DoE's inception, high school students' reading and math scores have not changed. In fact, in 1999, there was actually a decline in scores (I blame Limp Bizkit). And between 1996 and 2005, there was a similar decline in science scores.

But hey, science isn't even that important anyway, right?! During this four-decade poop fest, spending per pupil has risen dramatically. A study by Andrew Coulson at the Cato Institute shows that each student who graduated in 2009 was worth around $151,000 in federal spending; that's three times what it cost to get a kid through the public school system in 1970.[24]

Another primary goal of the DoE was "closing the achievement gap" in education by income, minority status, and education. This was a big seller when the agency was launched, but unfortunately, time has shown yet another DoE failure. According to Coulson's Cato Institute study:

> Test score breakdowns by family income are not available, but we do have something close: a breakdown by parents' level of education. This allows us to compare the children of high school dropouts to those of college graduates. In Reading and Science, the gap between these students has not narrowed in 40 years. In Math it has narrowed by barely one percent of the test score scale. So, here again, federal appropriations and the programs they have funded have failed to achieve their goals.[25]

Bottom line: More money doesn't necessarily mean better (or more equal) education. The DoE has failed miserably and should be dismantled. The time has come to change the way we oversee education in the United States.

The government tends to give its agencies really important titles, like the "Department of Education," so that their existence seems essential. But in reality, most of these agencies don't really do much at all, other than staff themselves with overpaid, pencil-pushing bureaucrats who try to force mandates on the rest of the country. Because if you have a fancy office in Washington, D.C., you know what's best for everyone else!

There is a psychological theory called learned helplessness, which basically states that you can teach people to be helpless and convince them that they cannot function without you. It happens a lot with battered women. Are we just battered Americans at this point? The feds have convinced the majority that we *need* them for guidance when it comes to education. What will we do without the Department of Education?! Where will we get money to fund our schools?! Who will make sure everyone is playing nice and fair if we do not have this ginormous bureaucracy looking over our shoulders?!

Well, what did we do before 1980? Give the money and the control to the states. A simple answer. But as you'll see, the government isn't really a fan of simple answers.

Mind Control

Just when you think the government couldn't make things any worse, along comes the new "solution" for education reform. It's called Common Core, a uniform curriculum for schools around the nation, and it's contributed big time to the downward spiral of education in America.

How bad can it be? *Really* bad. By attaching demands to federal money, Washington is attempting to control what every U.S. student learns.

According to the propaganda on the official Common Core Standards website, "Forty-two states, the District of Columbia, four territories, and the Department of Defense Education Activity (DoDEA) have voluntarily adopted and are moving forward with the Common Core."[26]

"Voluntarily adopted." Ha! What they aren't telling you is that, as a part of this so-called voluntary project, $4.35 billion was offered to states that signed on to Common Core under the guise of the "Race to the Top" grants.[27] Now, technically, any state could apply for that assistance whether or not they'd signed on to the feds' new program, but if they didn't, what do you think their chances would be of getting a taste of that cash?

This doesn't sound much like reform to me. It sounds like coercion. And at a time when we have entire districts of decrepit schools like Sasha's, the feds choose now to try and foist their new system on us using our own money as leverage.

So how did it work out for the handful of states that said no to Common Core? Virginia said no and then put in an application for their share of the Race to the Top funding. And guess what? *BZZT!* Aw, so sorry.[28] On the other hand, Rick Perry down in Texas said no to Common Core and added, *BTW, you can keep your money.* The governor said, "Texas is on the right path toward improved education, and we would be foolish and irresponsible to place our children's future in the hands of unelected bureaucrats and special interest groups thousands of miles away in Washington, virtually eliminating parents' participation in their children's education."[29] *Thank you, Rick Perry!* At least you got one thing right!

This bribe money was so enticing that some states agreed to sign up for Common Core *before* the curriculum was even completed.[30] These states had no idea what they were signing up for. All they knew was that a big pile of money would be involved. Kentucky was the first state to adopt the Common Core, sight unseen. What made them think that could be a good idea? People of Kentucky, take note. This is who is running your state.

The DoE tries to make Common Core sound sooooo appealing: Everyone will be treated the same, every state will have the same standards, blah blah blah!!! Let me remind you that it is *illegal* for the federal government to get mixed up with education, yet they've all but put the presidential seal on Common Core. And of course, the DoE is blatant about ignoring the Constitution with that funding carrot they dangle.

But the real problem with Common Core is the curriculum itself and the geniuses who came up with it. The Gates Foundation (run by Bill and Melinda Gates—a couple of billionaire bleeding-heart liberals) spent $200 million pushing the Common Core plan.[31] Microsoft will also be selling all the software each of the school districts uses to train teachers in the new standards.[32] They even unabashedly have a link on their website to assist with the "Tech Essentials for Testing Success," which describes in detail how schools using Common Core tests will need to spend tons of money on new Microsoft products. "For many schools, time is running out," Microsoft warned. "In a report issued by Smarter Balanced in 2012, it found that 56.1 percent of K–12 schools reporting were still running on aging Windows XP, which had an end of service (EOS) date of April 8, 2014. In the face of this looming cutoff of support, it's recommended by IT professionals to migrate to the new Windows as soon as possible."[33]

In an interview, Mr. Gates did a lot of hemming and hawing when asked how much he stands to gain from Common Core.[34] Making money is a wonderful thing, but using a philanthropic organization to further your profits at the expense of kids' education? Pretty shameful.

A 2016 undercover investigation led by journalist James O'Keefe reported more shady Common Core business practices: A $1.3 billion Common Core iPad contract was given to Pearson Education in a bidding process that was questionable, at best. Pearson sales executive Kim Koerber told one of O'Keefe's undercover journalists, "The contract was written for Pearson to win. All the companies knew that…Everybody knew that it was written for Pearson."

The group with the guts actually to stand up and take credit for Common Core is a think tank in D.C. called Achieve.[35] Its chairman, Craig Barrett, is also the former CEO of Intel and still a shareholder in that company.[36] All the Common Core student assessment testing will be taken using a computer, and Intel is the world's largest microprocessor manufacturer by far. It's hard to say exactly how much loot computer companies like Intel are set to rake in, but let's just go with a shitload. CNBC did a little breakdown of the top contract awards and threw out some estimates, and wow.[37] Let's just say that Common Core is a multi-*billion*-dollar business.

But let's ignore the conflicts of interest for a moment. This is, after all, about the kids, and unfortunately, the worst part about Common Core is the teaching methods. Parents around the country hate Common Core, complaining that the methods make no sense.[38] Even some celebs have spoken out about the insanity. After his kids came home with nonsensical Common Core math problems, comedian Louis C.K. tweeted, "My kids used to love math! Now it makes them cry."[39]

It's easy to see why he was so pissed. Take a look at a few nonsensical math problems from real Common Core textbooks (and if you think I'm cherry picking, just Google "Common Core math problems," and you'll see countless similar examples):

1. Overcomplicated "addition sequences" are used in order to find the answer to simple problems. Does the problem below make any sense to you?[40]

   Add 26 + 17 by breaking apart numbers to make a ten.
   Use a number that adds with the 6 in 26 to make a 10.
   Since 6 + 4 = 10, use 4.
   Think: 17 = 4 + 13.
   Add 26 + 4 = 30.
   Add 30 + 13 = 43.
   So, 26 + 17 = 43.

2. The following Common Core question was taken from a state exam in New York. Is it just me, or is this seriously confusing for no reason at all?[41]

   There were 54 apples set aside as a snack for 3 classes of students. The teachers divided up the apples and placed equal amounts on 9 separate trays. If each of the 3 classes received the same number of trays, how many apples did each class get?

A) 2

B) 6

C) 18

D) 27

So this is essentially asking what 54 divided by 3 is. What is the reason for the question's second sentence, other than to confuse students unnecessarily?

And Common Core's foolishness doesn't stop with math. Some of the curriculum's suggested nonfiction reading material is just plain pornographic. Sophomores at Buena High School in Sierra Vista, Arizona were assigned to read the Common Core–suggested novel *Dreaming in Cuban* by Cristina Garcia.[42] If you haven't read it, I'll save you some time. It includes explicit scenes of bondage and borderline violent sexual acts, which these high schoolers were asked to read out loud.

I don't know about you, but I felt a little awkward as a young teen having to read certain passages of *Romeo and Juliet* out loud. But narrating a sex scene in which the characters tie each other up, slap each other, and call each other, "My bitch," well, that would have left me just about as scarred as the characters—and with a total misconception of what a healthy sexual relationship was like.

This kind of situation is rampant with Common Core. A school district in Newburgh, New York, spent $6,000 on copies of another book recommended by the curriculum, *Black Swan Green* by David Mitchell. The plan was to distribute them to ninth graders, but administrators refused to do so after noticing the book's graphic contents.[43] The book's narrator describes his father's penis, as well as vivid details about a couple having sex. The words *dick*, *cock*, and *erect penis* show up on at least eleven different pages of *Black Swan Green*. Not exactly the kind of educational reading most parents have in mind.

In May 2014, William Baer, a father from Gilford, New Hampshire, learned about a sexually graphic book that had been assigned in his daughter's school under the Common Core standards. When he showed up at a school board meeting to address the issue, the board members cut him off and demanded that he "be respectful of other people."[44] When he refused to be silenced, a cop showed up and actually arrested him, handcuffs and all. Baer was ultimately charged with disorderly conduct.

There are several disturbing aspects to this story. First, Baer was never notified that his daughter would be exposed to explicit reading material, which schools usually do when it comes to sex ed and the like. He had to find out on his own. Second, of course, is that he was arrested because he had the *nerve* to be concerned about what was being taught to his own daughter! Clearly, he is one of those "educational anarchists" who wants to be involved in his kids' education. Slam his ass in jail!

With this kind of material making up the Common Core reading lists, all parents should be concerned. I don't have kids at home (unless you count my eight-pound Chihuahua,

Scrappy), but I can imagine that it's not exactly ideal to come home and find your fourteen-year-old child reading about a father's "erect penis." Seriously, how do you even broach the subject at the dinner table? "How was your day at school, sweetie?" "Oh it was great, Mom! We read about Hugo biting Felicia's nipples and leaving bruises on her upper thighs. Can you pass the mashed potatoes?"

No parent wants that for his or her children, but at least this whole mess carries a glimmer of hope. Lots of states are now realizing what a terrible decision this was, and one by one, they're now scrapping Common Core. Indiana and Oklahoma have already dropped out, and at the time of this writing four other undisclosed states are reviewing their stake in the program. Let's hope by the time you're reading this, Common Core will be on its way out and with it reading assignments about fathers' penises.

Thankfully, high school doesn't last forever. At least once your kid moves on to college it will be smooth sailing, right? Nope! If you thought that grade school was a study in frustration...

Higher (Priced) Education

Wait until you confront the catastrophe of college, and I'm not talking about that one night at Stinger's after the $2 Purple Nurple shooter specials. The higher education system is another example of how we get jerked around by the overreaching hand of the federal government. We all know how much of a hit in the wallet college can be, and you might still be feeling it. Tuition has ballooned by 500 percent over the last thirty years and doesn't appear to be dropping anytime soon.

Private and public colleges cost an average of $29,000 and $22,000 per year, respectively. Many of the more prominent universities, such as Tufts and Sarah Lawrence College, will set the family back by over twice that amount. These ridiculously fat price tags have led to the average college graduate walking away with more than $27,000 in student loan debt.[45] And if you want to attend medical or law school afterward, you can add a big fat zero to that figure.

But hey, it's cool. At least most of us can pay off our debt quickly, since we've all landed top jobs thanks to our pricey college degrees. Right? Wrong! A whopping 53 percent of new college graduates are either jobless or underemployed.[46] How often do you hear NBC or CNN reminding us of these figures? Way too much, right? Kind of a buzzkill. But what they never talk about is the federal government's role in exorbitant tuition fees and colossal student debts.

Government student loans and grants were created to help low-income families afford college. In principle, that's not a bad thing. But as they say, "The road to hell is paved with good intentions." About 95 percent of college students borrow money to pay for college, and most of them are borrowing from the government.[47] The federal government funds more than 70 percent of all student aid.[48] And just like that, government assistance does more harm than good. Essentially, any student can qualify for as much money as they need to cover their education, no matter how high the tuition. Sounds great, doesn't it? But what does this do? Are you sitting down? This enables colleges to continue to increase their rates, because no matter what they charge, students will always be able to find the means to finance it with money from our pocketbooks.

Washington bureaucrats have been pushing unlimited government student loans for years. At this point, we've all been programmed to believe that more money is the answer to all of our nation's higher education problems. President Obama has repeatedly stated that this student entitlement money is necessary to ensure that young people are getting the education they need, but he's simply failing to acknowledge the facts.

New research by economists at the Federal Reserve Bank of New York shows that government-sponsored financial aid helps colleges more than students (shocker).[49] In addition to federal loans, government-subsidized Pell Grants are given to low-income students. They are not repaid, and they're horribly inefficient. For each additional dollar given to these students through Pell Grants, their tuition actually *increases* by 55 cents. Put simply, each tax dollar that goes to Pell Grants will save needy students only 45 cents. Federal subsidized loans, which are income capped and go to low- and middle-class families, are even worse. They increase college tuition by 70 cents for every dollar given, essentially reducing them to charitable-sounding wealth transfers to universities. Using our money.

Once you look at the numbers, it's obvious that the federal government is hardly helping students by giving out "aid" like candy; rather, it's the colleges that are making out like bandits.

It's simple economics: when colleges see an increase in financial aid, they raise tuition simply because they can. There's no need for colleges to compete with each other on the basis of price. No matter what they charge for tuition, students will always be able to cover it with the help of the good ol' reliable government ATM.

And what, exactly, do universities do with all of this extra cash? Often, they spend it on vanity features and unnecessary amenities to make their campuses more attractive to prospective students. Overpriced universities around the country have installed lavish rock-climbing gyms, spas, karaoke lounges, hot tubs, arcades, and movie theaters on campus.[50] And guess who's writing the checks for all this fancy stuff? We, the taxpayers. The funds are not going to improved education but instead to the betterment of the amenities, all in a bid to justify the cost of tuition. It should also be pointed out that a lot of this money is going to private colleges; at least state schools openly admit that they rely on taxpayer money.

Universities are also spending the loan and tuition money on administrators—that is, people who sit at desks on campus and supposedly do stuff. (What stuff, you ask? I'll let you know when someone figures that out.) I'm talking about college deans, vice presidents, associate vice presidents—all with armies of assistants. In the last forty years, the number of these so-called college administrators has increased by 85 percent.[51]

Now, how do we fix this mess? The free market, duh! If the federal government scaled back on the loans, students wouldn't be able to afford many of the nation's most prominent universities. Cost would become a much bigger factor for prospective students choosing a university. Schools like Boston University, which charge almost $50,000 per year, would see their admission numbers fall drastically and might not even be able to fill all of their slots. BU and the others would be forced to lower their tuition rates and actually compete for the brightest students based on cost and quality of education—not just their lounges and spas.

For-profit colleges are also a big part of the problem, receiving significant amounts of funding from government-subsidized student loans. For-profit universities make up only 12 percent of all postsecondary students, but they account for around 25 percent of student-aid funds from the Department of Education.[52] Yes, your tax dollars are helping subsidize those cheesy University of Phoenix commercials. And tuition at these schools isn't cheap. For-profit universities have steep prices because tuitions at their nonprofit competitors are so high. University of Phoenix doesn't need to lower pricing much in order to be competitive in the marketplace, because the for-profit schools like NYU charge students nearly $64,000 per year to attend.[53]

Of course, financial aid should still be available to those who truly need it. But by subsidizing tuition for the majority of the nation's college students, the government is only driving up costs and lining the pockets of overpaid campus administrators. Until a change is made, college will continue to earn a big, fat F at living up to its promise of the American Dream for our nation's youth. Fourteen percent of waiters and 16.5 percent of bartenders in the United States have a bachelor's degree, with an average price tag of $120,000.[54]

Until Washington stops indirectly inflating the price of tuition, many degrees are simply not worth the cost. But hey, at least the 85 percent of students who end up moving back home after graduating college get to enjoy Mom's lasagna once again and help Dad clean out the garage. Mom and

Dad will just have to wait a little longer to convert their kid's bedroom into that new workout room.

Finding Common Sense on Common Ground

So when Tilly, the teacher's aide, says...

"If you love your teacher Ms. Johnson so much, don't you want her to have rights, too?"

You say: "I'm not against teachers' rights. I love good teachers. I'm against bad teachers getting rewarded by corrupt unions."

"Charter schools are just a gateway drug to privatizing all education and keeping the poorest kids out."

You say: "Some of the best charter schools are in the poorest areas. And if you have enough charter schools, you'll have enough room for every child: rich, poor, or otherwise."

"You want to cut the Department of Education? How the heck are we going to keep churning out the smartest and the brightest?"

You say: "You must think we still live in the 1950s. Globally, we're seventh in literacy, twenty-second in science, and twenty-seventh in math. Most kids today can't even name all seven continents. Nice job, DoE."

"Maybe you think all the 'interesting' people you meet nowadays are homeschooled because they're all rich kids who got to travel on Daddy's sailboat all over the place."

You say: "Homeschooling is not just for the rich. Haven't you noticed all the rich kids go to private school?"

> "Cutting federal aid for colleges will keep the poor
> kids from getting an education."

You say: "Students who are legitimately poor deserve federal aid, but there's clearly a problem when the government is funding *70 percent of all student loans.* To fix the broken system, we have to draw the line somewhere."

> "Shouldn't we listen to Bernie Sanders when he says
> a free college education should be provided to every-
> one, just like they do over in Europe?"

You say: "Nice idea, Bern—for countries like Denmark with a few million people—but with a country our size there's no way to pay for it unless we raise taxes to astronomical levels. Even then, you know the feds would mismanage the money and screw it up!"

CHAPTER 5

Wanna Start a Business? Bahahaha!

"B*tch, don't kill my vibe."
~ Kendrick Lamar ~

The American dream has always been to get an education, find a job, and become a productive member of society. Unfortunately, though, that just isn't feasible for many of us these days.

An old friend of mine has a mother, Linda, who used to be an alcoholic. Linda has been through hell and back multiple times, going in and out of rehab, and even jail— until she gave birth to my friend Steph in the early nineties and decided to turn her life around. Now mind you, it isn't exactly easy to get a job when you have a criminal record. And it's even harder to support yourself and a child when you don't have parents with the means to help you out and your child's father isn't around to help pay the bills. So Linda had a choice. She could either sit on her butt and collect welfare checks every month or press forward and try to make something of herself. After the umpteenth rejection by a prospective employer, Linda started thinking outside the box.

Turns out, Linda was not only entrepreneurial minded,

but she also had a knack for cutting hair. She turned one room in her tiny home into a hair salon, and it didn't take too long for the money to start flowing in. Linda would cut the hair of all of her friends and her friends' kids, and her friends' friends started coming to her. She was good at what she did and way cheaper than the legit hair salons in town.

Linda was merely being an entrepreneur, giving the market what it wanted. But as far as the government was concerned, she was operating in the shadows. Washington, D.C., has a habit of crushing any kind of entrepreneurship and getting in the way of innovation. Want to start a beauty salon? OK, but it will cost you thousands of dollars in licensing fees, so your salon lives up to the government's list of requirements. Yes, you need Uncle Sam's approval to cut hair and paint nails (as if they're an authority on looking fresh to death). You'll need a beautician's license, a business license, an LLC, business insurance, and a tax ID before you're legally allowed to cut the hair of paying customers, even in your own home.[1] Oh, and you'll also have to hire an expensive attorney to set up a tax structure, accounting procedures, and so on. In addition to federal regulations, some states have put in place additional restrictive (and expensive) rules of their own for those who want to become hairstylists.

Thankfully, Linda was never found out and punished by the government. But others haven't been so lucky. Jestina Clayton moved to Utah from Africa fifteen years ago. When she got to the U.S., she supported her children with money she made from hair braiding, a skill she learned in Africa. One day Clayton received an e-mail threatening to report her to the state's cosmetology board if she continued to braid hair without the proper permission. Upon contacting the board, Clayton learned that she needed to obtain a cosmetology license, which required two thousand hours of classroom time...even though none of the state's beauty schools even taught African hair braiding. The license can cost up to $16,000 to obtain. If Clayton failed to get the license but kept braiding anyway, she would be charged $1,000 for the first offense and $2,000 per day for all subsequent offenses.[2] How is a poor person expected to cough up $16,000 to run a small braiding operation out of their home?

Thankfully, Clayton's story has a happy ending. She sued the state in 2011, and a judge ruled in her favor, writing, "Utah's cosmetology/barbering licensing scheme is so disconnected from the practice of African hair braiding, much less from whatever minimal threats to public health and safety are connected to braiding, that to premise Jestina's right to earn a living by braiding hair on that scheme is wholly irrational and a violation of her constitutionally protected rights."[3]

Despite the epic ruling in Clayton's favor, there are still other U.S. states—including Utah, Iowa, Texas, and Florida— that require expensive licenses and lots of classroom hours to braid hair.

If you think cosemetology is the only field tainted by overregulation...think again! Illogical, and often expensive, burdens are placed on almost every entrepreneur. Want to mow lawns for some extra cash? Good luck with that. To start a landscaping business you need similar licenses as well as liability insurance for anyone who works for you. Is it any wonder that most landscapers work under the table? Our own government is almost encouraging us to break the law by making rules and regulations impossibly expensive to follow.

Even if you don't want to start your own business, landing a normal job has become insanely difficult, thanks to a government that penalizes companies with extra taxes and insurance requirements when they hire new employees.

Imagine that you own a small company with forty-five employees. Business is going well, and you'd like to bring on some new staff to continue that trend. Not so fast. Under Obamacare, employers with over fifty full-time employees are automatically forced to provide full health insurance to all their workers or pay a hefty penalty. So why make those new hires when it would mean shelling out hundreds of thousands and actually *reducing* your profits? It's easier to just not hire those new people.

And the politicians in D.C. wonder why our economy stagnates.

Look, everyone knows that there must be some level of regulation in the business world—we can't revert to the days of robber barons and kids dying in horrible smelting accidents. But the ridiculous, costly rules imposed on us today have gotten out of hand. For many of us, the government's insistence on sticking its nose into every business has made the American dream nothing more than a pipe dream.

The Birth of an Entrepreneurial Nation

Can you imagine the kind of courage it must have taken to leave your homeland and travel for more than two months on a wooden ship to establish a colony on what you thought was the edge of the earth?[4]

How many of us today would agree to do the same?

How many would leave all sense of security and stability behind and travel for months or years to settle eventually on a distant planet? Nope, sorry, you can't bring your smartphone. And, *no*, the shuttle will not have a Starbucks. Sadly, there are no skinny mochaccinos in space. Insanity, right? Think about how badly you would have to hate your life to give up technology *and* flavored coffee to travel to the Great Unknown.

Or could it have been an authentic entrepreneurial spirit that inspired the original colonists to give up pretty much all their prized possessions (luxuious seventeeth-century creature comforts like chamber pots and leeches) to venture into uncharted territory.

The first permanent settlers in America were members of the Virginia Company, and their mission was to try to find silver and gold as well as a trade route to Asia.[5] That was a huge deal back then. Basically, finding trade new routes between Europe and Asia would have been like Apple having a monopoly on selling computers to the entire world today.

These folks weren't freeloaders content to sit around waiting for someone else to take care of them. Oh, wait. Maybe it was because no one *was* going to take of them that they knew they had to make their opportunities in life. And even though they didn't exactly discover any long-lost pirate treasure buried on the New England shore (sorry, Jack Sparrow), many members of the Virginia Company did manage to survive a harsh winter, near starvation, and frequent attacks by the natives who didn't exactly appreciate these strange-looking invaders.

The colony eventually began to thrive after they started planting tobacco. *That's right.* They could starve (or live in their parents' basements, which would have made starvation a preferable option), or they could harvest a completely natural plant that happened to make folks feel good when they smoked it. The American Dream and the free market economy were born together. And that, my friends, was a beautiful thing.

But if you happened to be a participating consumer in a capitalist market by toking up before American History class in high school, you may have missed the part where the colonists were taxed up the wazoo on tobacco and tea, among other things, which was basically why we fought a revolution. But look at us now. Is our current federal government, with all of its taxation and regulation on small businesses, really any different from the colonialist rule of eighteenth-century Britain? And why did we fight a war for independence in the first place, if 250 years later we were going to roll over and succumb to another equally absurd bureaucratic power?

Capitalism: Over 60 Billion Served

Basically every time we allow the feds to impose their ridiculous regulations on private business, our Founding Fathers are rolling over in their graves.[6] George Washington owned one of the largest plantations of his time, producing wheat, rye, and barley (basically the trifecta of life-sustaining foodstuffs for all colonial peeps) before eventually expanding his operation to include a gristmill. The mill allowed him to process his grain into flour and then export it across the Atlantic.

Just like pot dealers who grow, harvest, and distribute

their own crop du jour, Washington had complete autonomy with his farming business and reaped generous rewards because of it. Benjamin Franklin, Thomas Jefferson, and Alexander Hamilton were successful businessmen, too, who carved out niche markets for themselves and flourished just like Washington in their pursuit of life, liberty, and earning lots of paper money with their pictures on it.

Sam Walton, the founder of Walmart, was born in Kingfisher, Oklahoma, in 1918.[7] It doesn't get any more humble than that. After college and a stint in the military (saving our butts from the Nazis in World War II), Walton began working in retail before eventually opening his first Walmart store in Arkansas. He saw a need and found a way to give the masses what they wanted. Cheap. He was a brilliant salesman and businessman, so much so that at the time of his death, Walton was worth nearly $25 billion and Walmart was the world's largest corporation.[8] Not too shabby for a boy from Kingfisher. No superpowers required, just a lot of grit and determination.

With roles models like these guys, how could we not have a country filled with self-made people ready and eager to grab the proverbial brass ring?

Remember *The Great Gatsby* from tenth-grade English class? No? How about the glitzy, hyper-stylized, cracked-out film with Leonardo DiCaprio? The story of Jay Gatsby is one most of us can relate to, because it involves a totally ordinary dude turning his life into something so extraordinary that he became a legend. A god. Who wouldn't want to be a deity if given the chance?

While Gatsby's fate wasn't exactly ideal (spoiler alert: the dude is shot in the back while chillin' in his pool), he does manage to carve out a pretty sweet existence at the top of the food chain right up until he's hunted down like Cecil the Lion. He didn't do anything wrong (well, except for maybe amassing millions through bootlegging and organized crime connections) and definitely didn't deserve to bite it while enjoying the fruits of his labor.

Gatsby deserves our admiration because he refused to accept his lower-class origins. Once he saw that it wouldn't land him the girl of his dreams, he hustled his ass off to make millions. That's a dream we're all sold from the day we're born. If you've grown up in America, you've most likely had to read *The Great Gatsby*, not to mention been inundated with media and societal messaging telling you all things are possible—just as long as you work hard and don't give up. And in a truly capitalist country, such dreams would be possible. In theory, we should be hearing about more billionaire playboys than just the fictional (albeit super hot) ones like Bruce Wayne, aka Batman, and Tony Stark, aka Iron Man.

In a truly free market economy, we would all have the opportunity to make our mark on the world, as large or small as we want. It would be a future of our own choosing, not that of some policymaker rotting away in a congressional catacomb.

Here's a story that may sound familiar: A suburban Chicago high school graduate named Joel was home alone while his parents went out of town one summer weekend. Joel had only his scheming friends and wild imagination to keep him company. Through a series of misadventures involving a prostitute, pimp, and Porsche, Joel came to be in desperate need of cash so his parents wouldn't find out about said hijinks. Answer me this: What's the best way to earn some fast cash when you know a ton of horny teenage guys and your new girlfriend knows a ton of call girls? Let's just say Joel wasn't in his school's Future Enterprisers group for nothing.

Turned out our boy Joel knew enough about economic theory to recognize the fortune to be made from the world's inexhaustible demand for sex. And through one fantastic night of turning his home into a brothel, Joel ended up earning enough money to not only make all his problems disappear but also make his dreams come true when his keen business skills so impressed a Princeton admissions officer that he was immediately accepted. Oh, yeah, and there was even time for some hot sex on a late-night L train.

There's your American Dream.

Okay, so you may have heard Joel's story before. He wasn't exactly a friend of mine, as anyone knows who has ever watched the classic capitalist film *Risky Business*, which starred a very young Tom Cruise long before he bought a one-way ticket on the crazy train and started jumping on and off couches.

But Joel's story, even though it's fictional, is an important case study in the intrinsic power behind the law of supply and demand. He didn't necessarily have to be selling sex to make a lot of money. It could have been anything. He could have sold lawn-care services or washed some cars. Would he have made thousands in one night? Most likely not. Some needs cost more than others.

We have to ask: Did Joel or his brilliant acumen for capitalism hurt anyone? Of course not. Prostitution is nothing more than a business relationship between consumer and a service provider. You got an itch? There's someone ready to scratch it. And why shouldn't they if it doesn't harm anyone else? Marijuana, tobacco, and prostitution are just a few remedies for the countless itches we all feel at some point in our lives. Who is anyone else to judge? Granted, these are all extreme examples of free market enterprise. I'm not necessarily recommending this business model for anyone ready to dip his big toe for the first time in the entrepreneurial pool. I'm just trying to make a point that will stick with you—markets work best when left alone so that any man, woman, child, or horny teenager can make his or her dreams come true.

A person or a company should be free to make all the decisions regarding the making and selling of a product, including how much they want to charge for it. Sounds like basic common sense, right? It's in your best interest as a business owner to make a quality product and sell it for a price people are willing to pay, because otherwise you can say good-bye to your business.

That's the beauty of competition in a free market. If you have to worry about your customers buying something that you sell from a guy down the street, you're gonna have to be a lot more creative in making your product really stand out at price that is affordable to your consumer base. It's a win-win for both the business owner and the customer when the business owner sells a better product at a better price than the competition.

Capitalism is the best economic policy for many reasons.[9] It results in maximum efficiency. Businesses, large and small, are constantly tweaking and reimaging even their best-selling products, because competition gives them an incentive to grab a customer's dollar before anyone else. Who wants to be left behind when someone else has come up with a better and more inexpensive version of the same thing? Capitalism also makes goods cheaper and more innovative, which is awesome for consumers.

I'm sure most of you have used the ride-sharing service Uber. Uber is faster and more cost effective than traditional taxi services—I use it to get from place to place whenever I travel. The app is a perfect example of capitalism at work: entrepreneurs, harnessing new technology, have created a more efficient, cheap way to go places. It's a beautiful thing. But of course, like that crazy ex who won't stop texting you while you're with your new boo, the government is trying to get in the way of Uber's success.[10] Hillary Clinton and other Democrats have already called for initiatives that would destroy it and other ride-sharing services, citing "workplace protections." Newsflash: *No one* is forced to work for Uber! The drivers volunteer. Many Uber drivers have told me they love their job thanks to the flexible hours and independence. Still, politicians like Clinton insist on backing the taxi cartel, which has been micromanaged by the government and typically provides inefficient, overpriced service. The taxi industry doesn't like competition—and neither does the government.

Not all consumers are looking for the cheapest deal, though. Some are more than willing to pay a little extra if it means they'll be getting something *cool* or trendsetting. Apple and Microsoft are great examples of slightly different forms of capitalism at work. Both Apple and Microsoft rocked the world of personal home computers, bringing an innovative and revolutionary idea to the marketplace. While Americans were clearly hungry for new technology in the eighties (and it's a beast that seems to never be satiated), they also greatly benefited from the fight between two of the greatest entrepreneurial minds in history. The intense professional competition between Steve Jobs and Bill Gates was fortuitous for us all, because their back-and-forth mind games over design and implementation produced an amazing variety in the kind of personal computers and smartphones we have to pick from, with just about every price point imaginable.

The free market is also good for workers. Free from the shackles of government interference, businesses are forced to compete for the best and most efficient workers. How do companies snag more effective employees than their competition? By offering higher wages, better hours, and more attractive benefits packages. Duh. Why do you think I left my first job, scrubbing vomit off of hospital walls, to take a job at the local diner in high school? Better pay, better hours. Many will have you believe that unions are responsible for the eight-hour workday. But in reality, this standard came about thanks to the free market. Henry Ford offered his employees an eight-hour workday and doubled their pay in 1914.[11] He did this to attract better employees than his main competitor, General Motors. What happened next? In order to retain its own talent, GM was forced to match Ford's hours and wages.

The glory of capitalism is that everyone—consumers and business owners—has the freedom of *choice*. Titans of industry can choose how to run their businesses, and people can choose how to spend their money. That's exactly how it should work and how it would work if only the federal government wasn't so damned determined to cockblock us all.

Who Invited This Geek?

Imagine you're out at a club having the most awesome night of your life when at the bar you spot the hottest girl/guy/tranny you've ever seen. The two of you lock eyes, and you're flashed with a megawatt smile, before the object of your desire gets up to meet you at the dance floor. You start dancing—this night is about to become the stuff of legends, when suddenly...

Your overweight and obnoxious friend taps you on the shoulder, and keeps tapping harder and harder. Eventually, you have no choice but to disengage from the ensuing ecstacy and listen to whatever the hell needs to be said in your ear. "We gotta go," your friend says. "I don't feel so well. I think I'm gonna puuuuuu..."

And in an instant, you're covered in green chunky slime, and all your hopes and desires for a perfect world are in the toilet.

Welcome to the wonderful world of government regulation!

We've become a nation buried in government oversight because at some point we decided to invite that weirdo in a unicorn T-shirt from down the hall to our epic dorm floor rager. Why, oh why, did we do it? Are we a nation of masochists as much as opportunists?

There seem to be two major reasons for regulation: Lawmakers are moronic enough to think they know better than us how the world should run, and lobbyists have figured out that special interest equals more zeroes on the ends of their paychecks.[12]

Take, for instance, the Dodd-Frank Act of 2010. Some do-gooders thought they would save us from the big, bad bank guys by ensuring another financial meltdown could never happen. The basic intentions of Dodd-Frank were easy to understand: improve transparency, stop banks from taking excessive risks, prevent abusive financial practices, and put an end to the practice of regulators euthanizing financial firms on the brink of disaster. It had the best of intentions, right? So it was totally the best bill for us to pass?

Um, nooooo...

When it was all said and done, Dodd-Frank became a cluster of regulations mired in clarifications that were hundreds of pages long. At 848 total pages, it was twenty-three times longer than Glass-Steagall, the reform that followed the Wall Street crash of 1929.[13] Think about that for a minute. The bill that was passed after the economic world crashed into a brick wall going 180 in the 1920s was minuscule compared to how policymakers reacted to the more recent market correction.

Lengthy, labyrinthine bills only make it easier for legislators to slide stuff through, totally undetected, to the complete benefit of their buddies (i.e., campaign donors). A litany of regulations benefits lawmakers and the folks or businesses bankrolling them. That's it. It does diddly-squat for us as private citizens.

Many economists now believe that because of government involvement in trade, private industry, and banking, the Great Depression went on way longer than it should have.[14] If we had just allowed the free market to do its thing, we wouldn't have needed a Second World War to bail us out of a financial collapse.

There's much to be learned from other countries as well. Ireland's economy was able to flourish once its tax burden and GDP fell. On the opposite end of the spectrum, Jamaica's insistence on social-justice legislation dramatically slowed economic growth when compared to its neighbor island of Barbados, whose government was less up in every one's grill.[15]

During recent decades no politician has remained completely out of the cesspool of regulation, but Obama was definitely one of the worst. In the first five years of his presidency, the Obama Administration issued 157 new major rules that cost Americans nearly $73 billion annually, taking the cake for government regulation in U.S. history.[16]

Congress doesn't get out of this smelling like a rose, either. Most business regulations can be traced back to agencies like the Federal Communications Commission (FCC) and the Securities and Exchange Commission (SEC), which aren't under presidential control. Increased economic regulations harm all of us in many different ways, including: slowing corporate expansion, destroying innovation, and hurting job growth.

Unfortunately, small businesses are negatively affected the most, because it's much more difficult for them to cover the varied costs of new laws. Big chains like McDonald's can easily afford the costs associated with increased regulation, but little guys, like the mom-and-pop diner down the street, usually have a hard time dealing with these new costs. In the end, big business often benefits from increased government interference while the little guys are squashed.

Besides, imposing any gratuitous policies on small businesses is a total affront to the very ideals we hold so dear as

Americans. Some of the most egregious legislation is passed under the guise of helping those less fortunate. But does it really do anything positive, or is the government actually doing more harm than good?

Minimum Wage: Support Your Local Teenager

So what about people on the other end of the capitalist spectrum? What about folks who aren't Donald Trump, born with millions that metastasize into billions more (yet seemingly with very little to invest in better hair), or even simple country boys like Sam Walton? According to a 2016 Huffington Post/YouGov survey, 66 percent of Americans favor an increase in the minimum wage.[17] While it's supersweet that people care about the standard of living for their fellow Americans, it also shows how clueless most folks are about the reality of what they're asking. Sounds to me like 66 percent of Americans believe in the Magic Money Fairy who waves her wand to make all of our problems disappear. I hate to ruin it for you if you're reading this and are under the age of ten (and if you are, your parents should be arrested), but there are no such things as Magic Money Fairies.

The federal minimum wage was the brainchild of President Franklin Roosevelt and signed into law in 1938 at the height of the Great Depression.[18] There's no question that was a dire period in our country's history. At the time, the minimum wage was twenty-five cents per hour (adjusted for inflation, it would be the equivalent of $4.04 today) and applied just to those workers who produced products that were shipped in interstate commerce. Which meant it applied to only about 38 percent of the workforce. Through the years, Congress has gone into hyperdrive and expanded the coverage and increased the rate until today the Fair Labor Standards Act covers about 85 percent of the labor force.

It's easy to see why politicians fall so easily into the welfare rabbit hole. No one wants to be perceived as heartless. But the reality is far, far from the perception. According to the Bureau of Labor Statistics, fewer than 3 percent of U.S. workers actually earn the minimum wage.[19]

The media loves to propagate the stereotype that people earning low wages are adults with large families to support. We're made to feel guilty if we don't pay a single mother $15 an hour for scrubbing toilets in a hotel because that would mean that an entire family would have nothing to eat for dinner each night but the stuffing from their couch.

This is nonsense, because hard data tells us otherwise.[20] The truth is that almost half of paid-hourly employees are teenagers (twenty-four and younger) and the vast majority of these kids aren't downtrodden and living hand to mouth. They typically come from families with an average income of $70,600.

That buys a lot of couch stuffing.

The other half of minimum-wage earners are twenty-five years old and up. Granted, the majority of these workers live near the poverty level. The important thing to remember is that of those living in poverty, only 25 percent want to work full-time and just 34 percent work full-time year-round. That's a pretty big deal. That means we're all being duped about who is actually being helped by messing around with the minimum wage. Definitely not just single moms working three jobs to make ends meet.

Let me ask you this: Do you think it's worth destroying your local economy, when businesses leave for another state with a lower minimum wage, so the teenager working the cash register at McDonald's can buy another Xbox? Minimum-wage hikes also price low-skilled workers out of the market. The mom-and-pop hardware store down the street likely won't expand and make those new hires they were considering if the cost of labor increases. But it's not just small businesses that will be impacted—many companies, big and small, will be more hesitant about hiring new employees for lower-level work if the minimum wage is hiked. No fast-food chain is going to pay its employees $15 an hour—the minimum wage being promoted by Hillary Clinton and other Democrats—to take orders. It's cheaper to lay off some of these staff members and have touch screens do their jobs instead.

The bottom line is that the minimum wage impacts our entire capitalist economy. It doesn't matter if you're a small business struggling to make ends meet or a national chain store; minimum-wage hikes hurt. A lot. Granted, the pain is actually far greater for the little guys. It's like the difference between being hit by a semi truck when you're on a bicycle or in a Humvee.

The problem is that money for an increase in the minimum wage has to come from somewhere, and it leaves just three options to choose from: investors (who would see lower profits), customers (we would pay more for products), and workers (companies would hire fewer people). Competition in the marketplace will determine who pays. If a particular market is rife with competition, a business will do whatever it has to do to keep prices at levels customers will still pay. So in that scenario, workers will have to be sacrificed to lower the bottom line. When a government program leads to people being laid off, how is it helping anyone?

It doesn't take a fancy economics degree to understand that enforcing a higher minimum wage will cost a business more money. And because individual states are allowed to establish their own minimum wage if they want it to be higher than the fed, businesses ultimately have to decide if they want to stick it out or cut and run for a different state where the minimum wage is lower. If it's going to cost more money to hire labor in Oregon than Texas, and all other industry factors are equal, then where do you think that company will go? *Well, hello, Longhorns!*

Take a state like Massachusetts.[21] Wages are high there, and so are prices. Few employers will have to spend a lot more on their workforce under a higher federal minimum wage, and few will have to raise their prices to make up the cost. But in a state like Mississippi, employers will have to raise their wages. That pretty much means the cost of a minimum-wage hike would be passed on to consumers in the form of higher prices.

That's not a big deal if it were only superrich people who were paying the higher prices. But that's never the case in poor states like Mississippi. It will be people in poverty who will have to pay more, forcing them to buy less with what little money they have. And if consumers are at all sensitive to prices, at least some of them will choose to spend less on labor-intensive goods and services now that they are more expensive. And if businesses have fewer customers buying less, that will most definitely reduce the number of minimum wage jobs available.

Democrats are currently pushing for a $15 per hour minimum wage. Why stop there? Why not make it $20 per hour? How about $50 per hour? Hell, why not $100 per hour? Seriously, where does the insanity end?! If we absolutely insist on setting a minimum wage, we would all be better off if state and local governments did so themselves, taking into account local wages and local price levels. Why not make it half of the median full-time wage in an area? That nuance alone would have made minimum wages ranging from $12.45 in Massachusetts to $7.97 in Mississippi.

But if you ask me, the best solutions for consumers, employees, and businesses is to lower the minimum wage to $0 per hour. After all, the Fourth Amendment states that business owners have the right to spend their property any way they please.

But the real question is: If minimum wage hurts people at risk for poverty or currently living in poverty, why do we insist on keeping it? It's seriously like a bad Lifetime movie about domestic abuse starring Tori Spelling and whatshisname. Let's turn the channel, already!

Killing Us (Not So) Softly...with Red Tape

As popular as shows like *Shark Tank* and *The Apprentice* are, the truth is our country is less of a friend and more of a frenemy to entrepreneurs. From 2008 to 2012, the number of small businesses that name government regulation and red tape as their greatest concern jumped from 8 percent to 22 percent.[22]

What if you're a college kid looking for a part-time job? Sounds simple enough. It used to be pretty common for a girl like me to find work as a nanny. It was great in a city like Boston. You weren't looking to make a career out of it, just some cash, while getting an education that would lead to bigger and better things. And the families you worked for could benefit from paying you out of pocket (forgoing all those taxes and Social Security contributions). It was a classic win-win scenario for both parties, with the client paying a little less than the going rate because it was cash and a nanny could be totally chill with the plan, because she wasn't having almost half her pay taken away by the government. Seriously, why would a nineteen-year-old babysitter need to pay into Social Security and Medicaid anyway? But in recent years, the IRS has stepped in, demanding their share of the profit pie.[23] If you pay someone more than $1,800 per year, they are considered your employee.

What's next? Filing a Schedule H on your 1040 for the sixth grader who shovels your drive? Why not demand a 1040 EZ from kindergartners selling lemonade?

The government loves to shit on dreams.

Funeral directors in a Louisiana parish had enough influence to get a state law passed stipulating that only licensed funeral directors could sell caskets. A yearlong apprenticeship and a passing grade on an "industry test" were required in order to get the license. Clearly, the policy was in place to drive away competition. Monks at an abbey in Louisiana, who hand-make their own caskets, literally had to fight in federal court to sell their products.[24]

Sorry, dudes of the cloth, you can't nail together some pieces of wood to make an empty box.

In a 2011 op-ed in the *Wall Street Journal*, Obama

acknowledged the problem of rampant regulation, writing, "Sometimes, those rules have gotten out of balance, placing unreasonable burdens on business—burdens that have stifled innovation and have had a chilling effect on growth and jobs."[25] He called for federal agencies to reduce the regulatory burden on small companies. But, unfortunately, very little was done to address the problem.

I can't say I'm surprised.

When fishermen are required to fill out reports on how much fish they catch even during weeks when they aren't fishing…I'd call that an unreasonable burden.[26] It's estimated that excessive government regulations cost $84 billion as a result of inefficiencies and higher costs to consumers. That's a boatload of fish, caught or not.

As big of a mess this is, there are solutions to be had.

Self-regulation is the regulation of an industry by its own members, usually by means of a committee that issues guidelines and sets standards that it then enforces.[27] These regulations are meant to reduce risks to consumers, increase public trust, and combat any negative perceptions held by the general public. Flexible regulations allow companies to operate more efficiently and minimize costs by giving them lots of options for innovation.

In other words, self-regulation lets businessmen and women do what they do best. *Business.* And the best part about this system is that people who actually work in the industry make the guidelines. Why would we ever think it's a good idea to have career politicians decide what's good for business? Only a handful of members of Congress have ever run a business.

Self-regulation also can help businesses work within their own moral beliefs or codes. You may not subscribe to their way of thinking, but then it becomes your prerogative not to apply for a job at their company or buy what they are selling. If a company feels morally compromised by having to provide birth control for its employees, which the federal government is constantly battling for, then it will greatly impact how it hires people. The ramifications of government intervention on business are as complicated as they are far-reaching. It's like trying to contemplate the Middle East crisis...or the Nicki Minaj–Miley Cyrus feud.

Again and again, all roads lead back to the beauty of a free market economy. It works spectacularly, because both the business and the consumer have a choice. In no other country would we have so many options on everything ranging from craft beer to cat food. And we, as well as our cats, are all the better for it.

It's in a company's best interest to continually self-evaluate for greater efficiency and innovation, because it will translate to higher customer satisfaction and profit yield. Do you think the only thing holding Linda back from giving shitty haircuts is the government telling her she can't? She has to keep her customers happy and coming back for more.

Check Your Good-Time Guest List

There is a time and place for everything known to man—including government. It has a very special role to play in the growth of our economy. It should enforce contracts, create a level playing field, and promote a few general rules (more like guidelines) for businesses. After that, entrepreneurs should have the freedom to do what they do best: innovate and take risks.

The United States has produced some supreme titans of industry. From John D. Rockefeller and Andrew Carnegie to Bill Gates and Steve Jobs, ordinary Americans have transformed themselves into the extraordinary because they were able to fulfill the needs of millions of people. They reached the pinnacle of their respective industries but, more important, stayed there because they were allowed to adapt and evolve their business models. If they had been held back by regulation and red tape, imagine where we would be in our lives. I don't know about you, but I'm picturing black-and-white TVs and cans of Spam.

Through it all, as our country rose to the top of the world economy, big government was nothing more than an obnoxious third wheel tagging along on a fun date, forever interrupting the conversation to talk about plantar warts or serial killers.

Look, there's no such thing as a free lunch. Ever. And you know when the government is offering to pay, you really need to be on the lookout for a shank in your neck. The feds may offer to pay for your meal and even go so far as to reach over and grab the check off the restaurant table, but when your back is turned as you head to your car in the parking lot, you'll be beaten and mugged with that very check dropped on your blood-soaked shirt.

Rather than focus on harmful policies, we should concentrate on generating faster economic growth that will cause wages to rise and create more opportunities for all workers. A sharply increased minimum wage will have a negative impact on employment, which translates to fewer jobs. Why don't we try to address income inequalities by investing in education and skills? Equip people with the means to help themselves.

Our nation was founded by standing up to a big bully named George III who wanted to tell us how to live our lives and demanded our obedience and hard-earned money. The colonists fought back, and many lost their lives to a cause they held so dear. Ever since, Americans have loved a good fight, particularly against tyrannical governments.

Finding Common Sense on Common Ground

So when Sally, the chatterbox down at the Laundromat, says...

> "Isn't Walmart the company that pays their workers
> minimum wage and doesn't let them work full-time
> because they'd have to pay them health insurance?"

You say: "At least those people have jobs—many are in rural areas where no other jobs are around. And if Obamacare didn't cost so much, maybe Walmart would hire more full-time workers!"

> "Capitalism may breed *optimum efficiency* but
> it doesn't breed optimum quality when we get sold
> low-quality, defective products made in Mexico."

You say: "Companies that make inferior products end up having inferior bottom lines and will soon be out of business. That's the law of the jungle—'*Kill* or be killed.'"

"How can you say capitalism gives us freedom of
choice when in 2016 our choice is usually between a
few giant conglomerates who own everything?

You say: "Those giant conglomerates were once small companies, too. Look, if Sally's Café wants to compete with Starbucks, then she should make better coffee, charge less, and provide better customer service. And it's the government that's holding back small companies, not capitalism! The little guys can't afford to keep up with the red tape and pay for absurd regulations, but guess who can? The big guys."

"You seriously don't think lowering the minimum
wage to zero is a good idea, do you?"

You say: "Why not!? Companies that refuse to pay their workers fairly won't be in business long, and the ones that do pay a good wage will have the happiest employees and best product."

CHAPTER 6

Regulation Nation

"What-eva...I do what I want!"
~ Eric Cartman ~

Unless you zoned out in chapter 5 after ingesting way too many vape hits, which I don't advise but is totally your prerogative, and *if you've been paying attention*, by now you should understand that more government interference in the free market usually results in less economic prosperity. Once you've digested that, digest this: Government interference doesn't end in the corporate world—no, no, no. Twenty-first-century bureaucrats love to stick their noses into all aspects of our private lives, regulating and banning seemingly anything that displeases them. You do realize this insidious form of legislative intrusion means you and I have less personal choice in life, right? So what is our generation going to do about it? Not your problem, bro? Really?

The struggle for personal freedom is not an abstract issue; it affects every American and has ever since our Founding Fathers created this nation. It's *real*—if you don't believe me, jump into your way-back machine and think about your own upbringing. If you're like most of us, your struggle for independence began long before you even left your parents' home. I personally fought for mine my entire life.

I've had an entrepreneurial knack since birth. Even as a mere tot, I loved the smell of money. I began obsessively collecting loose change around my house before I could do simple math. As I got older, I begged my parents to let me do chores. Kind of weird, I know, since chores are most kids' worst nightmare but I gleaned a special kind of thrill from earning a couple of bucks. Plus, it's not like I had anything better to do; I lived in the sticks of New Hampshire for chris-sake. My only friends were my Goosebumps books.

Before I did my chores, there was nothing I enjoyed more than haggling with my parents. *You want me to mow the lawn for $5, Dad? Get real. That'll cost you $10 at least... No? Okay, fine, let's meet in the middle at $7... Deal.*

I was a born negotiator, and as a result my piggy bank got heavier every month. Life was good; I was a youngster stacking *dolla-dolla bills.* My future was bright, but after a while my greedy little self yearned for more and more and more money. The ten bucks I was collecting each week for scraping mom's meat loaf off dirty dishes and scrubbing dirty toilets just wasn't cutting it anymore.

And that's when it hit me: I'd hold my own yard sale and sell my old crap at the bottom of my driveway. It was a stroke of genius. I found a few old card tables in the garage and gathered all my junk—some old stickers, a couple of Beanie Babies, a scratched Shania Twain CD, a half-used notebook (I tore out the scribbled-on pages... they'd never be able to tell). You get the idea.

I placed all my stuff on the tables and taped a huge SALE sign on one. Then I waited to rake in the dough, and waited. Remember, I lived in the boonies, so business wasn't exactly booming; I sat out there all day. The few customers I got were stay-at-home moms walking their dogs who bought something just to be nice. But hell, I loved it! There was nothing better than the feeling of closing a sale.

I started having these little yard sales quite often on weekends, and I enlisted my friend Amanda to help me. I was the main salesperson, and she was there for backup and emotional support. I learned the best way to make people buy stuff was to act cute. After all, only a coldhearted jerk wouldn't buy a $2 trinket from a smiling little angel! One summer I saved up for months to buy my own Nintendo 64—it was my first major purchase. I was *so* proud of that crummy little gaming system.

In the end, even though my "small business" never made me rich, it paid dividends. I learned a lot about entrepreneurship, fiscal responsibility, and the art of the sale. It made me a confident, self-reliant person and convinced me that it's good for kids to earn their own money instead of constantly having everything handed to them by Mommy and Daddy.

Apparently, though, the government doesn't agree with me. During the last few years, the government has launched a war against kindergarten entrepreneurs. Kiddos hosting their own little sales or lemonade stands have been shut down and even slapped with penalties for not acquiring the right permits. In 2015, two little girls in Texas had their lemonade stand shut down after a couple hours for failing to get a permit from the health department (#NotFromTheOnion).[1] *The absurdity!* The duo was trying to raise $105 to buy a Father's Day gift for their dad. Thankfully the girls found a loophole in the red tape: They were able to give away their lemonade and take donations.[2] Still, the whole situation is insane. Kids from all parts of the country who had the audacity to operate their own "unlicensed" goodie stands have drawn police visits and gotten their parents slapped with $500 fines. In one case, a city councilman even called the police on kids selling cupcakes.[3] What a d-bag.

Welcome to the Nanny State

Now that I've taken you on a trip down my own memory lane, I want you to remember your childhood. Did your parents ever bust you for wrestling with your older brother, or maybe a neighborhood kid? They probably told you to cut it out but you wouldn't, would you? It was so much fun… that is, until your arm got twisted or mom's favorite lamp was launched across the room. Maybe you bawled your eyes out while Mom or Dad used every ounce of their willpower not to yell. Your shenanigans probably got you a stint in kiddie prison (your bedroom) to think about what had just unfolded.

After you served your time, you most likely found a whole new set of draconian rules thrown down in your house, like, "No more monkey business of any kind inside!" Did you think your parents' reaction was a bit…extreme? I mean, all things considered, it was just a bit of harmless horseplay, no one got seriously hurt; the lamp was easily repaired.

Maybe you voiced your displeasure with the new rules, but Mom and Dad wouldn't hear it, so you went to bed wondering where it all went so wrong. Well, here's your wake-up call: The extreme ruling came down on your precious little head because it happened when your dad was reading the paper and your mom was on the phone long-distance with

Auntie Judy. They weren't concerned with you getting hurt; it was just easier for them to ban all monkey business than to have to monitor your every move to see if you were up to no good.

This, my friends, is exactly how our government rolls. It's called the *nanny state*, and it's here to smother you in maternalistic mismanagement and overregulation. The Cato Institute defines the nanny state as a collection of laws, regulations, and binding court decisions that send the very clear message that politicians and bureaucrats know more than we do about how we should live, take care of our health, and raise our children.[4]

It's so much easier for the Nanny to ban and regulate the heck out of everything than to look up from the newspaper and actually engage in the situation at hand. So now every American citizen is being treated like an annoying eight-year-old wrestling in the living room. Whether it's on the federal or state level, we're being infantilized to the point of absurdity. I don't know about you, but I like to think of myself as an intelligent adult, fully capable of making my own decisions. If I run across something in life that I don't quite understand, like computer circuitry or why Adam Sandler continues to be allowed to make movies, I know where to find the answers or who to ask for help.

The point is I have fully operating brain synapses firing on all cylinders, so I can take care of myself. I can get from point A to B without a court-appointed guardian. I know to look both ways before crossing the street and not to stick my finger in an electrical socket unless I want to end up looking like one of Lady Gaga's wigs. I know where to go to fulfill my basic needs, be it the grocery store or nail salon. I know staying out until 3 A.M. on a work night is probably not going to bode well for my productivity the next day. I don't need a bureaucrat to tell me that.

The Know-It-All, No-Nothing Congress

The thing is, these bureaucrats don't know any more than the rest of us, but they seem to think they're the experts who must save us from ourselves. How chivalrous of them to make every life decision for us from what we eat to what we can do to our own bodies. How many members of Congress have the training to tell us if genetically modified organisms are safe or the work of the devil? How many have studied mechanical engineering to understand the physics behind car seat belt safety?

Legislators are also notorious for lacking the patience for any sense of ambiguity. They hate unknowns, because that would require intelligent thought and careful consideration. It's much easier to ban lawn darts or Slip 'n Slides from every kid's summer vacation to-do list than it is to stand up to the fanatical whims of misguided consumer groups or concerned parents led by D-list celebrities playing doctor. It's far simpler to kowtow to the loudest squawkers, be they wing-nut constituents or billionaire lobbyists, than it is to be an arbiter of rational thought and reason. Our lawmakers are determined to ensure a risk-free world, even if it kills them . . . and us.

There's a reason why the Constitution begins with the words "We the people . . ." The Founding Fathers wanted American citizens to control their own lives. Our government was created to work *for us*, not against us with a never-ending set of rules and regulations. Are we really free if we have to cower in our basements to smoke a cigarette, watch porn, or have a sleepover with a well-paid friend? I'll answer that for you. You're about as free now as you were when your mom threw you behind the bars of your crib so she could finish watching *Dallas* in peace.

The federal government was never intended to be the supreme power of the United States. That's why we fought the American Revolution, folks. "The fed" was designed to secure our general welfare, enforce the Constitution, and do things like defend us from enemy attacks while playing nice with the other countries of the world. Big-picture diplomacy stuff that we as private citizens can't be bothered with because we have jobs and families and summer music festivals to attend.

That's it. That's all the federal government was conceived for, and in return it's our duty as Americans to govern ourselves and make good choices, which shouldn't be too hard because it's in our own best interest to do so. So every time we allow legislators to pass into law regulations that will "protect" us, we've just handed our asses—our *freedom* and our *individualism*—over to the government on a silver platter. And I don't know about you, but I like my ass—it gets a lot of compliments—and I would like to hold on to it.

Speaking of asses...I'm a big girl now. I don't need my parents to wipe mine or blow my nose, so why should I let some government bureaucrat do it? I grew up with strict parents; they were awesome, but at a certain point they had to let me live my life. They let me move hundreds of miles away to attend college and then hundreds more after I graduated.

I don't sleep in my childhood bed anymore, because my parents respected me enough to let me spread my wings and fly. I know that may sound cheesy, but the point is my parents raised me to be a self-sufficient, contributing member of society. They helped me more than they'll ever know by letting me make my own decisions. So my question is: If my own parents were able to let go, why won't the federal government?

Adding In-Salt to Injury

The nanny state will never let us sit at the adult table. Do responsible adults really need someone to take away their Cokes or hide their table salt like they were unruly children? This may sound like an extreme analogy, but it's closer to reality than you think. There is actually such a thing as *table salt regulation* in this country. New York's Health Department has proposed requiring all chain restaurants to add salt-shaker symbols on menus next to items that contain more than the recommended daily limit of 2,300 milligrams of sodium, or about one teaspoon of salt.[5] San Francisco, not to be outdone by its liberal comrades on the East Coast, wants to ban ads for sugary sodas on public property and even passed legislation to require health warnings on ads for sugar-sweetened drinks. Their measure also forbade the use of city funds to buy sodas.[6] Salt? Sodas? Seriously, people?

Sugar isn't the spawn of the devil. Sure, sucking down too much of it isn't good for you, but a little won't hurt you, either. Any nutritionist will tell you a little salt is essential to good health.[7] Adults need to consume sodium and water to replace the amount lost through sweat. There's also research

suggesting that salt is actually good for brain development—
it's the iodine in iodized salt that helps the body make thyroid
hormone, which is critical to an infant's brain development.[8]

Prick or Treat?

Unfortunately, nutrient regulation isn't the only area where
the government insists on sticking its big fat nose into our
lives. Some school officials recently decided to suck the fun
out of traditional holidays (sayonara, Santa, and eat shit, Eas-
ter Bunny). Students at a Pennsylvanian elementary school
were banned from wearing Halloween costumes because
school officials said they were making safety their top
priority.[9]

Safety from *what*? I don't know. The horror of inappro-
priate costumes like Slutty Sixth Grader or Friendly Neighborhood Serial Killer? When it comes to "safety," did these
Pennsylvania school officials think kids were going to trip
over their Jedi robes or pass out from lack of oxygen while
wearing their Dora the Explorer plastic masks? How many
kids do they think they're protecting? It's like the Grinch's
cousin couldn't find work tormenting the Whos in Whoville,
so he decided to run for a seat on the Pennsylvania school
board.

Along those same lines, another ridiculous attempt to
protect our country's youngest citizens resulted in flip-flops
being banned in San Juan Capistrano city parks. Were the
brilliant minds in San Juan Capistrano trying to prevent the
city from liability in case someone blew out their flip-flop in
Margaritaville? Good grief. I, for one, refuse to live in a world
where a government employee determines my footwear. I

think I speak for all women when I say there's no better way to incite fear and panic in the hearts of womankind than to mention the possibility of having a civil servant yank their shoes away from them. Don't you men know many of us womenfolk would rather sleep with our Manolo Blahniks than with most of you? There is no more intimate relationship on earth than the one between a girl and her shoes, so step back, boys, and leave us alone with our sole mates!

Another modern form of self-expression that's dangerously close to being violated like a Yorkshire terrier at an inner-city dog park is the freedom to tattoo. Some cities are now calling for a twenty-four-hour waiting period before people can get them, in a brilliantly titled but inherently flawed "Think Before You Ink" campaign.[10] I have a feeling they came up with the slogan and thought it was so awesome they needed to come up with a law to go with it. I mean, I like a good catchphrase as much as the next girl but did anyone notice this is "cosmetic skin adornment" we're talking about here? Just because the Nanny thinks we're being rash in our decision making doesn't mean she has the right to stop us from doing what we want to do...*to our own bodies*...right?

How far can this type of regulation go? I can tell you how far it's gone in the past. Not so long ago, getting body art was outlawed in New York City (from 1961 to 1997).[11] It's one of those early egregious examples of city officials making bogus claims (by linking tattoos to a minor outbreak of hepatitis B).

And the *mother of all government interference with our bodies* would have to be the antichoice laws that prevent women from having early-term abortions. I can't think of any greater example of a bureaucrat literally sticking his dick in my business than being forced to give birth to a child against my will. Seriously, what do these old geezers know about my personal life circumstances? They have no clue about my current living situation or what my future plans are. They don't know my dreams and aspirations. But now, through overregulation, they've become active participants in how I'm going to live my life? They get to make a choice that will affect every moment of my life until my dying day? In the nanny state strangers get to determine *the course of your life*. If that doesn't chill you to the bone, I don't know what will. This isn't some bad sci-fi thriller starring Bruce Willis and a barely-clad Milla Jovovich running from Big Brother while maneuvering through high-speed airborne-car chases. No— this is *your life*.

The Mayor of Nannytown

Have I got your attention yet? Because moral condemnation aside, the concept of complete strangers working in an ivory tower in Washington, D.C., and making decisions about what I can or cannot do to my body is insulting at best and criminal at worst. It's nothing short of insanity that we live in a country where the former mayor of New York City thought it was perfectly acceptable to browbeat New Yorkers into taking the stairs instead of an elevator by posting signs all over office buildings with the admonishment "Burn Calories, Not Electricity. Take the Stairs!"[12]

Subtle, dude. Real subtle.

But he wasn't done, not by a long shot. Mayor Michael Bloomberg became a nanny-state icon when he ruled New York City more like a day care than the fifth largest city in the world. During his twelve-year reign, Bloomberg got so ban-happy he all but made New Yorkers walk around with pacifiers in their mouths. He did things like trying to ban the sale of sodas and other sugary beverages larger than sixteen ounces.

Now it's totally obvious that our country has gone pear-shaped by packing on more than a few extra pounds. There's no way to sugarcoat it (or deep-fry it in a vat of lard at the state fair); we, as a nation, are a bunch of fat-asses. And the more we talk about it, the worse the problem seems to get, but snatching a Big Gulp out of out of Chubina Fatsorelli's sausage fingers is not the answer. There's evidence to suggest a ban would actually increase the use of sugary drinks.[13]

Suppose the sixteen-ounce soda was verboten and you could only buy ten ounces—but you wanted *more*. What would you do? You might be tempted to buy two 10-ounce drinks so you end up drinking *more* than you originally intended. When it comes to scratchin' that sugar itch, if someone wants to drink their weight in Mountain Dew, mark my words they will drink it, and ask for seconds.

Bloomberg's proposed legislation was oddly selective. Restaurants, sandwich shops, and movie theaters were forbidden from serving supersized beverages. But other businesses like 7-Eleven and Starbucks, with their caffeinated milkshakes and high-calorie coffee drinks, were given a pass. This made about as much sense as using Italian words for small, medium, and large coffee sizes (I'm looking at you, Starbucks mermaid). The fundamental problem with this type of regulation is pretty much that everything in excess is bad for you, so where do you draw the line? Banning things can become addictive—look at the bloomin' mayor. I don't think he wanted to stop until he'd wiped the behind of every New Yorker.

You can't even escape Mr. Bloomberg's reign of terror by running into the bathroom. If you're a woman who has ever nearly peed yourself while waiting to use the restroom at a major concert or sporting even, good ol' Mayor Bloomberg was there to save you like a knight in toilet paper armor. Dubbed "Potty Parity," his legislation to ensure a two-to-one ratio for women's restrooms in new public venues including bars, restaurants, and concert halls was passed by the New York City Council. Thanks…I think?

In his three terms in office, Bloomberg nearly busted a nut trying to ban just about everything from serving trans fat in restaurants to loud headphones. Check out all the other fun stuff he banned at some point during his tenure, on this hit list compiled by Gizmodo:[14]

- No smoking in commercial establishments like bars and restaurants (2003)
- No smoking in public spaces (2011)
- No cigarette sales to those under twenty-one (2013)
- No sales of "flavored" tobacco products (2009)
- No smoking e-cigarettes in public spaces (2013)***
- No cigarette in-store displays (2013)
- No cars in Times Square (2009)
- No cars driving in newly created bike lanes (2007–2013)
- No cars causing congestion below Sixtieth Street in Manhattan (2007)*
- No speeding in residential "slow zones" (2013)

- No high sodium levels in processed foods (2010)**
- No Styrofoam packaging in single-service food items (2013)
- No sodas larger than sixteen ounces (2012)*
- No collecting yard waste and grass clippings during certain times of the year (2003–2013)
- No organic food waste from landfills (2013)**
- No commercial music over forty-five decibels (2013)
- No chain restaurant menus without calorie counts (2008)
- No posting of signs in "city-owned grassy areas" (2013)
- No non-fuel-efficient cabs (2007)
- No new cabs that aren't Nissan NV200s (2013)*
- No greenhouse gas emissions (2007)
- No government buildings that aren't LEED-certified (2005)
- No non-hurricane-proof buildings in coastal areas (2013)
- No black roofs (2009)**
- No construction cranes over twenty-five years old (2013)
- No No. 6 and No. 4 "heavy" heating oils (2011)
- No cell phones in schools (2006)
- No more than two terms for city elected officials (2008)*

* Overruled/appealed ban
** Suggested/voluntary ban
*** Proposed/pending ban

In case you're worried that you still might have to check your Big Gulp at the Lincoln Tunnel, never fear, my Classic

Cokeheads. The New York State Supreme Court struck down the soda ban. In a twenty-page opinion, Judge Eugene F. Pigott Jr. of the New York State Court of Appeals wrote that the city's Board of Health "exceeded the scope of its regulatory authority."[15] At least someone had some common sense for once, but that rarely seems to be the case these days. Seeing rational thought come out of a court ruling in 2015 is like spotting Leonardo DiCaprio at a wedding chapel or Jessica Simpson in a turtleneck and flats. Americans rarely witness their tax dollars being spent on safeguarding their personal liberties. It's far more likely you are paying to have them taken away.

The Long and the Short of It

While government spends way too much time regulating Slurpees, sodas, salt, and tattoos, there are more serious vices that are simply banned. Prostitution, gambling, and pornography drive blood to our extremities for a variety of reasons. And while our society has taken a hard line on the immorality of engaging in these activities, it hasn't seemed to deter these practices. Sex workers have been around since the dawn of man and, more important, woman. And whether or not we find it to be a nasty practice done by perverts, the sex industry won't be disappearing anytime soon.

Prostitution continues to flourish everywhere, but who is getting rich off it? It's certainly not the working girls. It's usually some Tony Soprano–esque crime boss running delightfully named strip clubs like the Bada Bing. And who gets hurt? Just about everyone but the crime boss. Why?

Since prostitution is illegal, everyone involved in the

industry is driven underground. This affects not just the industry workers, it affects us all—even the good wholesome families in suburbia. How? When sex workers can't receive adequate medical care, that results in somebody's daddy bringing home a supersexy case of syphilis for Mommy.

Now let's just dream for a minute and think about what would happen if we dropped all the regulations and let the horny men run wild and free. What if prostitution were legal? Working girls would be able take a more preventative approach to their health care as well as seek help when they needed it. And hey, if you had government-run brothels, you could tax them up the wazoo and make billions.

The Netherlands is a great example of a country that understands the far-reaching benefits of decriminalizing everything from paid sex to drugs. Prostitution has been legal in Amsterdam since 1988. The Dutch have a violent crime rate far lower than that of New York City and have found that regulating the sex industry reduces human trafficking, forced prostitution, and exploitation of children.[16] That's right, legalizing everything has made their society *better*. Dutch prostitutes pay taxes on their income and get tested for sexually transmitted diseases regularly. The city of Amsterdam has been so pleased with the system that in 2007, a bronze statue memorializing "working women" was erected (pun definitely intended).[17]

I truly believe other vice industries like drugs, pornography, and gambling could be regulated with similar results. We could bring these billion-dollar industries out into the light and it would be no different from Colorado and Washington State legalizing marijuana, which has proven to be a huge success in both states.

When any activity is driven underground, the bloodsuckers will come to feast. Even if this is all foreign to you, don't be fooled into thinking vice crimes don't impact your life. The truth is whenever organized crime gets involved in an activity, even law-abiding citizens can get dragged into the mess. Innocent people get in the line of fire all the time.

The ultimate question of how far the government should be allowed to go in their endless pursuit of smothering our liberty is whether we should be allowed to pursue our own deaths. What gives the government the right to decide if you can take your own life?

Brittany Maynard came to national attention last year when she fought a very public battle to have the right to die with dignity.[18] Diagnosed with a rare form of terminal brain cancer, Maynard simply wanted to die on her own terms. She was not depressed; she was not being rash or ill informed. Maynard simply wanted to alleviate the suffering of herself and her family. Death is not pretty, and living with a terminal illness is perhaps the most brutal fate one can have. Our society is so concerned with giving inmates on Death Row a humane form of execution, what about the general public? Why can't Americans have the right to leave this world on our own terms and not as a slobbering, vegetative mess? It is because euthanasia makes a few bureaucrats squeamish? So sorry my death makes *you* uncomfortable...

Maynard made her choice with considerable thought and care, and she still had to move to Portland to take advantage of Oregon's Death with Dignity Act, a law that allows doctors to prescribe lethal drugs to patients with less than six months to live (if a second doctor agrees). Currently only California,

Oregon, Washington, Vermont, and New Mexico allow for the terminally ill to take their own lives.[19] There is a cooling-off period of fifteen days in each state, so no one is allowed to make a decision like this lightly. As difficult and horrifying a choice it is to make, the one saving grace is the person gets to make the decision for herself, which was exactly what Brittany did, and I applaud her for it.

Although Brittany's final wishes were met, many others around the country are not so lucky, which is just plain sad. I can't think of a more perverted way for the government to intrude in your life than by forcing you to live through a debilitating chronic condition that physically and mentally wrecks you and your loved ones beyond all recognition. Competent adults are allowed to make other momentous, irrevocable choices like having a sex change or an abortion (for the moment and really only in certain states). People deserve the same control over their own death. It's my party, and I'll die if I want to.

Too Many Rules Don't Make Us Safer

Government regulation not only does not make our lives any better, it actually undermines our pursuit of happiness. Studies have shown treating people like babies can turn our brains into pablum. If you take away someone's free will and ability to use common sense, they start acting like real idiots. If you don't have to take responsibility for your own actions, it impedes brain development. Think about it: When you were growing up, rational thought didn't come naturally. It took practice—lots and lots of practice—like any other skill in life, such as learning to read or play the piano.

The bottom line is if you want to be good at anything, you have to be free to do it often and experiment until you get it right. It's good to fall on your ass a few times when you're learning to ride a bike. Baby birds learn to fly better when Momma bird isn't catching their fall, and so do we. We learn faster that way; we're more careful and deliberate when we know it's us and us alone who will pay the price if we screw up.

It may sound counterintuitive, but it's human nature to take *more risks* if we know we won't get hurt. Want scientific proof? A geezer named John Adams (not *that* John Adams), world renowned for his research in risk assessment, has determined that seat belts aren't as helpful as we've been led to believe.[20] He studied eighteen different countries with mandated safety belt laws and came to the shocking conclusion that seat belts had no effect on the safety of people and even *increased* road accident deaths. It's true. Adams found drivers took more risks when they had seat belts, airbags, and antiskid brakes to protect them.

It stands to reason that if you have a net beneath you on a tightrope, you're gonna push yourself harder, but try walking on that same tightrope with no net and you're totally gonna cut down on the number of flips you do.

I'm not suggesting we do away with seat belts entirely. I do think young children should be forced to ride in car seats, because they can't make a rational choice in the matter. But in terms of the adults in this country, I believe seat belt laws have veered off the Rational Road. If I don't want to wear a seat belt, why should I be forced to? If I'm willing to take that risk and am not threatening anyone else, why shouldn't

I be allowed to decide for myself? Like Gwen Stefani sang, with a 1920s finger-wave bob, *It's my life. Don't just walk in.*

Shit Happens...Then We Regulate the Hell Out of It

Life gets messy sometimes. Things come flying out of left field, and we can't always have on a mitt or a helmet or even a condom. We can't possibly predict all the thousands of potential scenarios when an individual moves from point A to B, because—sorry, gamers—we don't live inside a PlayStation where every action has an ascertainable result. To suggest otherwise is insulting to every citizen of this country and to our Founding Fathers, who brilliantly devised a form of government that allowed people to live free and sometimes die through their own choices.

All the regulations we are forced to swallow on a daily basis don't make us perfectly safe. We're not robots or computers. We're all human, and we all make mistakes. Accidents still happen. Children still get hurt on school playgrounds. Surgeons still chop off the wrong leg during surgery. Planes still crash, as do automobiles. Our humanity ensures we will always have errors in judgment, people will always be willfully negligent, and others will even intentionally harm others. Government regulation will never end human error.

Yet in a capitalist country like ours, it will always be in the best interest of a business (or employer) to consider what is in the best interest of their customers (or employees), because that translates into greater revenues. Our nation has reached the maximum saturation level for regulation, but people still get hurt and die in freak accidents. Right now, somewhere in

America someone is burning her tongue on scalding hot coffee. Someone else is ingesting half his daily caloric intake by slamming down a supersized soda larger than a bathtub. And guess what? We're still functioning. Somehow we're managing to make it through the day.

In the end, the road to hell is paved with good intentions. Despite the best intentions of the Dudley Do-Rights in Washington, not to mention the litigators hoping to buy summer homes and matching sailboats in the Hamptons, there are loads of unintended consequences of living in a nanny state. Something's got to change. But it's going to take action, not just words. We need to spit out our federally issued pacifiers; it's not a good look for anyone over the age of two.

Finding Common Sense on Common Ground

So when Kathy, the Starbucks barista with a lip ring, says…

> "Don't you think we need *some* regulation to keep us safe?"

You say: "Of course, but when it comes to regulating things like tattoos and soda, we've crossed into an Orwellian nightmare where the nanny definitely doesn't know best."

> "The nanny state is needed to protect the idiots in this country from themselves."

You say: "Ever heard of the Darwin Awards? They're given out to the people who have the stupidest deaths, and you never hear anyone wishing those geniuses are still around, do you?"

"You want to get rid of seat belts? Really?"

You say: "I'm not saying get rid of them; I'm saying get rid of the laws that force adults to wear them—if I want to make like a bug and go splat, who am I hurting but myself?"

"Giant companies aren't looking out for the best interests of their employees, they're just trying to turn a profit for the fat cats in power."

You say: "Don't you know a happy worker makes the best products? Piss off your people and you can kiss your profits good-bye, fat cats!"

"Why hate on laws that will help our country become less obese? We're all gonna die of diabetes if we keep slamming down Big Gulps."

You say: "Even a government-mandated nutrition plan won't stop the couch-sized couch potatoes from getting their fat on, so why pass laws that will never work?"

"Will you at least admit Bloomberg's 'Potty Parity' law, mandating two public female toilets for every one for men, is a good one?"

You say: "OK, you got me—even though it's paternalistic as hell, that one I don't mind! Then again, I'm not a business owner."

CHAPTER 7

The Problem with Free Money

"Don't care how, I want it *now*."
~ Veruca Salt ~

Please go to a search engine and look up "Matthew Lesko." You'll know it's him when you find yourself rapt, confused, and staring into the face of a Riddler even Batman wouldn't touch. You may have already spotted Lesko in one of his late-night infomercials. He wears a suit covered in question marks. He yells a lot. Wild gesticulations, fistfuls of money, and flying spittle are his shtick. If you have one of those cable packages with entire blocks of infomercials, he'll eventually haunt your nightmares, shrieking at you about "FREE MONEY!!!"

Lesko specializes in four things.

1. Selling his books and products, mostly through infomercials
2. Claiming his books and products will help you tap into huge wealth streams (unclaimed governments funds, i.e, "free money")
3. Calamitous sartorial choices
4. Yelling and shrieking

Like the ouroboros, forever swallowing its tail, we'll circle back to the shrieking question mark man soon enough.

First, let's go shopping. I was in a Walmart recently (yes, I shop at Walmart, and I'm proud of it!) when I noticed something disturbing in the checkout line. No, not the magazine cover with the fifty worst celebrity beach bodies. It was the woman in front of me.

You know the type. Michael Kors handbag, OMG shoes, and a blouse neither you nor I could afford. Perfectly manicured nails tapped away on her new iPhone, which I'm surprised she could even see with her Prada shades on and her nose stuck high in the air.

When the teenage cashier's voice interrupted her texting with the total and she reached into her bag, I was expecting one of those fabled AmEx "black cards." But out came an Electronic Benefit Transfer (EBT) card, and with one swipe, she paid for all of her items with government welfare!

Now, for all of you who have been too busy watching Honey Boo Boo reruns or reading those trashy magazines to notice what's been going on during the last couple of years, EBT cards are the modern version of food stamps—and an astounding number of Americans now depend on them.

It was at that exact moment in Walmart when I realized just how far-reaching and out of hand the welfare state has become, all thanks to the granddaddy of our never-ending helplessness, Franklin Delano Roosevelt.

I'm sure you've heard of him, and how "great" he was, plenty of times. Left-wing zealots in the media and in higher education are constantly pounding it into our heads that FDR single-handedly rescued our country from economic depression with his heroic New Deal (possibly while riding on a white horse and wielding a fiery sword, depending on whom you ask).

What FDR actually did was jack up our taxes and establish legions of federal programs—think rent control, Social Security, and unemployment payments. While the Deal may have been a quick fix for the Great Depression, it set a seriously scary precedent of long-term government dependency, taxpayer-subsidized goodies, and the "gimme gimme" culture that is more prevalent today than ever before.

Now let's go back and look at Matthew Lesko and his question-mark suit. Do you know why he continues to make his commercials? Because it's worth his time. And who makes it worth his time? The people who buy his line of crap. And the people who buy his crap are the people who want a quick fix, an easy answer, and free money.

We all know there is no such thing as free money. But too many of us, as demonstrated by the longevity of Lesko's career, click and buy anyway, hoping for the easy way out.

And sometimes, we get it. But folks, none of that is sustainable, and we've been feeling the impact ever since the New Deal.

In 1932—just one year before Roosevelt took office—the highest income tax rate that anyone in the country had to pay was 25 percent. Just thirteen years later, America's top rate income tax was 94 percent.[1] *Ninety-four percent!!!* Where is the incentive to work all day when you're giving virtually all your income to the feds, who will inevitably redistribute it to their special-interest buddies and waste it on failed dependency programs?

Many contemporary liberals hold the view that the federal government has the answers to all economic and political problems. There is no evidence of this. And it was FDR and his New Deal who provided the building blocks that helped give rise to this foolhardy, throw-caution-to-the-wind liberalism.

We can thank the FDR school of thought for the explosion of disability payments, despite the fact that the United States has only become safer every year (we'll get to this later, but see Steven Pinker's *The Better Angels of Our Nature: Why Violence Has Declined*), food stamps, Obamaphones (yes, those are real), unemployment payments with no work requirement, and what is sure to be known as the single biggest government failure of our time—Obamacare.

Here's the basic gist: The New Deal set the precedent for the mess we're in today, and unfortunately for the generations that followed (including us), this bankrupt way of managing public policy has only gotten worse—and worse.

Oh, SNAP: 1 in 5 Americans Are on Food Stamps

Of all the welfare programs to choose from (and there are tons), the booby prize of our modern entitlement culture would have to be food stamps. Dubbed by the U.S. Department of Agriculture (USDA) as the Supplemental Nutrition Assistance Program (SNAP), food stamps have grown into an expensive and bloated failure. Again, I get it: If tragedy strikes or someone loses his job unexpectedly, a *temporary*, effective, and efficient safety net to help struggling Americans put food on the table undoubtedly makes sense. But as it stands now, SNAP is straight-up broken.

How bad is it? Well, nearly 43 million Americans now receive food stamps, and that number had increased by 13 million since President Tax-and-Spend Obama took office.[2] Take a look at the photo of the crowd at Obama's inauguration. It was in the neighborhood of 2 million. Now multiply that crowd by 23 and consider *just how many people are on food stamps.* That means about 20 percent of U.S. households are receiving food stamps, and some states lean more heavily on that crutch.[3] Oregon ranks number two in food stamp enrollment with about 20 percent.[4] The current leader, at 23 percent, is none other than our nation's capital, Washington, D.C.[5]

Are you ready for the real kicker? Forty percent of Americans on food stamps are *obese.*[6] Yes, our tax dollars are literally being used to fund Pop-Tart addictions across the nation. (But at least they have Obamacare to subsidize those doctor's appointments for their type 2 diabetes.)

Here's how SNAP works (I'm assuming you aren't on food stamps): Recipients receive an EBT card, which looks and functions just like your everyday debit card but is supposed to be used only to purchase food. Yet it's been documented again and again how recipients are able to swipe the card and get cash instead, supposedly for food and food alone, but come on. Give a burnout, a junkie, an alcoholic, or a sex addict a thick wad of free cash, and how do you think they're going to spend that money? Buying broccoli, avocados, and peaches? Not really. They'll be spending it on drugs, booze, and hookers.

Now, don't get me wrong. I'm not here to tell you how to spend your hard-earned cash. That's completely up to you. I believe wholeheartedly in your right to eat pink-slime-filled fast-food nuggets, wash them down with malt liquor, and indulge in a pack of cigarettes (just don't blow your smoke in my face). I'm not your mother. I'm not going to follow you around yelling, "Eat your green beans!" Hell, if you want to take the money you earn from teaching kindergarten and spend it all on blow, that's your prerogative. But when we're talking about money that comes from hardworking taxpayers—that's an entirely different story. I don't know about you, but I'm not busting my rump in the office every day to pay for some junkie's next fix. But sadly, thanks to SNAP, we all are.

Don't expect SNAP to downsize anytime soon. Despite spending an eye-popping $74 billion on food stamps in 2014, the USDA is making the case that the program needs *more* funding.[7] This is another danger about creating a big, fat federal government. Not only do our citizens become dependent, but the institutions themselves—these "departments"—have a vested interest in their own survival. And they're never satisfied with what they get.

The USDA is so set on expanding SNAP that in 2011 alone it spent over $43 million to advertise food stamps.[8] It makes me wish *Mad Men* had run for another forty years so I could have seen Don Draper come up with the perfect pitch for the program:

"Snacks. In the original Greek the word for snacks meant 'crunchtastic.' It was a twinge you felt in your waistband. That doesn't mean you have to feel the old wound in your wallet. The EBT card is a scrapbook. It reminds you of all the things you've ever tasted…and that you'll taste in the future. It returns us, with a poignant ache, to a time when our mouths were full of snacks. And we can do it. We can go home...to a place where our mouths are always full."

On the other hand, perhaps it's a good thing that Matthew Weiner ended the series. Nevertheless, government-produced, slick, colorful commercials are out there enthusiastically *encouraging* people to sign up for the subsidies. No, thanks! Sorry, Uncle Sam, we don't want your corrupt handouts.

By the way, shouldn't getting on welfare be *dis*couraged? And remember, it's our tax dollars that pay for all of this. These commercials portray food stamps in a wholly positive light. Government efforts to distribute food stamps should not demean or denigrate recipients in need—fair enough. But we need a better balance between safeguarding the dignity of these recipients and making them feel that SNAP assistance is an unending and unqualified right.

That "gimme gimme" entitlement mentality promoted by the overgrown SNAP program has gone international—there are even SNAP ads targeted at illegal immigrants! Yes, you read that right. Your hard-earned tax dollars are spent on encouraging illegal aliens to get on the dole in a joint effort between the USDA and the Mexican government.[9] We have actually produced and sent Spanish-language fliers to the Mexican Embassy, telling Mexicans that if they cross our border they can receive SNAP without having to declare their immigration status. Emphasized in bold and underlined, the fliers say, "**You need not divulge information regarding your immigration status in seeking this benefit for your children.**"[10]

WTF? And when you compound this with what we've been shelling out for all the Central Americans who have been flooding the southwestern United States in recent years, we're effectively climbing on top of an economic powder keg and lighting the fuse.

It's not like the USDA is diligent with SNAP funds, in general. In 2013 alone, the department spent $6.2 billion improperly—$2 billion of that was spent on food stamp over-payments.[11] Oops.

If that wasn't enough (is it ever?), SNAP is also riddled with fraud. This is not cynical fatalism. It is not pessimism to describe a negative situation realistically. The fact is, any-thing that can be exploited will be. Exhibit A, Walmart lady. Though it might be difficult to believe, the Queen of Walmart is not the worst example of welfare abuse. Lots of recipients trade in their food stamps for cash, allowing them to use that money for whatever the hell they want: booze, illegal drugs, cigarettes, even donuts and Twinkies.

Many of these transactions take place on Craigslist. One such posting in the Atlanta area read, "I have $500 worth and it costs $350 cash. No I will not do half!"[12] It's win-win—the original SNAP recipient gets cash, and the buyer saves a couple hundred bucks at the grocery store. And what does our government do to address this issue? A big fat nothing.

The USDA has done a terrible job enforcing its "food only" regulation—the rules have basically become just squishy guidelines. Especially since the program has a "cash assistance" program that lets recipients use their EBT cards to take out cash at ATM machines. As a result, food stamps have been accepted as payment for lots of items that will make you go "whaaaa?" Here are just a few of the many, many things you can buy with your EBT card:

- **Taco Bell and KFC.**[13] Hey, deep-fried shit still gets your stomach full.
- **Dildos, thongs, and condoms.** Kiss My Lingerie in Louisiana was approved to accept EBT cards as payment in 2014.[14] If I'm going to be kissing Southern Fried unmentionables, I don't want them to come from the government.
- **Strip teases.** A FOIA request several years ago revealed that welfare recipients were using their EBT cards to withdraw cash near infamous strip clubs and jiggle joints.[15] Erections are free and easy to come by, but apparently we need to subsidize them.
- **Bail.** Felons have reportedly used their food stamp benefits to pay their way out of jail.[16] Is this, or is this not, the lamest "jail break" in history?

Here's another disturbing SNAP tidbit: McDonald's encourages and helps its employees and their families sign up for welfare—most notably, food stamps—through its "McResource" program.[17] Imagine that you go in to a job for your new staff orientation and right out of the gate your HR manager is talking to you about the glamorous lifestyle of *welfare*. Why, why, why? Isn't the purpose of an employer to provide *gainful employment*?

This is employment without the gain.

It's simple: McDonald's can pay lower wages if more of its employees are on food stamps. We taxpayers are subsidizing a good chunk of every fast-food worker's salary, leaving the savings for McDonald's.

Walmart does the same thing. Not only is the retailer our

nation's largest private sector employer, it's also the biggest consumer of taxpayer-subsidized welfare. Its employees are the single biggest group receiving taxpayer subsidies. The average Walmart worker receives $1,000 per month in welfare.[18] America currently hosts about five thousand Walmart stores and clubs. That's a lot of working welfare recipients.

And it's not just big chain companies that are doing this; lots of little guys are taking advantage of us taxpayers for their corporate gain, too. The summer after I graduated from college, I met an old roommate for lunch who had just landed a job working at a nonprofit in Boston. She was going on about how shitty the pay was but then added, "It's cool though, they're helping us sign up for food stamps. At least I won't go hungry!"

So now we're paying for college just so graduates can end up on food stamps.

Is hiking the minimum wage the answer to these problems? Hell, no. We went over why that never works in the last chapter. The only real solution is to downsize the mammoth food stamps program. If we do, Walmart, McDonald's, and other corporate giants would be forced to increase salaries to retain employees. Besides, the fact that 20 percent of American households receive food stamps at this point should be proof enough that it's currently far too easy to qualify for the benefits.

The biggest fundamental problem with SNAP is that the program is fundamentally counterproductive because it discourages work. When a recipient starts making too much income, they lose the benefit. The incentive to find a job— the basic need to feed yourself and your family, to work or starve—is wiped away. No wonder enrollment continues to grow with no end in sight. Most traditional Democrats and old-school lefties assert that food stamp use is up because the economy has tanked, but that's simply not the case. Food stamp spending nearly doubled years ago, *before* the current recession. The program's budget rose from $19.8 billion in 2000 to $37.9 billion in 2007.[19] And then add on what we've experienced since Obama became president.

If you're looking to foster more productive and independent generations to come, this is one of the most pressing issues facing our nation today. Yet it receives almost no coverage from the mainstream media. So what's it going to take for the media and the rest of us—the voters—to wake up? Are we going to wait until one-third, one-half, or maybe even three-quarters of us are receiving food stamps?

Since the market crash in 2008 and the advent of the so-called Great Recession, we Americans have become obsessed with the "1 percent" and the "99 percent"—or better still, the 1 percent *versus* the 99 percent. Isn't it about time we turn our focus to how much the 20 percent on SNAP are taking from us, the 80 percent? Isn't that a statistic worth raising placards and protesting in our public parks?

And let's not forget the great and powerful Oz, I mean overseer, the U.S. Department of Agriculture (USDA). Clearly a byproduct of the Washington political mindset, the USDA thinks they have the answers to all of life's problems. And it's not just with SNAP. In all their wisdom, USDA bureaucrats have heavily regulated and subsidized the agriculture industry for decades, scaring American farmers away from real free trade until they come running to Washington, seeking help. If you thought the American farm industry was a bastion of true capitalism, think again.

For decades now, Democrats and Republicans alike have continued to increase the power, reach, and purse of the USDA, with no end in sight. According to their own office, the department "provides leadership on food, agriculture, natural resources, rural development, nutrition, and related issues." Well, do you know what the latest tab was for that "leadership"? Try $146 billion.[20]

In 1862, President Abraham Lincoln established the USDA at the outbreak of the Civil War and at a time when over 50 percent of Americans were farmers. Since a great deal of American agriculture was based in what was then the Confederacy, the Union couldn't afford failed crops. Lincoln's idea was to provide the farmers with good seed stock and solid information about agriculture, soil, and seasons. It was, in a way, a matter of national security. Lincoln referred to this small, focused, new agency as the "people's department," and it was initially headed by a commissioner without cabinet status. Oh, how times have changed.

Today fewer than 2 percent of Americans are farmers, yet the USDA has ballooned in size and scope. Cash payments *alone* to farmers cost between $10 billion to $30 billion each year.[21] The average farm household income is $87,289—way above the average American household.[22] Farm subsidies do not make economic sense, but farmers have strong armies of lobbyists, so we taxpayers continue getting stuck with these enormous bills.

It doesn't end there. Legislators from rural farm states who want in on this pork have made deals with those from urban states who want subsidies for welfare programs like SNAP. In the end, the deal-making politicians spread the wasteful spending across various districts and political party lines—and into the pockets of their special business interests.

A few years back when I had just started out as a reporter, I discovered footage of the USDA's "Cultural Sensitivity Training," in which government employees were instructed to bang on tables and chant, "The pilgrims were illegal aliens."[23] (Could there possibly be a less catchy chant?)

During this "sensitivity training," conducted on a government contract by a guy named Samuel Betances, workers were also told not to use the word *minorities*. Betances and his firm were paid almost $200,000 for this "training." And do I need to remind you who paid for it? That's right, suckers like us.

The lion's share of the USDA's steadily growing budget goes to other endeavors, such as regulating agricultural markets, enhancing food safety, and providing food assistance and nutrition advice. This all sounds fairly high-minded and noble, but the USDA has become yet another department that keeps expanding its waistline—just like the Pentagon and most other federal government departments. Except in this case, what began with protecting seeds has mutated into a bureaucratic behemoth that pays corporate farmers billions in subsidies and creates dependency among millions of Americans via SNAP.

Was this really Lincoln's intention? My bet is that he'd be one of the first calling for the Department to be revamped in light of such revelations, and maybe even, I don't know, *sent out to pasture.*

Mo' Money, Mo' Problems

Ever felt a little depressed? There's an itch between your shoulder blades that you just can't reach, yet you're single and thereby have no one to scratch it (or to love, for that matter). Maybe you're counting the hours until your rent check bounces, because despite your ability to vote, drive, and retain a stack of credit cards, you still suck at math. You probably wish you had just stayed in bed, but you're out of sick days and worried you'll get fired if you try to take just one more. We all go through rough patches in our lives, some tougher than others. What can you do other than buck up and force one foot in front of the other?

Well, you could get *paid* for being down in the dumps! That's right, Uncle Sam will cut you a check every month if you say you're too depressed to leave the house and go to work. Honestly, they should start sending me money ASAP, because even most movie previews get me crying.

"My ex's new girlfriend just posted a hot picture on Instagram.... She's so much hotter than me, I'M DEPRESSED!"

"OMG I gained five pounds this week... SOOO DEPRESSED!"

"I dropped my iPhone in a parking lot and the screen is cracked... DEPRESSED!!!!!!"

My mommy tells me I'm a just drama queen with "white girl problems," but it's depression, dammit! I want my check!

I would never willingly become a drain on the system. But there are lots of other folks with their hands out; currently, 8.8 million Americans receive disability checks from the government.[24]

I first discovered disability payments for depression back when I was a youngster in New Hampshire. Rebecca, a middle-aged woman who lived in my dad's neighborhood, told my dad that she had severe depression. So bad, in fact, that she was collecting disability because of it. Rebecca revealed that she hadn't had a normal job in years; she was simply "too depressed" to make it into an office each day.

Here's a thought: Maybe she was depressed because she hadn't had a reason to leave the house in years! I imagine that staying at home day after day, with no job to give you purpose, would actually make depression a lot worse. I'm no psychologist, but I'm pretty sure most of us would be climbing the walls with depression and anxiety if we lacked a sense of purpose. I know there are plenty of cases of actual severe depression that really does hinder normal day-to-day activity. But given that a person's subjective claim that he or she is "mentally incapacitated" is enough for that person to start collecting disability every month, it's easy to imagine how hundreds of thousands of Americans game the system.[25] And besides, do we really want to be using our tax dollars to pay able-bodied people to stay home and watch *Bachelor* reruns year after year? Thanks, but no thanks.

Disability payments are doled out by the Social Security Administration under the name of Social Security Disability Insurance (SSDI). And as with most mammoth welfare programs, paying for these benefits ain't cheap, people. The cost of the program was $144 billion in 2013—yes, we're literally shelling out hundreds of billions to pay people not to work.[26] And that has nearly doubled what it cost ten years ago.

As the spending increases indicate, the number of Americans on disability also continues to skyrocket each year; since 2008, the number of individuals receiving these benefits increased 20 percent.[27] There is currently one person collecting disability in the U.S. for every thirteen people working full-time.[28] The number of recipients has exploded since 1968, when one person was collecting the benefits for every fifty-one people working full-time. These troubling stats would lead you to believe America is becoming more dangerous and unsafe everyday—or why else would the number of "disabled" folks be growing so steadily?

Actually, our nation has only gotten safer over the years. Back when relatively few Americans were on disability, a larger percentage of the population worked in factories and had blue-collar jobs that often involved dangerous physical labor.

Today, most working Americans have office jobs, and as a population we suffer from fewer disabling conditions than we did in the past.[29] Advances in technology and research have given birth to superior medicine and resources to help the sick and disabled. As a result, our average life span is longer than it's ever been.

So why are disability payments skyrocketing?

The Social Security Administration argues that the growth in disability spending is due to the mass retirement of baby boomers. But that's not the whole story. Researchers at the National Bureau of Economic Research discovered that only 13 percent of the recent growth in the disability program among men was due to the aging population. For women, it was just 4 percent.[30]

The real culprit is relaxed eligibility, making it easier than ever to collect disability benefits. And before you start blaming Obama, here's a dirty little secret that you'll never hear from the Republicans: Ronald Reagan is the one who relaxed the eligibility requirements. Yup, that's right—Ronald

Reagan, the right's poster child for traditional, small government conservatism.

In 1984, under Reagan, Congress passed the Social Security Disability Benefits Reform Act (SSDBRA...don't you just love a good government acronym?).[31] Under SSDBRA, the government is required to place more weight on applicants' own assessments of their disabilities, especially when it comes to physical pain, and to loosen the screening process for various mental illnesses.

Translation: If you tell your doctor that you're in pain or depressed, or that your back hurts—even if there's no way to prove it—you can get disability benefits. Easy as store-bought pie.

Reagan clearly didn't foresee the consequences of this provision when SSDBRA was passed. When he signed the bill into law, he proudly said, "It maintains our commitment to treat disabled American citizens fairly and humanely while fulfilling our obligation to the Congress and the American taxpayers to administer the disability program effectively."

One reason the number of disability recipients has increased so drastically since Obama took office is because after the recession of 2008, many people who had trouble finding jobs realized they were eligible for the benefits. These folks had been eligible since Reagan signed the SSDBRA, but many didn't know it until they were out of work.

It also doesn't help that the size of government payouts for disability has increased substantially over the years.[32] And then there's the fact that Americans of all ages who qualify for the disability benefit also automatically receive Medicare.

The value of Medicare benefits also continues to balloon, simply increasing the incentive for out-of-work Americans to get on disability. Why schlep it to your shitty job answering phones and doing dull paperwork all day when you could be paid to stay home eating Fritos and talking to your dog? Did you see *Million Dollar Baby*? After making it big in boxing, Hilary Swank's character surprises her enormously overweight and lazy mother with a house. She immediately protests that if she has a house she can't collect disability. "Maybe you could get a job," offers her daughter.

"You know I watch my stories in the afternoon," Mom replies.

This life of ease can be yours with a simple trip to the doctor's office for that pesky shoulder pain you've been having.

Wasteful spending aside, the saddest part of this situation is that the explosion of the program may actually hurt those who are genuinely sick or disabled. There are Americans out there who truly do need assistance because of crippling disabilities, but the present system does a disservice to those folks. Many able-bodied Americans are currently gaming the system, collecting disability checks for life. This makes it difficult for the Social Security Administration to direct resources adequately to those who actually need it. And since the SSDI trust fund is set to go broke soon, the only way to ensure that the legitimately disabled get assistance is to reduce spending and tighten the eligibility criteria immediately. It's time we got rid of the rampant abuse in the disability program before the people who need it most become the ones losing out.

Someone's Gotta Pay for My Fifteen Kids

A family friend, Jack, owns thirty to forty low-income prop-
erties in New Hampshire. Most of the places are falling
apart, with peeling paint, ripped-up carpets, and the telltale
lingering cigarette stink that screams, "Nobody cares." Jack
often told us horror stories about tenants who wouldn't pay
rent. Keep in mind that a lot of these tenants weren't nice,
wholesome families with two kids and a golden retriever;
many of these folks were drug dealers and others who had
serious criminal records. Sometimes Jack brought a baseball
bat with him for protection when collecting rent. Oftentimes,
they still wouldn't pay, and Jack was forced to evict them (not
so quick or easy a process).

. After several years of doing this, Jack finally figured out
a way to make these problems go away: He began renting,
almost exclusively, to tenants on Section 8. Section 8 recipients get up to $2,200 per month from the government to
pay for their rent. That's more than most people can afford
on their own. Section 8 became the government's solution to
public housing buildings, which are notorious for being crime
ridden.

The program is great for landlords like Jack. Dealing
with Section 8 tenants eliminates the annoyance of having
to deal with unreliable tenants who don't pay rent. Section 8
rent checks show up in the mail every month on time, since
Uncle Sam is technically the tenant. The system also benefits
landlords, because it allows them to jack up rent prices—the
government doesn't make the effort to ensure that each property's rent is set at a fair price.

But Section 8 often harms the same people it's intended to help (shocker). If you make too much money, you lose your Section 8 benefits. So if you get a job and start earning an amount that disqualifies you from Section 8 funding, you may end up paying more for rent and reducing your disposable income substantially. Needless to say, I wasn't shocked when Jack told me that he almost never sees one of his tenants leave the program.

Many Section 8 recipients work under the table to avoid losing the rent money. Others decide to simply not work at all. The program, which has no limit on how long recipients can receive the benefits, is literally creating generations of families dependent on Uncle Sam.

Our own government is miring people in permanent poverty by rewarding them for not working. By subsidizing people to stay in poverty, the government enables the most vulnerable in our society to remain dependent. In thirty-five states, welfare pays better than minimum wage.[33] Why go out there and work your ass off flipping burgers when you can sit on it at home eating Cheetos and make more money doing it? The current welfare system provides such a high level of benefits that low-skilled workers are better off financially if they choose to not work at all. If you really wanna live large on welfare, move to Hawaii, which offers over $60,500 per year in benefits, not to mention the beaches and year-round sunshine.[34] *Hell-oha*, that's more than the average household income in the United States! Recipients also do well in Washington, D.C., and Massachusetts, where annually they can collect $50,820 and $50,540, respectively, but without the palm trees and balmy weather.

And even with all of this money going out, welfare doesn't do much to end poverty. If anything, it's like a life support system for keeping people poor and unemployed. The numbers don't lie. Taxpayers spent nearly $800 billion on ninety-two federal programs to help the poor. Yet the poverty level remains only 2.5 points lower than it was when President Lyndon Johnson declared war on poverty in 1964.[35] Clearly this system of perpetual victimhood and government dependency isn't working. Here's an idea: Instead of spending hundreds of billions to keep poor people in poverty, why don't we invest some of that money in things like effective teachers in our public schools and training programs? As the old saying goes, give a man a fish and he'll eat for a day; teach a man to fish and he'll get off his Cheeto-dusted ass.

It's painfully obvious that welfare needs to be downsized across the board. At the time of this writing, nearly 50 percent of U.S. citizens receive some sort of financial assistance from the U.S. government.[36] That's half the population!

Unfortunately, welfare is on the fast track toward more and *more* and *MORE* expansion, and many Americans don't seem to notice this problem hurtling toward us like a money-sucking meteorite. Today, many are of the opinion that Uncle Sam is obligated to provide for the every need of all Americans. Gallup polling shows that about half of Americans support an expansive government as opposed to a limited one.[37] And 19 percent support a *very* involved government that "should take active steps in every area it can to try to improve the lives of its citizens."

Having money in the bank, a house to live in, food to eat, medical care, a cell phone, and fast WiFi—these are all things that many Americans now believe are fundamental *rights* that the government has an obligation to provide. Gone are the days when hard work was mandatory to put food on the table for your family. And is it really necessary to point out that when a government provides every need of its people, that's called Communism? I shouldn't have to explain why *that* doesn't work.

This kind of entitled mind-set reminds me of that glorious Britney Spears single called "Gimme More" (yeah, the one she released the same year she went psycho and shaved her head). Poor Brit. In her prime she was the perfect pop-princess diva-goddess all-star that every nineties girl aspired to emulate.

And speaking of more…

A few years back, a woman named Angel Adams garnered national attention. Adams, who was thirty-seven years old at the time, had fifteen kids. Her fiancé, the father of ten of her children, was in jail. Adams believed that the system failed her even though her food, her furniture, and her $800-per-month rent was all being paid for by Good Samaritans and the government. But that wasn't enough. "Somebody needs to pay for all my children," Adams told a local news station.[38] "And all my suffering. Somebody needs to be held accountable, and they need to pay."

Um…*somebody* needs to pay? Maybe that somebody should be Adams! And I shouldn't have to point out the many ways to protect one's self from giving birth to more than a dozen children. These poor families are given incentives to reproduce though. Each little baby they pop out bumps up their benefits.

This kind of sickening entitlement should make every American furious. There are plenty of needy Americans out there who are struggling to make ends meet; many of these folks are embarrassed and ashamed that they are on government assistance, and they will do everything in their power to get off of it as fast as they can. *Those* are the people who are supposed to benefit from our welfare system. *Those* are the people we all want to help. Not people who are unwilling to work and think they deserve everything for nothing.

The crazy thing is that it's not just Americans who think our government owes them something. So do people from around the world. The United States is a beacon of hope, where all kinds of people can come and take their shot at the American dream. It's a wonderful thing. But when people come to our country and demand to have their every need subsidized by hardworking taxpayers, things start to go south.

And statistics suggest that America's generous welfare system is attracting illegal immigrants with their hands out. As of September 2015, 87 percent of illegal immigrant families were on welfare.[39] There are also reports indicating some immigrants migrate to the United States illegally and then have children in the country just so they can bank on these benefits.[40] It's crippling our country, not to mention that it completely ruined that Britney song for me. Most anthems are shouted by activists who want change, but this one is just whined in between commercial breaks.

Gimme, gimme more. Gimme more. Gimme, gimme more.

Gimme, gimme more. Gimme more. Gimme, gimme more.

Gimme, gimme more. Gimme more. Gimme, gimme more.

Gimme, gimme more. Gimme more. Gimme, gimme more…

How the Hell Did We End Up Here?

In a nutshell: Most federally managed welfare programs—whether SNAP, disability, unemployment, or the Obamaphone program—have negative unintended consequences, despite good intentions.

So how did it get this bad? The Founding Fathers wanted to promote general welfare by allowing the government to legislate law for the common good of its citizenry. But there's no question that they'd roll over in their graves if they could see the swollen welfare system in place today, taking from some and giving to others.

In an 1816 letter to his respected friend Joseph Milligan, Thomas Jefferson wrote:

> To take from one, because it is thought his own industry and that of his fathers has acquired too much, in order to spare to others, who, or whose fathers, have not exercised equal industry and skill, is to violate arbitrarily the first principle of association, the guarantee to everyone the free exercise of his industry and the fruits acquired by it.[41]

It doesn't get much more direct than that. Jefferson was wise enough to predict happiness and prosperity for the nation, so long as it could "prevent the government from wasting the labors of the people under the pretense of taking care of them."[42] (For a fascinating look at the evolution of Jefferson's thinking I highly recommend *American Sphinx: The Character of Thomas Jefferson* by Joseph Ellis.)

Jefferson is often quoted by modern conservatives, He was, after all, a member of the Democratic-Republican Party, which political scientists today call the first Republican Party. Democratic-Republicans opposed a powerful centralized government, fearing it would lead to monarchical tendencies. They demanded that authority be given to the states, instead.

So given that Jefferson was a small-government guy, it doesn't come as a shock that he was explicit about his disdain for a welfare state. What is more surprising, though, is that Jefferson's political foes—those belonging to the Federalist Party—were also quite clear in stating their opposition to the government taking from some to give to others. There's something innately commonsense in the highly reasonable stance of, "I earned this and I want to keep it."

John Adams was a staunch Federalist (in case you slept your way through eighth-grade history class, he was also the second president of the United States). He believed that a strong centralized government could prevent tyranny. (The word *tyranny* has an antiquated ring to it, so as a more modern, Orwellian, and chilling alternative, consider tyranny as *totalitarianism*. If you're in a totalitarian state, it simply means that there's no way to opt out. Think monarchies, North Korean regimes, Scientology, and so on.)

Adams clearly opposed the welfare state. In his 1787 published work, *A Defense of the Constitutions of Government of the United States of America*, he wrote:

> The moment the idea is admitted into society that property is not as sacred as the laws of God, and that there is not a force of law and public justice to protect it, anarchy and tyranny commence. If 'Thou shalt not covet' and 'Thou shalt not steal' were not commandments of Heaven, they must be made inviolable precepts in every society before it can be civilized or made free.[43]

Adams and Jefferson make the same general point: The redistribution of wealth by the government would not yield freedom or prosperity. Nothing confusing there, right?

There's so much yammering and handwringing about what the Founders actually intended. But when it comes to handouts, it's crystal clear. We're lucky enough in this case to be able to go right to the source: the Constitution. The Constitution's general welfare clause outlines simple, and very specific, duties of the federal government.[44] All other powers are left to the people and to the states.

James Madison, generally regarded as the "father of the Constitution" and its principal author, said, "With respect to the two words 'general welfare,' I have always regarded them as qualified by the detail of powers connected with them. To take them in a literal and unlimited sense would be a metamorphosis of the Constitution into a character which there is a host of proofs was not contemplated by its creators."[45]

Thankfully, for much of U.S. history, the Supreme Court treated the welfare clause the way the Founders wrote it. There wasn't any reason not to. In a 1905 ruling, the Supreme Court even wrote that the Preamble of the Constitution—in which the "general welfare" is referenced—"has never been regarded as the source of any substantive power conferred on the Government of the United States or any of its Departments."

Well, that all changed in 1933 when FDR became president and introduced the New Deal (that thing we touched on earlier in the chapter before you took a time-out to follow your favorite celebrity down a Twitter black hole). The New Deal helped us get out of the Great Depression, but in the long run it paved the way for the modern welfare state.

FDR was the first U.S. president who saw the Constitution as a "living, breathing document." Translation: He thought that he could interpret it any way he wanted to interpret it, to make it mean anything he wanted it to mean.

Remember the rules from *Animal Farm* that the pigs kept perverting to the point where we got paradoxical maxims like "All animals are equal, but some are more equal than others"? The rules and phrases were as malleable as Play-Doh.

It reminds me of when I was in high school and my mom would say, "Make sure you come home early," as I left for a Friday night party. Of course, I never listened and would end up rolling into the driveway around 11 P.M. She'd be all pissy about it, reminding me that she had ordered me to come home early, and I'd come back with some snide remark like, "I *did* come home early. Everyone else is staying at the party until at least one A.M. I was basically the first one to leave. It was a misunderstanding! I had simply *interpreted* what you said to mean, come home early *for a Friday night.*" It never worked, and I spent a lot of my teenaged years grounded. No regrets, though—that was how I ended up so good at *Farmville.*

FDR thought he could twist the Constitution by interpreting meanings that weren't explicitly written in the document. Unfortunately for FDR and his grabby political descendants, *words mean things.* It is painfully obvious when someone is willfully twisting a phrase to suit his or her own ends.

The Supreme Court justices at the time weren't on the same page as FDR. Despite the adulation he's been receiving for decades, the president initially had a tough time getting major parts of the New Deal legislation passed. The justices were weary of an activist government and held strict constructionist views, meaning they applied the text of the Constitution only as it is written. (Makes sense, right? Get thee to a *Webster's Dictionary,* nation, and heal thyself!)

Despite the overturning of many of his programs by the courts, FDR vowed that he would do whatever it took to end the Depression. He explicitly said in his inaugural speech of 1937 that if the powers given to him under the Constitution were not enough to do what he wanted to accomplish, he would simply give himself more powers.[46] You know, kind of like a king, or a tyrant, or a Big Brother type from Orwell's worst imaginings—exactly the sort of thing our forefathers came to America to avoid.

An insight about tyranny comes from one of Aesop's animal fables, "The Wolf and the Lamb." A wolf meets a lamb in a field and decides he wants to eat him, but how, oh how, can he justify it?

Their conversation is illuminating:

"Last year you grossly insulted me," says the wolf.

"Indeed," bleated the lamb, "I was not then born."

Then said the wolf, "You feed in my pasture."

"No, good sir," replied the lamb, "I have not yet tasted grass."

Again said the wolf, "You drink of my well."

"No," exclaimed the lamb: "I never yet drank water, for as yet my mother's milk is both food and drink to me."

Upon which the wolf seized him and ate him up, saying, "Well! I won't remain supper-less, even though you refute every one of my imputations."

As always with Aesop, there's a moral, which in this case has an uncanny relevance to our discussion: *The tyrant will always find a pretext for his tyranny, and it is useless for the innocent to try by reasoning to get justice, when the oppressor intends to be unjust.*

Boom. You can't reason with or placate people who have already made up their minds. You need to know that for most of the New Deal's myriad legislative programs, at least some parts of them were pushing the limit or over the line of any reasonable notions of constitutionality. FDR intimidated justices, packed courts, overstepped at every turn, and used the presidency as the means to bring about his utopian vision no matter what the costs.

Roosevelt's goals were the three Rs: Relief, Recovery, and Reform. Alliteration does have its charms, but ending Great Depressions was not one of Roosevelt's accomplishments. We have the Second World War to thank for that.

The New Deal gave birth to a never-ending, ever-expanding welfare state, where the government has taken on the role of our ineffective, fumbling caretaker. Although this notion was never the intent of our nation's founders, it is now accepted by many Americans that it's the responsibility of the feds to take from some to give to others. At least Robin Hood stole from the rich to give to the poor. In this case, we're all being robbed.

A Poorly Tended Lighthouse

The situation is grim, but there are solutions. It's not too late to turn things around. Welfare cuts need to be made across the board. When over half of the population depends on monthly checks from the government, something is wrong. There are too many people taking advantage of the system, and it's time to nudge these folks back into the work force.

It's critical that we create enforceable work requirements for able-bodied welfare recipients. I know it sounds harsh, but if recipients were forced to get out there and work (or at least mandated to attend job training) to receive benefits, their families would be better off in the long run. We've already seen success with work requirements on the state level.

In October 2014, Maine Republican governor Paul Le-Page implemented a work or volunteer mandate for able-bodied adults without dependents to receive food stamps. Those who did not complete the work or volunteer requirement were denied the benefits after three months.

The result? An astounding 70 percent drop in enrollment in SNAP.[47]

Another solution: We could tax welfare benefits, most of which are currently tax free. This has worked relatively well in Sweden, a nation known for its generous welfare system. If recipients were paying into the system, they would be likely to support an efficient government.

And let's not forget education. Education level plays a large role in determining who receives welfare. Investing in good teachers—and having the ability to fire bad ones (see chapter 4)—would go a long way toward equipping young Americans with the skills they need to be self-sufficient down the road. We have to be giving people opportunity, not handouts.

These are all relatively easy and simple reforms. Why isn't Washington taking the necessary action?

As Americans, we pride ourselves on giving everyone equal opportunity and helping the most vulnerable in our society. The Statue of Liberty, a symbol of hope that's recognized around the globe, promises a better life to those who come to our shores: "Give me your tired, your poor, your huddled masses yearning to breathe free." But Lady Liberty holds a torch, not a welfare check.

America has served as a beacon. We have shone brightly to guide other countries by our example and ethos. But lately we've turned that beacon of liberty into a poorly tended flame that threatens to flicker out completely if we don't start fixing things soon.

Finding Common Sense on Common Ground

So when your sweet little aunt May says...

"You want to downsize welfare? How heartless!"

You say: "I don't want to downsize welfare. I want to super-size self-sustainability! Can you think of any downside to helping people get back into the workforce, and off the government dole? (Which, in case you forgot, is financed by our tax dollars.)"

"Welfare has kept millions of poor people fed and clothed when they have nothing else."

You say: "Some people definitely need and deserve welfare. But welfare has also kept millions of able-bodied Americans stuck in perpetual poverty. And that number continues to grow with each generation raised to accept such limitations. When does a temporary accommodation become a permanent or semipermanent crutch?"

"More Americans are on food stamps because of the 2008 recession."

You say: "I've heard that, too, but it's just not the case. The food stamp program ballooned years ago, *before* the current recession. These are hard, verifiable numbers for anyone who's willing to look objectively, they're not abstractions. Here are a few places you can check out. This is all public knowledge: factcheck.org, publicagenda.org, etc."

"Obesity is a disease. Some people just can't help it."

You say: "Sure, but there are always better choices that every single one of us can make. If everyone tried to even be a *little* healthier, the amount of money the government would save in payouts would be staggering. This doesn't have to be all or nothing. If everyone made *one* healthier choice a day, we'd all benefit."

"Disability abuse has been rampant since Obama became president!"

You say: "I hear that a lot, too. I think a lot of people would be surprised to learn that it was Republican hero Ronald Reagan who drastically relaxed the eligibility requirements to receive disability. And if we're talking about disability abuse, we can't separate it from the characters of the abusers. We can't blame any one president for the thousands who have gamed the system over the years."

CHAPTER 8

Party! Party! Party!

"I hate everyone."

~ Grumpy Cat ~

While working as a reporter in Texas, I was dispatched to Dallas to cover the 2014 Texas GOP Convention. Let's just say it was an experience I'll not soon forget. During my short stay in the Lone Star State, I was quickly clued in to a well-known fact: Texas Republicans are truly their own breed. Whatever you may think about Republicans...well, let's just say that everything really is bigger in Texas. They don't just feel uneasy about the abortion issue; they *hate* abortion. They don't just think that we should govern with morality; they want to stock every classroom with Bibles. It's not that they're suggesting we don't say the word *gay*; they want us to take action to save us all from the abomination.

I knew all this going into the convention, but still, I tried to keep an open mind. And let me tell you, actually being there and immersed in that culture opened my eyes—in a big way. I looked over a sea of thousands of cowboy hats as the smell of leather boots engulfed me. I suppressed the urge to cover my ears as the deafening chants of *"USA! USA!"* rose to a crescendo when Rick Perry took the stage

Issues like spending and regulation, much to my surprise, weren't really discussed—the focus was placed squarely on social issues. When the main speeches concluded, the portion of the crowd that was interested scuttled off to a smaller room to discuss the official platform of the Texas GOP. Party delegates and members of the public were invited to voice their opinions on a variety of issues to determine how the platform would read. After a lengthy conversation about how "life matters" (translation: If you're a pregnant woman, your life doesn't matter because you're essentially stripped of all rights to your own body), gay marriage came up. Texas was one of the dozen or so states that still hadn't legalized it at the time, so I wanted to see what the GOP had to say. I could see how it could be a tricky issue for them. After all, the gay vote is pretty well established and sizable.

The discussion started with one gray-haired church lady babbling about how legalizing same-sex marriage would criminalize "her" Christianity (exactly how would that work?) and how gay people are essentially akin to murderers and rapists. Then there was a parade of more gray-haired church ladies, all of whom emphatically declared they were "deeply offended" that someone would even want to marry another person of the same sex. I rolled my eyes and didn't think much of it. I'd heard this kind of bigoted gobbledygook from the Texas Republican Party before. Then a teenaged boy I'll call Ryan spoke up.

Ryan said that he was a conservative and that he believed in many of the basic principles of the Party, like reducing taxes and making it easier for businesses to flourish. But he wanted everyone to know that he could no longer be a part of the Republican Party because of what had happened to his older brother.

Ryan's brother, now in his twenties, had come out as gay a few years before. Their family was very traditional and religious and, putting it mildly, his parents did not take the news well. They believed that being gay was a *choice*, like a hair color or a piercing. Their son had made this sinful choice and needed mental help. So the parents sought out conversion therapy to "help him become straight" and "heal his emotional problems." As part of this therapy, the brother was forced to accept that his feelings were evil and a sickness.

Well, guess what? The "counseling" didn't work—and when he turned eighteen and the parents still hadn't gotten the results they wanted, they cut him off from the family completely.

Fighting back tears, Ryan continued his story. "I haven't seen my brother in over two years." Describing the horrific impact that the therapy and estrangement had on his family, Ryan begged the Republican Party to consider a different stance. Ryan's words were emotional and moving, and his pain at the loss of his brother was palpable. I thought for sure the room of people would show compassion and there'd be some crack in the veneer. Incredibly, they all sat there staring at him, with arms crossed and scowls on their faces.

Beyond disgusted and feeling physically ill, I had to leave the room. Later, back at my hotel I started doing research. I found out that reparative therapy was not just approved but *endorsed* by the Republican Party of Texas! I also discovered that the "Log Cabin Republicans," a group of gay conservatives, wanted to attend the conference but were denied the right to have a booth. The official reason was that they "do not embody the Party's platform."[1] I'll say they don't. Their steadfast belief in limited government, free markets, personal responsibility, and individual liberty seems worlds away from what the current Republican Party has morphed into.

Is it any wonder that no young person wants to be called a Republican? Especially when the party platform is about as fresh as that green thing in the back of the fridge that nobody can identify (and nobody wants to smell) anymore?

You know, I used to be a Republican and proud of it. I loved wearing my elephant pin and representing the next generation at local rallies. What first attracted me to the party was being told, as a kid, that the Republican Party— you know, the guys who brought you Abe Lincoln and Teddy Roosevelt, Dwight Eisenhower and Ronald Reagan—was the party of states' rights and individual initiative, the party that let Americans be Americans. Republicans were against federal waste and opposed to creating an underclass dependent on government handouts. They believed that Washington, D.C., was too big, the federal government too bloated, and that a lot of the important decisions should be made at the state and local levels, if by any government at all. Amen, guys. I'm all for that. So where did that go?

Sorry for the sour grapes, but the Republican Party, as it is today, does not stand for youth, and it doesn't represent people like me. As with the Democrats, what we're dealing with here is a group of old-school, entrenched blowhards who somehow dare to call themselves "representatives." But just whom do they represent?

Beware of Wolves in Republican Clothing

These days, most of our Republican representatives fall into one of two equally horrible categories. There are the RINOs (Republicans in Name Only), the George W. Bushes, John McCains, and Marco Rubios of the party. The hawkish guys who think the world's problems can be solved with a nuke, and that cowboy-boot-wearing, gun-toting Westerners have the responsibility to save the rest of the world from those eeeevil Muslims.

Please. RINOs are about as big-government as you can get. They yap about "downsizing Washington" but want to inject billions upon billions into the DOJ like shady, back-alley butt implants, all in the name of public safety. These guys are the kings of scare tactics. It seems like every election cycle they give us a new country that we're all supposed to hate, and if we don't beef up our military—right *now*—Country X will find a way to nuke us all. The RINOs allege that the only way America will be safe is if we open up more military bases around the world and put more boots on the ground. Hah! Remember the iron triangle we talked about? We know their motivation.

Then there are the religious loons, the so-called Religicans. These are the Rick Santorums and Mike Huckabees of the Party. Just like the RINOs, these idiots claim they want to get government out of our lives but then advocate for the exact opposite. They yap endlessly about abortion, gay wedding cakes, and why every drug user in America should be locked up. They aren't on a mission from God; they're on a mission to control everything about the way we live, even the things we choose—and have the full legal right—to do in our own homes.

Now, there's nothing wrong with having a little religion in your government—as long as it's your religion. But if the government wants to adopt a god you don't believe in and practices you find disagreeable (and sometimes physically harmful), well then, there's going to be a problem. That's why my man Thomas Jefferson fought so hard to keep church and state separate. And especially today, with our country being one of the most diverse in the world, it really makes no sense to want to impose a religious agenda.

Let's make a deal, all you representatives of the Religious Right. Read the First Amendment to the Constitution, take a history class, and maybe then we'll consider voting for you.

And then there's President Donald Trump, who ran as another type of Republican entirely—but one that the youth vote got excited about. With his rhetoric about deporting millions and banning Muslims from entering our country, it's no surprise that he received only 37 percent of the youth vote.[2]

Meanwhile, with these nimrods at the wheel, the GOP wonders why the youth isn't flocking to join their party. It's pretty obvious, isn't it? The frustrating thing, and what perhaps makes it harder just to discount them summarily, is that many of the religious loon types actually have small-government stances on taxes and other fiscal issues, but as we saw in Texas, those topics are rarely mentioned.

Of course, there are a few sensible, small-government conservatives in Washington (how ya doin', Rand Paul?), but these guys are consistently belittled and overshadowed by the powerful RINOs and Religicans. Unfortunately, our political system incentivizes Republicans to fall into one of the two categories. It's much easier for them to raise money by drumming up support from the religious base and other major donors by harping on hot-button social issues and inciting fear using terrorism (Trump, anyone?) to distract us from the real issues. Heaven forbid they address the problems of budget sequestration or the coming entitlement tsunami. No, that just isn't as sexy.

Do as I Say and Not as I Do

So, if the Republican Party is so bad, does that mean we should all be Democrats?

Snort! Oh, man. I crack myself up sometimes.

If you've paid any attention up to this point, you know how disastrous that would be. Even though big-government policies championed by liberal Democrats *sound* nice, they are usually destructive as hell in practice. Democrats basically "buy" votes by promising citizens government goodies: free food, free phones, free Internet, free college, free cash, and other irresistable-sounding "entitlements." Then they conveniently never talk about how all of this will be paid for. It's like planning a luxurious tropical vacation with a boyfriend who never gets off your couch. Sounds fabulous, but you know you're going to end up footing the bill.

Just like the Republicans, the Democrats will say or do anything necessary to climb that same greasy pole of power. Lying is the norm in D.C., and sometimes the lies are downright criminal. But instead of being shunned by society or locked up, like normal criminals, members of the political class get away with it.

Hillary Clinton was caught blatantly lying multiple times.

Remember when she tried to blame the Benghazi attack on a YouTube video? Thanks to State Department documents, we now know that was a bigger lie than when I promised my mom I wouldn't sneak out past curfew on prom night.[3] Only, I got grounded for life, and Hillary faced zero consequences. And we now also know that she flat-out lied about using a private e-mail server to send sensitive national security e-mails while she was Secretary of State. Keep in mind that this is the woman who received the Democratic nomination in 2016. As a woman myself, man, I'd love to see a Madam President, but this ain't the chick.

It's not just the lying. Politicians seem to come from a group that doesn't think the rules apply to them. Republican congressman Michael Grimm from New York pleaded guilty to felony tax evasion in 2014, causing him to resign from office shortly thereafter. Former Speaker of the House Dennis Hastert, another Republican, pleaded guilty to providing $3.5 million in hush money to cover up wrongdoing in his past; Hastert was allegedly trying to hide the sexual abuse of a minor from decades ago, when he was a high school teacher.[4] And it's not just Richard Nixon who had a fondness for illegal surveillance. Laura Richardson, a Democrat from California, was found guilty on seven counts of violating U.S. House rules by improperly using her staff to campaign for her, destroying the evidence, and tampering with witness testimony.[5] Even presidents are corrupt.

When Barack Obama worked for the law firm Miner, Barnhill & Galland in 1996, he sued Citibank for not making toxic loans mandated by the Community Reinvestment Act.[6] Then, after becoming president, his administration sued Citibank for having made those exact same loans. Another glorious role model for the kids. You can grow up to be president some day! Just get really good at lying and cheating, and generally being the type of little brat who drives Mommy to drink.

Which may very well be the root of the problem. The power of political office tends to attract just the kind of people we *don't* want representing us. What kind of person voluntarily goes through all the trouble of campaigning—which usually requires giving up your normal day job, taking a low salary, and living in roach-infested America's Best Value Inns while on the trail—all without an ounce of certainty that he'll win? Sure, sometimes it's people who are actually passionate about effecting change in our system for the good of the people. Most of the time, though, it's narcissistic asshats more interested in their own celebrity status than the well-being of the people they're elected to serve. There's an old adage that politics is like Hollywood for ugly people. It's up to us to make sure we elect those who actually have substance—the Depps and De Niros, not the Steve-Os and Snookis.

The Two-Party Trap

In a lot of ways, the Ds and Rs are just the same wolf in different-colored sheep's clothing—and the similarities go far beyond their constant lying and sense of entitlement.

Take Hillary Clinton and Jeb Bush—each of whom represents the Establishment wing of their party—for example. The two couldn't be more different, right?

HAH!

Besides the fact that they both hail from political dynasties and look smashing in pantsuits, these two have a whole lot more in common. They're even funded by some of the same megadonors. More than sixty of the richest Americans contributed to both of their campaigns—from racetrack owners to bankers to hedge fund managers.[7]

But the commonalities don't stop there. Here are a few other ways in which Hillary and Jeb appear eerily similar:[8]

- They both supported mass National Security Agency (NSA) surveillance and the Patriot Act.
- They both support the failed War on Drugs.
- They both support bailing out big banks.
- They both support the dangerous Trans-Pacific Partnership Agreement.
- They both support the death penalty.
- They both do a wicked Adele at karaoke. (Or so I heard from those on the campaign trail.)

I could go on, but the point here is that two political figures, each of whom supposedly represents the pinnacle of their respective parties and complete *opposite* ends of the political spectrum, are actually quite similar.

Both also have blatantly corrupt corporate ties. And I'm not just talking about receiving generous donations from super PACs. I'm referring to the toxic mixture of corporate interests and government policy. Jeb served on the board of five major companies that have faced class-action lawsuits, some of which involve fraud, while Hillary was on the board of directors of Walmart for six years.[9] She also hired a former Monsanto lobbyist to run her 2016 presidential campaign. Can you say conflict of interest?

Don't get me wrong. There's nothing bad about candidates having a background in the private sector. After all, if they're going to run the world's largest economy, they should know how to run a successful business. But there's definitely cause for concern when politicians get supercozy with monster corporations. Remember the Obama Solyndra scandal?[10]

Back in 2009, the green-energy, solar panel manufacturing company received a $535 million loan from the federal government. During a highly publicized visit to Solyndra's headquarters, Obama proudly declared that the company was "leading the way toward a brighter and more prosperous future," which is liberal-speak for "financially unstable"—a fact that Obama's Office of Management and Budget reportedly knew at the time the megaloan was issued.

Why would he spend taxpayer money to make such an obviously bad investment? Billionaire George Kaiser, whose family foundation was one of Solyndra's main investors, was also a major Obama fund-raiser. What's even more insulting is how adamant Obama was about getting big money out of politics during his presidential campaigns—like he could just say it and we'd be gullible enough to believe him. In November 2007, he said, "I am in this race to tell the corporate lobbyists that their days of setting the agenda in Washington are over. They will not drown out the voices of the American people when I am President."[11]

Uh-huh.

Here's the bottom line: The Republican and Democratic Parties both suck big-time, and have been pulling fast ones on the American people for decades. They don't offer us hope, and they don't offer us change—they just offer the same old dirty, corrupt tricks. They lie to us, they deceive us, and sometimes they even break the law—all to further their own political careers or fatten their wallets.

The two-party system has caused us as voters to make inaccurate assumptions about candidates just because they have an *R* or a *D* next to their names on the ballot. Newsflash: Not every Republican will lower taxes, and not every Democrat will end our foreign entanglements. This is why we have to open our eyes and diligently examine all politicians before giving them our votes. And that doesn't mean choosing the one with the million-dollar smile or the one we'd most like to have a beer with.

The good news is, we appear to be stepping up to the plate. Many American voters are waking up, realizing how corrupt the two-party system has become, and making their voices heard at the polls. In 2016, Libertarian Gary Johnson received more than 3 percent of the popular vote. I know, I know, 3 percent doesn't sound like much—but that's 4 *million* votes "stolen" from Clinton and Trump. The 2016 election was the strongest showing in twenty years for independent candidates.[12]

In the 2012 presidential election, former Texas congressman Ron Paul practically started a revolution among voters who were fed up with the political status quo. Even though Paul ran as a Republican, he openly gave the finger to the establishment and didn't comply with the Party platform, which reeked of dirty money. Bucking the party system, Paul represented a different breed of conservative.

I'll never forget when, during a 2011 Republican primary debate, the congressman made the case for legalizing drugs. "You have the right to do things that are very controversial," Paul said. When the moderator tried to discount the idea, saying, "Are you suggesting that heroin and prostitution are an exercise of liberty?" Paul turned his attention to the audience. "How many people here would use heroin if it were legal? I bet nobody would," he said. With a strong dose of sarcasm, he continued, "Oh yeah, I need the government to take care of me. I don't want to use heroin, so I need these laws."[13]

The crowd burst into applause. Meanwhile, the RINOs standing next to him onstage began sweating profusely.

It was clear that despite all the attempts to downplay him, Paul had mass appeal. He ended up placing third in the Iowa caucuses with 21 percent of the vote, and second in New Hampshire with 22 percent.[14] Not too shabby for a "fringe" candidate.

It's no surprise that the Republican Party did everything possible to take out Paul. Just days before the Iowa caucuses, Paul had a commanding lead in all the polls. Yet establishment Republicans in the state, like Representative Steve King and Governor Terry Barnstad, tried to convince the public that a vote for Paul was a wasted vote.[15] These same individuals tried sabotaging the Paul campaign by claiming the congressman would lose to Obama if the GOP nominated him. It seemed like everyone hated Paul—*except the voters.*

We saw the same thing in the very next presidential election cycle, but it was Bernie Sanders shaking up the Democrats' status quo. Representing the antiestablishment, Sanders was even beating Hillary in many polls, despite the media constantly belittling him.

These alternative candidates are striking a chord with voters' growing disgust with the political class. Many of them end up settling for what they see as the lesser of two evils, begrudgingly casting a vote or even staying home on Election

210 Government Gone Wild

Day. But a growing number are actually stepping outside of the traditional red-versus-blue dichotomy and voting for a third party. Bucking the two-party system makes sense in many ways. Only two choices? We wouldn't accept that with shoes, so why with politics?

But just like the Rs and the Ds, third parties come with their own set of problems...

The Hippie, Neocon, Democrat Chick

My mom is a Democrat and my dad is a Republican (yep, you guessed it, they're divorced now), and I never completely agreed with either of them when it came to politics. I was usually able to find nuggets of value in each of their ideologies, but a lot of the time, when they got to rambling, I'd be *this close* to asking for a DNA test. I vaguely knew of alternatives to the mainstream Big Two, but I never really explored them as a kid.

That all changed when I was a high school student, and I heard Ron Paul speak at an event in New Hampshire. Prior to attending this speech, I was made to believe that Paul was a tinfoil-hat-wearing loon. The mainstream media portrayed him as a crazy man whose ideas were highly dangerous to the nation. But I knew enough about the libertarian philosophy to see that it aligned—at least somewhat—with my own views, so I showed up at Paul's speech to see what the man had to say.

As he went on about the state of the nation and what he thought needed to change, I found myself thinking, "This makes so much sense!" The general gist I got from his message was: Live the way you want to live, do whatever you want to do—just don't harm others while you're doing it. It was like a lightbulb went off for me. Isn't this why the Founding Fathers started the country in the first place? Amazing. It was as old—and as new—an ideology as we Americans could have.

I left the speech stunned. I had finally discovered the political party for me: I was a Libertarian!

For the next few months, I sought out the online libertarian communities and integrated myself as much as possible. I jumped into conversations on Facebook, Twitter, and in the comment sections of online news articles. I even started my own blog and Facebook page called *The Libertarian Chick*. Yes, I was fully on the Libertarian Party bandwagon, and I wanted everyone to know about it.

As time went on, however, I became disenchanted with the Libertarian Party members I conversed with. I noticed a general anger among them and an inability to entertain any ideas that didn't align exactly with every last plank of the Party. Even loyal followers of my blog sent me nasty messages when I published posts that weren't "Libertarian enough." I have gotten cranky e-mails calling me "The Tea Party Chick," "The Republican Chick," "Democrat Chick," "hippie chick," and others that are way too mean to include in this book (my mommy is going to read this!). And it was no different on my Facebook page. When I posted an article about government welfare I was a "heartless neocon." When I expressed support for Senator Ted Cruz I was "bought out by the Republican Party." When I posted about legalizing hemp I was a "left-wing nut job."

I began to notice this kind of griping going on outside of my immediate circle, too. It was at Libertarian Party rallies and fund-raisers. It was in the greater online community. The mind-set seemed to be that if you didn't agree with every aspect of the Party platform, then you weren't really a Libertarian. How the hell does that kind of epic closed-mindedness come from the party of freedom? Even the Big Two (or more accurately, the Entrenched Two) each have a wide spectrum of folks who can call themselves Democrats or Republicans. How was this progress?

This oppressive conformism became especially real to me when I was blocked from the official Libertarian Party Facebook page. (Yes, they blocked the Libertarian Chick— isn't that ironic?) During the 2012 presidential campaign, the page featured an article promoting a flat tax. I wrote a comment stating that Republican primary candidate Herman Cain also supported a flat tax. I was by no means trying to endorse that wackadoo; I was simply pointing out that, like the Libertarian Party, he supported a flat tax.

Within seconds I got bombarded with rude comments, telling me I had no business being there to "spew my Republican filth." At first I thought it was just a few crazies who were attacking me (it was the Internet, after all), but the nasty remarks kept coming fast and furious. I tried defending myself with comments of my own, but it was pointless; I was outnumbered. Later that day, when I went back to the page, I found out I wasn't able to post comments anymore because an administrator had blocked me.

God forbid that anyone express an opposing opinion in a political forum (*gasp!*).

The Libertarian Party has a big problem on its hands. The doctrinaire nature of its members—requiring litmus tests on such topics as immigration, tax policy, government spending, and social issues—is largely why they have been unable to effect major change. It is clear that Libertarians are principled people. They have strong convictions, which is what led them to break out of the two-party system in the first place. But clinging to these convictions without allowing any dissent is what hinders them from getting anything done.

I have spoken to many sanctimonious Libertarians who say they will *never* support any candidate other than <<Insert Name Of Some Abstruse Libertarian Party Representative Nobody Has Ever Heard Of>>. Like that could do any good. And anything positive I might have to say about a mainstream candidate who might have some libertarian tendencies but isn't running with an *L* next to his or her name usually sends them into a full-blown hissy fit. Doesn't sound a whole lot different from being locked into the two-party system, does it?

Libertarianism is supposed to be about embracing individualism. That means all voices should be welcome at the table—even those that don't conform to every last one of the Party's planks. But unfortunately, the stubborn dogmatism has made "Live the way you want to live" OK only if you're living the way the Party wants you to live. And in that way, the Libertarian Party has become no more representative than the Republicans and Democrats.

Paul-Bot

Now don't get me wrong—there's a lot about the Libertarians I love dearly. I still write my blog, *The Libertarian Chick*, and I try to abide by the "live and let live" philosophy. But

I'm not—and never will be—a card-carrying member of the Libertarian Party.

Other third parties are just as bad, too. Even the über-utopian Green Party has problems, and I've experienced them firsthand. In college I briefly became involved with the Green Party Club for a solar energy event. I mean, who outside of an Exxon-Mobil boardroom can argue with promoting alternative energy? But my experience with the students in the club can only be described as awful. They knew I wasn't left leaning on many issues, so they made it clear right away that I wouldn't be socially accepted by them—even though I was volunteering at their club meeting to help them! The members knew about my blog and continually referred to me as "Paul-Bot." Not that I really care (again, I heart Ron Paul), but still, it was annoying. And when the week of the big event rolled around—surprise, surprise—they "forgot" to invite me to the club dinner. The club members made it clear that because I wasn't fully on board with their entire agenda, I would never be accepted by them and would always be treated like an outsider. Aren't hippies supposed to be open and inclusive? I was on the exact opposite side of the aisle from the Republicans, yet I found myself stuck in the same old BS.

It doesn't matter so much which political party you align with. Just the act of subscribing to an established political philosophy and trying to fit into a large group can be problematic. Political parties inevitably lead to groupthink, which is basically what happens within a group when the desire for harmony with the people around you results in irrational thoughts and actions.

William H. Whyte Jr. first coined the term *groupthink* in the March 1952 issue of *Fortune* magazine:

> We are not talking about mere instinctive conformity—it is, after all, a perennial failing of mankind. What we are talking about is a rationalized conformity—an open, articulate philosophy, which holds that group values are not only expedient but right and good as well.[16]

We've all fallen victim to this kind of mob mentality at one time or another. Back when I was a junior in high school, a girl in the popular crowd inexplicably took an interest in me and invited me to a sleepover with her friends. Ironically enough, this gaggle of girls was known as the Group. Given my social status at the time, this was an exciting event for me. I knew I was in when Claire, the Regina George of the Group, invited me to their chat room on AOL Instant Messenger a few nights later (what we used pre-Facebook). This became a nightly routine; we would all log on and gossip for hours.

These girls had something to say about everyone, and most of it was mean. I had never been much of a gossiper (who the hell cares if Mindy gave Jeff a blowjob in the movie theater last week?), but I was desperate to impress the Group, so I went along. I started saying things I wouldn't normally say. When one girl would hurl an insult about how ugly her ex-boyfriend's new girlfriend was, I'd jump right in, trying to top it with an even nastier comment. The meaner my comments were, the more the Group seemed to like me. It was a disturbing bonding experience.

A couple weeks later, during a nightly chat-room session, one of the girls brought up Hannah, a girl in our grade who was known for being socially awkward and wearing weird clothes. *"That girl has a face only a mother could love. Did you hear that she lost her virginity to Mike last week? Apparently he screwed her while his mom was home. What a slut."*

Hannah and I had become friends that year when we were paired as lab partners in biology (nothing brings people together like desperately trying not to fail a class in which you are both mentally challenged). She was an aspiring fashion designer with an inexplicable love for old thermoses and black tea. An oddball for sure, but I was an oddball too. Inevitably we had become close.

A few days before the Group brought her up during the chat room, Hannah had told me all about the incident with Mike while we pretended to be working on our lab. She described how awkward the whole thing was and that she regretted it. Of course, I promised not to tell anyone. Cross my heart and hope to die.

I valued my friendship with Hannah. But in that moment, in the chat room, the only thing on my mind was impressing the Group. And without thinking, I typed something to the effect of, *"Haha! I'm lab partners with her. She told me ALL about getting banged by Mike."* I then proceeded to tell the girls all the dirty details.

Within a matter of days, everyone in our grade knew. Hannah became a laughingstock and a "whore." And of course, it eventually got back to her that I had been the one who'd spilled the beans. She never spoke to me again, aside from short exchanges necessary to finish our bio lab.

I had fallen victim to the social pressure of groupthink. Because I was so desperate to fit in with the Group and feel a sense of conformity and safety in numbers, I'd tossed my morals right out the window.

And FYI, my status as a member of the Group didn't last long. Eventually they found out that I was really a nerd who spent most Friday nights watching *Futurama* reruns with my dog, and I never heard from them again. Oh, well.

The exclusive mind-set I experienced in the Libertarian Party and the Green Party seemed to be symptoms of the same phenomenon: Even though many of these third parties pride themselves on being alternative and individualistic, loyalty to the group usually results in the loss of independent thinking. After all, raising controversial issues or disagreeing with the group could result in being ostracized.

Sounds kind of like a cult, right? Did you read George Orwell's novel *Nineteen Eighty-Four* in high school? In case you did not, it takes place in a totalitarian superstate called Oceania, where the government controls and sees everything. Citizens of Oceania are supposed to speak "Newspeak," a language created and controlled by the state with the goal of stamping out individuality and self-expression. A vital part of Newspeak is "doublethink," when people accept two contradictory beliefs at the same time.

Psychologist Irving Janis, famous for his study of groupthink, would often refer to Orwell's novel when explaining what happens in group situations:

Groupthink is a term of the same order as the words
in the newspeak vocabulary George Orwell used in
his dismaying world of 1984. In that context, groupthink takes on invidious connotation. Exactly such a
connotation is intended, since the term refers to the
deterioration in mental efficiency, reality testing and
moral judgments as a result of group pressures.[17]

All of this is to say that when people feel allegiance to
any party—whether it be to the Democratic Party, the
Republican Party, the Libertarian Party, the Green Party,
the Communist Party, or the United States Pirate Party (yes,
that's a real thing)—they are vulnerable to falling victim to
groupthink.

Orwell wrote *Nineteen Eighty-Four* way back in 1949,
which goes to show that people throughout time have been
pretty consistent in their desires to band together in order to
feel safe, be it from prehistoric saber-toothed tigers or illegal
aliens crossing the border. Whenever we feel threatened by the
unknown, our natural instinct is to follow the path that promises the best chance for survival. Many times in world history
that basic urge has led to folks handing over their freedom in
exchange for security. So it's not hard to see how Orwell could
conjure a story about the horrors of totalitarianism, a direction
one could say our own government is headed in today.

These Shoes Rule; These Shoes Suck

You may have heard the expression that everything old is new
again. It's a pretty common refrain when it comes to fashion trends, but can also very easily be applied to the current

state of our two-party political system. Hemline lengths and round- versus pointed-toe shoes have gone in and out of fashion favor through the centuries and always seem to put women squarely in camp Goodie Goodie Two Shoes or Wicked Witch of the West. It all depends how designers decide to make us march down the runway to the beat of *their* drums, never our own, because that would be bad for business. If everyone started deciding for herself that she no longer wanted to be a slave to trends and began following her own sense of personal style, instead of emptying her wallet every three months when the start of a new retail season signals the need for a whole new wardrobe, the clothing industry would topple off its stilettos and fall to its knees.

Unfortunately, our country's political party system has more in common with the fashion industry than just the billions of dollars at stake.[18] It, too, relies on people blindly following what the "experts" tell them. It's a self-supporting ecosystem, in which the greatest power is derived from politicians feeding off Americans who don't ask questions or demand to be heard. Individuality and independent thought are the death knell to the two-party system every bit as much as to the fashion industry.

And, likewise, everything old is indeed new again when the mere notion of a party system is just as repugnant to so many of us today as it was to the Founding Fathers. Having witnessed the eighteenth-century version of hate ads and personal attacks on the European political stage, the drafters of the Constitution had every intention of dissuading Americans from joining in the same orgy of power and influence.[19] If we're going to turn this thing around and get America back on track, perhaps we'd all benefit from taking a few history lessons as well.

Finding Common Sense on Common Ground

So when Debby, your annoying coworker, asks...

"You're not a member of any party? What planet are you from anyway?"

You say: "I'm from Planet Freedom; I don't align myself with any party because they're all flawed and corrupt. I don't fall for groupthink because I think for myself!"

"So what do you stand for anyway?"

You say: "I stand for independence from government intrusion and personal freedom. I'm ahead of my time and waiting for the rest of you to catch up with me!"

"So you recommend young people not vote for anyone?"

You say: "No! Use your brain and make the decision that is right for you. If I tell you who to vote for, I'm as bad as the groupthink brainwashers who are dividing the country."

CHAPTER 9

Our Unprecedented Opportunity for Success— or Jackassery

"YOLO"

~ The Internet ~

My shoes were soaked as I hurried along a Boston side-walk, wet with slush left over from the snow we had gotten last week—even though it was April. I was already twenty minutes late to meet Rob at Samurai, a hip sushi joint on Boylston Street. Oh, well, it's not like I cared too much. This was a Tinder date, after all. Yes, I will admit it: I have used Tinder, and I am not ashamed! If you're under thirty-five and you haven't used it, you're lying.

Anyway, I didn't really know much about my date at this point. All I knew was that his name was Rob and he was an MBA student at the Sloan school at MIT. It seemed promising, but you never really know what you're going to get with Tinder.

When I finally arrived, I was thirty minutes late. Rob had texted me earlier, saying he would be in a white shirt with a red tie. Scanning the room, I saw a bunch of trendy-looking couples, but no Rob. Then finally, in the back of the room, I spotted a man wearing a white shirt and a red tie—but that couldn't be him. He looked...old.

Before I could look away and duck back outside, he waved me over. Crap! He saw me. As I got to the table, though, I don't know if it was the dim light from the old-school incandescent bulbs, but he wasn't necessarily bad looking. In fact, he was pretty sharp.

We ended up staying there for over four hours, until they closed. We talked about everything: our families, school, his obsession with rare coins, my passion for ending the Fed. You know, the usual. Rob turned out to be an interesting guy.

Surprisingly, it ended up being a pretty great date. Instead of ending in a blacked-out Uber ride home at 3 A.M. like I hear most Tinder dates end, we shared a quick kiss after dinner. I headed home, knowing that I wanted to see him again.

As soon as I got home, I called Bagels. Bagels is my best friend from high school, who got his nickname when he was caught stealing—yup, you guessed it—a bagel from the local grocery store in ninth grade. We all have our vices. Even though we ended up going to colleges in different cities, we still talked almost every day.

I told Bagels all about Rob and how much I liked him, and Bagels got right to work researching Rob on Facebook, Twitter, Tumblr, Instagram, Ancestry.com (standard procedure after all my dates). When I was really into a guy, there was nothing more pleasurable than obsessing over every post and picture he put up on social media—and analyzing it all with Bagels. (*"He just posted a picture online with this weird girl. Who the hell is that bitch??? Oh wait... I just went to her profile... It's his sister."* That kind of thing.)

We looked for Rob on Twitter but found nothing. It was a little odd, but I didn't think much of it—maybe he just wasn't that into Twitter. I knew he had a Facebook account—we were already Facebook friends. It was fairly inactive, though, with very few pictures or status updates. It had enough to keep us busy that night, but there was nothing really worthy of freaking out over.

As the week went on, I texted Rob several times, trying to initiate another date. His responses were always flirty, but he wouldn't commit to another meet-up. Strange. If he was as interested in me as he had acted, why wouldn't he want to go out again?

Then on the following Sunday, I saw that he posted a rare status update on Facebook, something to the effect of, *I'm going to the Boston Common for the afternoon. Look forward to taking in the nice weather!*

Of course I called Bagels immediately.

That was when Bagels came up with a genius idea: I would go hang out at the park, just to read or do tai chi or something, and "accidentally" run into Rob. What a coincidence that I was there, too! The plan was perfect. Besides, hundreds (probably thousands) of people go to the Boston Common every weekend, and this was the first nice Sunday we'd had since winter—so it wouldn't seem odd at all that I would be there.

Long story short, I never spoke to Rob that day. When I got to the park I saw him from afar pushing a stroller. The woman with him—his wife, no doubt—appeared to be in her late thirties. I managed to leave the park, in shock, before he spotted me.

Later that evening, when reality set in that Rob was a creepy married man, I sent him a text, confronting him: I had seen him with his family, and he was an awful, awful person for going on a Tinder date with me. Three hours later, this is the exact text I received in response: *Do not contact me again. I am 42 years old and never had an interest in you.*

Of course I was mad as hell. There he was, a married man, trying to pick up girls half his age on Tinder. And I knew he looked old, but forty-two? Seriously?! Still, after catching Rob I also felt empowered in a way. I had literally caught a man trying to cheat on his wife, and it felt strangely powerful to call him out on it. To this day, Bagels and I still refer to him as Rob 42.

Now, I could have done without meeting Rob 42, but thanks to apps like Tinder, Facebook, Instagram, and Twitter, I've actually met and connected with lots of cool people. My old roommate and I had our first conversation on Twitter; one of my longest romantic relationships was with someone I met on Facebook; I am able to keep up with Bagels, and other old friends around the country, on Snapchat; and in the case of Rob 42, I have Tinder to thank for one of the best cocktail party stories of my life.

Recent rapid advances in technology have allowed us to connect in faster, more efficient ways than ever before. But it's not just communication that has changed—it's our entire way of life. Thanks to massive open online courses and other online resources, you can now get a great education from a top university—even MIT or Stanford—from the comfort of your own bed. Not to mention, you can do it while Facebook messaging your bestie and checking out cat memes on Reddit. How awesome is that?

These days, Americans are insanely good at multitasking and processing information—faster than we ever were before. Sure, a fair number of us have attention deficit disorder, but we don't really *need* a long attention span when we can learn calculus in our underwear at home, and politicians are making their presidential announcements with no more than a tweet and a snappy YouTube video. Yes, what was unheard of only a few years ago is now standard, and we're set to take full advantage of it.

You've heard me complain about how closed-minded and isolated some folks can be. Well, with high-speed Internet becoming the norm and traditional cell phones being phased out in favor of smartphones with data plans and social media preinstalled, we have the means to combat that. The Internet has made it possible for almost everyone to meet, learn, argue, debate, discuss—even idiots and lowlifes like Rob 42 and Clinton 45. There's no arguing that we're a connected society (and if you feel compelled to, just leave your thoughts in the "comment" section). Today, we can see, hear, and gossip about everything everyone else is doing. It has never been easier to be an informed citizen than it is today.

And politics has been altered forever by the rise of social media. Back in the day, political campaigns were simple: The more places that a candidate physically visited to give rousing speeches, the more people would be willing to vote for them. It was a total money game, and those who couldn't ante up simply got flushed out. But now the tide has turned.

Politicians with smaller budgets actually have a shot at winning elections by connecting directly with voters to spread their message (though if I get one more e-mail from a politician with the subject line "hey," I may scream).

And as voters, we can easily push out the unqualified jokers—every election has them—by simply fact-checking them on Google. Hell, we don't even need to watch the speeches live anymore. We can catch the videos on YouTube or Vimeo, on our computers while reading up on the candidate's gun control policy, or even on our iPhones while waiting in line at the polling booths. There's absolutely no excuse for us to be uninformed.

So listen up, folks: An Internet storm is brewing, and it's the perfect time for us to change America. It's up to us to harness technology to not just play the political game, but to take it over.

The Rise of the Hoodie Geek

Fortunately for us, there's still time to take the government by the balls and squeeze until the dysfunctional bureaucracy cries uncle. It's not enough just to vote anymore. Don't get me wrong—voting is vital to creating change. But your voice, your opinion, is just as important. And today, there are plenty of ways to make your voice heard and change the screwed-up system.

Think about it this way...

Aren't we the lucky ones who get to support old people in the lap of luxury as they face mass extinction? Yep, just like the dinosaurs, but without the potential for a theme park (it'd be *way* too frightening to see a Hillary Clintonasaurus chasing after you in your car's side-view mirror). Instead of paying for an amusement park, you'll pay into Social Security for your entire working life and never see the benefit of it (if you have no clue what I'm talking about, you'd better go back and read chapter 2). Right now, you're out there hustling in the workforce so that millions of old farts can spend the next twenty years playing golf in Florida and lounging on the beach in too-revealing swimwear.

Doesn't that piss you off? Overexposed cellulite aside...it should! Get pissed and get loud. Use some of the same medicine that the boomers did back in the day when they were unwashed hippies and thought they could change the world, one peace march at a time. Fortunately there are better ways of telling our legislators that we're sick of eating their bullshit sandwiches. If there's a government program that reeks of entitlement or just plain stupidity, we need to let them know.

The reason we don't have to despair is because it's never been easier to use the tools our generation has created and developed to our advantage. We've been mocked and ridiculed for our use of technology. Now it's time to show the world that we're more than our Candy Crush scores.

If you're over the age of ten, you've probably heard that the mainstream media is biased. That phrase shouldn't be shocking. But do you understand the mechanics behind the expression? Traditionally, the type of people who gravitated toward journalism as a career came from educated, liberal backgrounds. And if a reporter came from a liberal East Coast family, how do you think she was going to frame a story? It would only be natural for that person to feel most comfortable in a position of servitude toward the politicians who mirrored her own principles.

Many journalists have admitted point-blank that they were coerced into slanting their stories in ways that were favorable to liberals, while also painting devil horns and a pitchfork on stories about conservatives.[1] I mean, when you have a network nightly news anchor who starts telling bald-faced lies about his experiences as a reporter covering the war in Iraq, clearly, these folks are used to making stuff up. And feel quite comfortable doing it.

Do you know what finally brought the truth to light in the case of Brian Williams's deceit? Interestingly enough, it was social media. The soldiers involved, the ones who actually put their lives on the line for Williams's butt, spent many years unsuccessfully fighting the bogus story he was sharing publicly about coming under enemy fire. No one listened. These brave men were not heard until Facebook and Twitter were launched and the truth was given a voice.[2] A voice that could not be ignored. Not even by the liberal media. The world, and by extension the world of social media, became ours for the taking.

It all happened not so long ago in a galaxy far, far away... called Harvard, where a nineteen-year-old student named Mark Zuckerberg started Facebook. Was it a completely new idea? Did he reinvent the wheel? Hell no. He was a college kid. There was beer to drink and girls to obsess over when they turned him down for dates.

But he did do something pretty extraordinary. He took an idea that already existed (a web-based school directory that was being used at most Boston-area colleges) and trans-formed it into the virtual place to be if you wanted to connect or be connected with.[3] The coolest part is that Zuckerberg started it all from his dorm room in a hoodie and flip-flops.

He didn't have to pretend to be an adult in an expensive suit with a mortgage and country club membership. Zuckerberg, before the age of twenty, started a networking revolution without ever leaving his dorm room. Even better, the dude made a fortune doing something he loved, and he is now worth an estimated $44 billion. He's currently the seventh richest person in the entire world.[4] He makes the blowhards on that old show *Lifestyles of the Rich and Famous* look like sad little hobbits.

Did I mention that Zuckerberg was a college dropout? You know someone else who dropped out and made a ton of money riding the tech train? Jack Dorsey, the guy who made us all into obsessive "Twits." Dorsey left New York, where he was a student at NYU, to follow his passion for coding in California, where he founded Twitter. What Dorsey lacks in fortune (estimated at more than $2 billion) next to Zuckerberg, he more than makes up for in *GQ* cover boy points.[5] The dude is smokin' hot, with or without all the zeroes attached to his bank statement, and he proves that nerds have come a long way since the old pocket protector days. No longer marginalized for being different, techies are now ruling a universe of their own design.

What did you do this morning after breakfast?

My point isn't to make you feel sad and pathetic that you're still in college or have just graduated and haven't founded a billion-dollar tech startup. Not everyone can kick it Zuckerberg style. Or else everyone would. Just like everyone can't be a mad genius coder who looks like Channing Tatum.

The way to be heard in today's world is through media, be

it social or otherwise. That's how we communicate and run our lives. Technology has brought us closer and also amped up the volume on our thoughts and opinions. So it makes total sense that social media, specifically, has become a powerful and essential tool in starting revolutions worldwide.

Gone are the days when Paul Revere had to bust his hump riding on horseback in the middle of the night to spread the word that the British were coming. And he wasn't talking about One Direction getting their rocks off.

Revere was a complete and utter badass. So much so, that he was employed by our Founding Fathers as a messenger to deliver news on matters of life and death for the colonists. Fast and accurate information was essential to the vast network of farmers throughout New England. Sadly, Revere hasn't had a TV show dedicated to him yet, but I do think he deserves more time in the spotlight.

Effective as Revere was at getting the word out that the king's troops were coming, he only had to reach a small audience over a relatively short distance. What if he had had to reach millions of people across an entire country?

What would have been impossible in 1775 is the norm today. Through social media outlets, we can reach ridiculous numbers of people living at the ends of the earth. With a little typing, and the click of a mouse, we can let the world know our thoughts on the latest Kylie/Tyga fight, or share an Instagram snap of the sushi we had for dinner (as if anyone but us cares). Sure, a lot of the messages we send are silly and unimportant, but the power of social media can be harnessed to effect real social change, too.

When the Middle East began to implode five years ago,

young people took to social media to bring worldwide attention to their cause. Demanding a better life with greater respect from their governing bodies, they knew the best way to communicate with each other and the outside world was through blogs, Facebook, and Twitter.

The so-called Arab Spring began in December 2010, when a Tunisian street vendor set himself on fire in protest for his mistreatment at the hands of the government.[6] He was just a self-employed merchant who was harassed by the local police and denied assistance by higher authorities when he begged for help. That one act of protest was the start of large-scale civil unrest that quickly spread across the Middle East and North Africa.[7] Citizens of countries like Egypt, Syria, and Yemen were fed up with living under autocratic regimes that clearly didn't care about their well-being. They were tired of being silenced and forced to follow laws that they had no part in creating.

When they finally decided that they couldn't take the abuse any longer and wanted their collective voice to be heard by the world, what did they do? They took to social media to spread the word on their revolution. Facebook, Twitter, and personal blogs provided not only an outlet for their anger but also a logistical tool for exchanging information and planning demonstrations. Facebook pages like "We are All Khaled Said" were created to generate support and organize demonstrations.[8] For the first time in centuries, the voices of ordinary Arabs were heard.

Now you may be wondering what someone in Tunisia setting himself on fire has to do with you. You may be pissed off at American government policies, but you're not looking for a Bic lighter to make your point. Fortunately for all of us born in the United States, we haven't had to resort to such extreme acts.

Your greatest weapon is your voice. And with the help of social media, we can be heard more loudly than ever by the people in power. We can be so loud, in fact, that it's impossible for them to say they didn't hear us. We have a record of what we've written and when and how many likes or retweets we've received. Those numbers speak a language that politicians understand. We may not have the strength in financial numbers of the lobbyists and personal-interest groups who are taking over Washington, but we can more than make up for it in the numbers of like-minded people determined to be heard above all the noise. We're lucky that despite the mainstream media's ability to screw up the facts and circumnavigate the truth, we can still be heard.

In 2009, when Barack Obama was inaugurated, the Tea Party movement was born. It became wildly popular and very quickly spread through the use of social media. The movement started with the angry rants of three stay-at-home moms on their personal blog.[9] They garnered a tremendous amount of support because they were able to bring together so many different people from vastly different walks of life all across the country. How'd they do it?

Technology was particularly helpful for a group that didn't want to limit itself to a party platform and wanted to remain flexible about its future course. How else would businessmen in New Hampshire, college students in Colorado, and retired oilmen in Texas be able to form such a powerful coalition? The Internet connected them all.

And then there's Twitter. I've had many great exchanges

with politicians by simply tweeting about them or retweeting something they may have said along with my own response. You'd be amazed how quickly some very public figures will get back to you if they think you've made an interesting point or maybe said something that they want to add to (or if you've managed to piss them off enough to prompt a response).

Our government was founded on the principle that our leaders should represent us. They are supposed to be our proxy in the legislature. To do their job well, they must have their "doors" open to us when we want to talk.

Unfortunately, for a very long time, the bureaucracy of big government acted as a barrier between politicians and their constituents. If you wanted to be heard, you would have to write a letter and send it through the postal service, and who knew if it was ever received or read and, if it was, by whom? Maybe an intern in between coffee runs? Those poor kids work their butts off for a decent job reference, but they're not exactly the audience you're looking for to change policy.

Do you know how popular and widely accepted Twitter has become as a platform for publicity and accessibility? So popular that Barack Obama has finally conceded that maybe he should be doing some of his own tweets.

Back when Obama was running against Mitt Romney in the 2012 presidential election, the future president pretty much ate his opponent's lunch by boasting 22.7 million Twitter followers over Romney's measly 1.8 million.[10] Obama also had 32.2 million likes on Facebook, while Romney could barely crawl to the finish line with 12.1 million. Did Obama win the election just because of a savvy social-media strategy? Probably not. But it certainly didn't hurt his chances.

Throughout his presidency, Obama has harnessed new platforms to target messages to audiences that normally wouldn't pay attention to politics. During his second term, he even compiled a fourteen-member staff for his White House Office of Digital Strategy (yeah, that's a thing), which is larger than George W. Bush's entire press secretary's office was in 2005.[11]

And then there was Trump's love affair with Twitter during (and after) the 2016 presidential campaign. Trump rightly complained about the bias of the mainstream media, but he was able to cut through the spin and speak directly to the voters using his own social media accounts.

Obama has been successful at building what's called *brand awareness*. Just like Apple and Starbucks, our politicians require sophisticated marketing strategies.

Not everyone is so slick and manufactured, though. And thanks to social media, candidates who aren't prepackaged with artificial sweetener can attract attention from a well-informed consumer. Ron Paul is a terrific example of a lesser-known political figure who has gained traction on Twitter. I mean, c'mon, it shouldn't be too shocking that the president of the United States has the most followers of anyone in the political arena right now, with nearly 24 million currently.[12] But Paul is true rock star for making it into the top ten list with more than half a million.

A medical doctor, now in his eighties, who served in the Air Force and National Guard, Paul entered politics as a congressman from Texas, all the while continuing to deliver babies. This guy is the real deal, and he also appears much more youthful and dialed into what our generation is looking for in a leader than many much younger politicians. Paul is exceptional in that he recognized very early on, while the Internet was in its infancy, how important it was to connect with younger generations. If a presidential candidate like Ron Paul, who is completely outside of the traditional two-party system, can cause such commotion on social media, *what's stopping you?*

Freedom and democracy are constantly evolving. And just as the world continues to change as rapidly as the casting on the *Real Housewives of Anywhere*, our politicians have to keep up if they want to hold our interest. I've mentioned before that we are fantastic at multitasking. It's given us almost superheroic powers of discernment, because we're great at weeding out the bullshit. Politicians now have to make their ideology short and sweet and straight to the point. Because who has the time or interest to read a two-hundred-page dissertation on the true meaning of the Second Amendment?

According to a Pew Research Center survey leading up to the 2014 midterm election, 16 percent of registered voters follow candidates for office, political parties, or elected officials on a social networking site.[13] That number may not seem super impressive at first glance, but keep in mind that it was a 10-percentage-point increase from the 2010 midterms, when only 6 percent of registered voters did so. One-quarter of registered voters now get political news on their cell phones.[14] Millennials specifically are getting news about politics and government mostly from social media. Roughly 61 percent say they get their political news from Facebook.[15]

We're better and more efficient at using that news in our daily lives. We would be chumps for not recognizing this and using it as leverage in public debate and discourse. Social media allows for what's called a *participatory democracy*.[16]

That means we the people hold all the power in politics, because we spread the word to family and friends about candidates or positions we approve of or want to annihilate. Just as a friend may recommend a killer bar on Instagram or Facebook and you decide to check it out for yourself, word of mouth from those you trust will be the most persuasive sales pitch in the world.

To Blog or Not to Blog

There are several monumental decisions we all have to make at some point in our lives: where we choose to attend college, whom we marry, where we live, and whether or not we have the balls to start a blog. Yes, blogging is not for the faint of heart. And only the strongest will survive, but if you do, you could become legendary. I mean, let's be real: Not everyone can score a sweet reality-TV gig. And truth be told, there are so many reality shows around now, what are the odds you would ever be noticed, anyway?

Blogs are different.

First of all, you have complete control over your image and expressed ideology. That rarely happens in a mainstream job. Usually you're selling yourself by toeing the company line. They sign your paycheck and expect you to be a repre-sentative of *their* brand, not *yours*. But your own blog, or one that you start with friends, is completely proprietary, which is probably Latin for *keep your hands off my shit*. You're totally free to go off on any rant or whim that strikes your fancy. It also allows for an in-depth expression of your personal ideology.

While social media is great for sending out short, witty

sound bites or information, it it's not effective for long-format discourse. To really get into the meat and potatoes of an argument or belief system, you'll need to write more than 140 characters. And skip the hashtags in a blog, by the way. It's like showing your thong at the opera. No one will be impressed.

But what if you're not ready to go completely solo and develop your own site, you ask? Well, fortunately for you, there are dozens of ultrapopular, firmly established sites that are usually in desperate need of new material to publish. The *Huffington Post*, Breitbart, and *Politico* are just a few examples of reputable outlets that can enable you to get your opinions out there and make a name for yourself.

The great thing about having so many options is that there's a blog for just about anyone having just about any belief system. Republican, Democrat, Libertarian, Green— or maybe you just feel superpassionate about cows having the right to graze on real grass. There's probably a site for that. If there's a blog dedicated to Ugly Renaissance Babies, I think you can find a niche fan group for that, too.[17]

Isn't that what this country was founded on? That we're all equal and free to believe what we want, including our right to view bad art? The real question is whether or not you are ready to truly put yourself out there and make a difference in the world. And if not you, then who? Zombies and power-hungry rednecks, er, I mean, the federal government and the people who run it. Doesn't sound good any way we slice it, does it?

Anyway, by now it should be obvious that emerging platforms are changing our society, changing the political game as we know it, and presenting opportunities for marginalized voices to be heard. But simply understanding new technology isn't enough—it's critical to equip oneself with certain skills to thrive in this brave new world and make a truly significant impact on the political system.

Charisma Is Everything...Just Ask Nixon

Charisma is everything. I'm going to say that again. Charisma is *everything*. Because we live in a world in which people can rattle off the names of the entire Kardashian clan before they can name a single member of the Supreme Court, the cult of celebrity is not only thriving—it's a multiheaded monster.

Our society has made it perfectly clear that we're easily swayed by slick trickery. If you're halfway good-looking, with a great smile, and can say a few words in front of a camera, you're golden. And that has everything to do with the presence of a television in every living room in America.

When John Kennedy and Richard Nixon (two dead guys whose names should ring a bell) engaged in the first televised presidential debate in 1960, they forever changed the rules of campaigning.[18] Kennedy was a dashing, young senator with All-American looks and a gorgeous, young wife on his arm. It was almost as if Brad Pitt was running for president with Angelina Jolie by his side. Nixon looked old, unattractive, and (even worse) like a total curmudgeon. Add in the fact that during the live debate, he began sweating, and then his stage makeup (which had been pancaked on) began dropping off his face. It was an epic fail for Nixon. Although, truth be told, he did make a comeback and went on to win the presidency twice, no doubt because of even less appealing opponents.

Now if Nixon had been running for office just a few decades earlier, his appearance and charm, or lack thereof, wouldn't have mattered in the slightest. Back then few people met or saw candidates in person. Voters were completely at the mercy of the print media. Sure, there were drawings (in the early days of our country) and then eventually photos for people to match up with the names they were reading about, but personality and charisma had very little to do with how people voted. And while it's great that we have more access to political candidates today through extensive multimedia coverage, it's also created an entirely new set of problems, because we want everyone we see on TV to be a celebrity. We expect politicians to look and act like movie stars, because they appear on the same screens as real entertainers do. We're far too easily swayed by glitz and glamour. Quite frankly, it's embarrassing. We're better than this, people. We're adults. And, hopefully, educated and passionate about creating a better future for our country. We shouldn't be making life-altering decisions based on whatever shiny object or talking bobblehead with bad hair captures our attention.

At the time of the first GOP debate of the 2016 presidential election, it was the most watched cable news telecast in history (only to later be outdone by the first presidential debate). Of the coveted viewing demographic (adults ages 25–54), it averaged nearly 8 million viewers, yet another cable news record. Why was this debate in particular so wildly popular, especially more than a year before the actual election, when the playing field included nearly twenty hopeful candidates?[19]

What attracts and repulses us in equal measure time

and time again? *Celebrity*. We all tuned into the debate *to watch what happens live* (ideally with cosmos and our best gay pals), because Donald Trump had created a carnival sideshow that couldn't be passed up. Some say he meticulously built his brand on buffoonery, because it got him lots of attention in a very crowded room. I say he's a marketing genius who knows how to connect with voters in the modern world. After the first GOP debate, Trump dominated headlines worldwide. Why? He has that certain je ne sais quoi that the American public loves to watch, radiating strength through a powerful presence. Love Trump or hate Trump, you know who Trump is. He's made himself one of the most famous men in the world, and it all comes down to charisma.

So, yeah, Trump is proof that politics is changing forever. Other candidates would be smart to learn from him. By harnessing creative showmanship, they can now get the attention of voters who normally wouldn't listen. Imagine if a politician like Gary Johnson, former Libertarian Party candidate for president, had gotten across his message using the Trump method—libertarianism would probably spread like wildfire.

And make no mistake: Charisma isn't just important for politicians. It's also critical for us everyday folks who just want to make our voices heard. Let's say you're passionate about increasing access to birth control. Your cause will get a lot more attention if you parade around the streets with mega-sized condoms than it would if you stood on a corner with a tiny boring sign. Remember, it's all about making people listen by getting their attention and making a bold statement.

The bottom line is that presentation and style are just

as important as ideas these days. You may hate it (how *you* doin', Jeb?), but that's just the way it is.

Arm Yourself with an Education...Not an AK-47

It's also easier than ever to educate yourself and call BS on what the mainstream media is hell-bent on forcing you to believe. Through the miracle of the Internet, you can do your own sleuthing to find out if a politician's record matches his or her campaign platform. You can also keep informed on what new socialist-inspired program the government is introducing today and hoping you won't notice. C'mon, use that search engine for something more than finding out what Taylor Swift song lyrics were written about which ex-boyfriend. Or to figure out how to get bong water stains out of the carpet. Again, it's never been easier or comfier to learn everything you've ever wanted to know about government policy but were afraid to ask.

Make sure you're following and "liking" candidates and programs on Twitter and Facebook that mirror your political slant. There is a nonstop deluge of information in my newsfeeds each day. Can I get to it all every day? Not likely. But it's the best way I know to stumble on the truly significant.

There's something so awesome about learning new things about topics I didn't yet know interested me. The Internet can lead to many happy discoveries. And while I sometimes wish I could unsee a few things like genital warts (don't ask) and a close-up of a spider's eight eyes, I honestly feel I've come across some really cool things that have brought the world around me more into focus, with the benefit of only two eyes.

The simplicity and accessibility of social media has everything to do with innovators who wanted the same thing their entire generation wanted. The only difference was their genius ability to make it happen. People like Mark Zuckerberg and Jack Dorsey had us in mind as they worked on their ideas because *they were us*. Just as their finished products are like another appendage for our generation, because they were created by one of our own.

It was young kids in dorm rooms or living on the fringes of society who did these things. They didn't cost a fortune to develop, and they weren't the products of a dozen old white men sitting around a conference table with spreadsheets and drawing boards. And now the greatest power of social media is its intrinsic nature to be a great equalizer throughout society. College kids, stay-at-home moms, and celebrities are all on equal ground and can easily communicate with each other without any awkward social barriers.

Through the effective use of social media, entire totalitarian regimes have been toppled at the hands of angry citizens. Just how effective is this method of protest? It's so effective that countries like China and Vietnam have either completely banned its usage or severely limited its availability.[20] Other countries like Egypt and North Korea monitor it very closely. Clearly they feel threatened. These authoritarian states aren't stupid. You don't get to subjugate millions of people by accident. You have to be shrewd and manipulative, and you have to crush individual thought completely. The best way to keep people down in the modern world is to take away their voice and their ability to connect with others. By taking away access to social media and the Internet, governments are wiping out their greatest threat—an individual's freedom to participate on the political stage.

Remember, you are only as free as you choose to be. If you decide to stand by while our government continues to decide what is best for you, then you're really handing over your freedom.

We have the chance to become the truly greatest generation. We may not be fighting Nazis like our grandparents did, but we do have to take a stand against something just as sinister. We're fighting zombies (the federal government) and power-hungry leaders (corrupt career politicians). Let's seize the opportunities we have to exert our power over these dangerous foes!

Finding Common Sense on Common Ground

So when Ethan, your hippie neighbor, says...

"Your digital call-to-arms is inspiring, but how can one person change anything when half a billion people are oinking into cyberspace at once?"

You say: "Movements are always started by one person; you just have to cut through the static and make yourself heard. You'll be surprised how much attention you get online if you make sense in a senseless world."

"What if I'm not attractive and have no personal charisma? Should I just hide under the covers and cry?"

You say: "Just because you don't look like ScarJo or have the slick oratory skills of Barry O doesn't mean your voice can't rattle some cages in the digital world. Remember, a beautiful mind can be a beautiful thing."

"Isn't it too late to change anything when the system is rigged to benefit the ones in power?"

You say: "Thankfully, our corrupt government is full of mortal old men who will retire or die one day. Our time will come, so get ready; you can be part of the solution if you get off your Xbox and give a damn!"

"I've got better things to do than vote."

You say: "Like what? Play Cards Against Humanity while Rome burns? If you don't care enough to vote, you have no right to complain about the government we have. Remember: No one is looking out for your best interests in this life, except *you*."

CHAPTER 10

What We Can Do to Fix America Now

"Real patriotism is a willingness to challenge the
government when it's wrong."
~ Ron Paul ~

The political divide is bitter right now. I can't think—and
I have tried—of a time since the North and South were at
each other's throats when things were so insanely partisan. I
know Democrats who literally will not associate with Republicans, and vice versa. If we can't to talk to each other, we're
in trouble. So let's talk, thoughtfully and with purpose.

Politics is a brutal business. I had no idea how brutal until
I put my voice out there:

*"What a shrill, stupid little cunt. I guess conserva-
tives are right when they say their wives and daughters are
worthless and stupid."*

*"Little miss cheerleader speaks with all the experience
and intellect of a spoilt little girl who has never had to go
wanting for anything in her life except for perhaps a pony
when she was little."*

*"Tate, who has never worked a day in her life, hates it
when poor Americans get too much food. Fascist twat."*

These are all real comments on my articles and videos online. Back when I first started my blog, comments like these really bothered me. Being the target of such mean-spirited public yet personal comments is embarrassing.

Speaking out about my beliefs meant I had to hear or see comments like these. It made it hard to get excited about continuing to write. But encouraging words from my parents—as well as some positive comments from other readers—gave me the strength to keep pressing forward with the blog, where I'd always felt freer to sound off loudly, with real conviction.

In my "real" life offline, though, I was relatively quiet about my political views, especially while I was still in college. I could only imagine the reaction from my peers at Emerson would have been if they had discovered I wasn't a full-fledged liberal. It's one thing to be the target of nasty comments online, but another thing entirely to risk your social standing in your own tight-knit community.

During the first few years of college, I never spoke out about my political views. I kept them all online. It was as if I had a double life, with two separate identities: online and off. Nearly everyone at my school was liberal, flagrantly so. It was the kind of campus where you might be called a bigot if you *weren't* wearing an Obama T-shirt in 2011. So my peers just assumed I was left leaning like them. It wasn't even a question.

But as the presidential primary ramped up in 2011, it became harder for me to stay silent. The more passionate my peers became about Obama, the more I wanted to speak up.

Finally, I couldn't keep my opinions to myself anymore. I

got home one evening, and wrote a column about fiscal versus social issues—I had become frustrated at my peers' tendency to hyperfocus on things like gay marriage while not caring at all about other critical issues like government spending.

This time, though, instead of posting the article on my blog as usual, I submitted it to the school paper. The following week, there was my article, in print. This was it, I thought. I had ruined my social life at college. I would forever be known, from this day forward, as the heartless, conservative bigot on campus.

I went online to look at the digital version of the article and waited for the negative comments to come in. After a few minutes I refreshed the page, and was shocked to see several comments.

The first one was a negative comment, attacking me for being insensitive. Blah blah blah, the usual. But the next few comments shocked me.

One student wrote, "This is a fantastic article, and I'd love to see and hear more debate at Emerson about fiscal rather than social issues facing this debt-ridden country."

When I walked into class that afternoon, a few students who had read the paper came up to me with similar comments. Some said that although they disagree with me, they thought I had valid points about political discourse on our campus. Others said they agreed with everything I wrote.

I couldn't believe it. There were people that actually *agreed* with me at Emerson; they just hadn't spoken out. Maybe they were like me, and feared being ostracized.

After that experience, I made it a point to be their voice. I became a vocal advocate of liberty on campus. Although this sometimes led to people making negative assumptions about me, it also made me realize there were lots of people who felt the same way that I did—they just didn't want to be the one to speak out.

My point is that it's up to each of us to stand up for what we believe, even if it's scary and even if our views might not seem popular. Sometimes it just takes one person sounding off to make a difference. And sometimes the person to show you the obvious is the last one you'd expect.

'Til the Fat Lady Sings

It was the summer of my junior year in high school. I had just gotten my license, my unsightly acne disappeared, and my boobs had finally reached a perky C cup. This was living. I unknowingly wasted my best summer on trashy reality shows like *Rock of Love* and, possibly worse, *Flavor of Love*. For all of you who were too busy doing important and/or cool shit during the early 2000s, these alarmingly vapid shows consisted of drunken bimbos fighting one another (via staged contests like playing touch football in the mud in their underwear) to hook up with the featured B-list celeb, Bret Michaels or Flava Flav. That summer of promise is mostly a blur of wigs and fake nails flying everywhere, and a whole lot of slurred, tear-filled cursing. It was epic. And whenever I wasn't watching *Whatever of Love*, I was working my part-time job at the local video store (this was long, long ago when Netflix was new and DVDs weren't being used for coasters).

One day while I was playing *Farmville* at work but trying to appear busy, a guy came over to check out a DVD. Instead of heading home to watch the film, he continued to talk—and flirt—with me for an hour. His name was Cole. We agreed to go out for coffee that weekend.

I arrived at the coffee shop with low expectations. To my surprise, after our two-hour chat, I found myself attracted to Cole. Yeah, he was edgier than the guys I usually liked, but he had a bad-boy way about him that I found alluring. He had that "I don't give a f**k" attitude that I'd only ever encountered in fiction. Cole told me he was a musician and he "didn't believe in school." He told me that after high school, he planned to skip college and travel the country in a van with his guitar. Our coffee date led to a second date, which led to a third date, and so on. Pretty soon, I was drinking the Cole Aid.

Cole and I got pretty serious that summer. When I wasn't at the video store I was with him: listening to his band practice, watching him play Xbox, and generally just chilling. Sometimes he would ditch me at the last minute for his friends, or to do something with his band, but the more douchy Cole was, the more I wanted him. He was different from anything I had known, and within a matter of weeks he became all I cared about. I was obsessed.

Summer eventually ended and I found myself back in school. But my mind wasn't there. I didn't care about my calculus honors class, the homecoming dance, or even about catching up with my old pal, Bagels, who had been out of the country that summer. Each day I just got through school as quickly as possible, and then immediately rushed over to Cole's house. As the weeks went on, though, he started ditching me more often. The more he slipped away, the tighter I clung to him.

Meanwhile, my peers at school were focused on choosing colleges and retaking the SATs. My mom tried desperately to connect with me—she was worried about my recent change in behavior, but I wouldn't open up to her about what was going on. My entire life—my friends, my family, and school—was crumbling around me, but I didn't care. I was too busy watching Cole blow smoke rings and serenade me with Kurt Cobain covers.

One day early that fall, I went to Cole's house after school. Cole's mom, Barbara, greeted me at the door—Cole wasn't home. Like always, I made a million excuses for him in my head: "He probably had an urgent meeting with the band and forgot to text me." I would simply wait at his house for him to come home like a good girlfriend.

I sat at the kitchen table, and Barbara started chatting with me. She was a scary-thin woman, with deep, stress- and cigarette-induced creases on her forehead. I'll never forget the huge, superobnoxious sparkly bumblebee pin she used to wear on all of her shirts. After some small talk, there was an awkward silence—we had run out of things to talk about, I thought.

Barbara looked across the table at me and said: "Why the hell are you with my son?"

I had no idea how to respond to that, so I said nothing.

She continued, "I used to be like you. You're from a good family, you're smart and pretty, you could go off to a good college. My son is a deadbeat. You're throwing away your life if you stay with him. He doesn't treat women with respect. I know this is going to hurt, but you seem like a good girl, so you should know this. He's cheated on you, at least once that

I know of—with that girl in his band, Tessie. You should get out of this while you can."

The rest of the conversation was a blur. I just remember staring at that big, ugly, sparkly bumblebee pin. *He had cheated on me. With that disgusting emo guitar-wrangling Tessie, who probably didn't even wear deodorant. He didn't love me and he never would.*

It was like being hit by a freight train. I left the house before Cole showed up. I never saw him again. He didn't seem to care when I called him and said the relationship was over.

The next few months were rough. My heart was broken, I was behind in the college application process, my grades that quarter had lowered my GPA, and my friends felt hurt and abandoned. I was eventually able to get my life back on track and repair relationships, but it wasn't easy.

As much as her words stung at the time, Barbara gave me the wake-up call I needed. "I used to be like you," she'd said. Despite the ugliness of the epiphany, her willingness to speak up came from a place of real compassion. Barbara knew my cautionary tale, because she'd already lived it. She was stuck with a bad ending, but I was not.

Somewhere in the back of my mind, I think I knew all along that Cole was cheating on me. I think I knew that he wasn't really that into me. But I didn't want to acknowledge reality. It was easier, and it felt better to keep living in a fantasy world where I had this badass, alternative, rock-star boyfriend who was crazy about me. At one point, during the height of my Cole obsession, I had even started thinking about not going to college so that I could travel the country with him and his guitar. Again, thank you, Barbara!

My moment of closure came a few weeks after the breakup, when Bagels and I were driving around after school. I had just finished my burger from McDubs (what we used to call McDonald's to psych ourselves out of the fact that we were making the worst possible food choice). We drove by Cole's house, and I gloriously chucked my Mickey D's bag full of trash out of the window and onto his lawn. Looking back, I realize that was more of an immature "f*ck you" to Cole's parents than to him, but I think Barbara would have understood. In that moment my act of littering felt perfect. It was healing. I was completely done with Cole and ready to get back to my life.

The general state of America today reminds me of the same stupid daze that I was in while dating Cole. We're on the fast track to self-destruction, but no one really seems to care. Because frankly, it takes zero effort to be apathetic yet a lot of work and thought to actually give a shit about the direction our country is heading in.

Apathy and ignorance are effortless. We all like things to be easy sometimes. But even though we know the situation isn't great, it's easier to take for granted that some political party—maybe the Republican Party, maybe the Democrat Party—will turn things around after the next election than it is to do something ourselves. We need a helluva lot more than one sassy Barbara stepping up and steering us clear of imminent danger. It will take the entire lot of us. We need a collective coming to our senses.

After reading this book, it should be more obvious than Caitlyn Jenner's new boobs that we have serious problems facing us—and they aren't conveniently going to disappear if all we rely on is more BS from D.C. It's going to take vigilance, awareness, and actions from us hardworking Americans to get things back on track.

Each and every one of us needs to Barbara up (nicotine stains and big-ass bumblebee broach optional). It's time to shake our sleepwalking friends and loved ones awake.

Easier said than done. Politics, civics, and real change take work. Who wants to work?

Most of this battle will be getting people interested in politics, despite all the competition for their attention. It's far easier to spend time keeping up with the Kardashians than with politics and current affairs. But we've got to make people listen—we've got to make them care—if we have any chance of correcting course.

The best way I know to get people invested in something is to help them see it compassionately. I've mentioned the need for a compassionate government a few times, but let's talk about what that really means.

How do you define *compassion*? Take a minute and think about it.

When I hear most people talk about feeling compassion for someone, it's often something more akin to pity. "I just felt so sorry for her because she's having such a hard time. Poor thing." Beneath every expression of pity-masquerading-as-compassion is the statement *I'm glad that's not happening to me.*

I mention this because we do not need a government that pities us. A government that feels sorry for us. Government officials who look at the plight of their constituents and say, whether sotto voce or out loud, "Wow, glad that's not me, but good luck to the little folk!"

Sadly, I think that's what we have.

Compassion literally means "to suffer with someone." To go through it with them. Someone with real compassion for you has put herself in your shoes, pictured step by step what it would mean to experience the same pain that you do. While practicing compassion, they do not feel sorry for you—in a sense, they *become you*.

This is what I mean by a compassionate government. A governing body whose leaders have taken the time to really suffer along with its citizens. A compassionate government produces policies that show this level of understanding, not policies that enable continued stagnation and diminishing returns on the future.

Picture your representative. Do you believe she really knows you? Do you think she's put in the thought and time to step into your shoes? Imagine whatever your idea of a campaigning politician is. Is it someone who really gets you or is it someone saying what she needs to win?

We both know the answer.

But there are still things we can do despite the politicians we are stuck with for now.

Get Involved at the Local Level

One summer I got a part-time job working as a videographer for the local access television station in my town. Back in the day, I had a plan to go into film (it was all part of my elaborate scheme to get famous and marry Johnny Depp), and this job seemed like a good place to start.

The job was the opposite of exciting. My first assignments

consisted of covering local events and school concerts (*wooo-eeee*).

A few weeks into the job, I got sent to film a nearby town hall meeting. I was expecting the usual snooze fest, but what ensued was a big surprise. After some speeches from town officials on budget issues, the floor opened up to residents. People from all over town showed up to express their strong opinions on how the town was spending its money. Some pissed-off residents even made a point to personally stick it to their elected officials.

What I witnessed was a dialogue between the officials and the public. There were some issues that prompted strong disagreement, but each side heard the other out and most of the time a middle ground was forged.

Each side listened. Each side compromised. Each side *thought*—they didn't just react.

This is what government is supposed to be all about. Unfortunately, "of the people, by the people, for the people" is only a reality on the local level; many of the bureaucrats in Washington, D.C., couldn't care less about what their constituents desire.

Want to make some meaningful changes? Then get involved and make your voice heard right where you are. Take part in grassroots, direct governance, which is more efficient and effective than politics on the national level. Whether you see quick results is irrelevant—it is apathy that is killing us.

Almost everyone, even the most self-absorbed among us, has opinions on hot-button national issues like abortion and gay marriage. Yet many of us can't even name one of our state and local representatives. They say ignorance is bliss. It can be, but not in politics. If you don't care enough to be informed, you forfeit your outrage when decisions get made that affect you.

State and local government have control over the taxes we pay, the schools our kids attend, our roads, and even the water we drink. So make sure you get to know and support candidates you believe will do the best work in your community.

Take New Hampshire, where I grew up. One thing that rocks about living in the "Live Free or Die" state (besides that fabulous slogan and the fact that Walter White spent one episode of *Breaking Bad* there) is that there's no sales tax—it's one of just five states where this is true. You may think state politics aren't important, but if the wrong boneheads were elected to state office, they could easily implement a sales tax in New Hampshire. Then, BOOM, you're paying an extra 5–10 percent on everything you buy. So much for my yearly trip back home for Black Friday shopping.

A state's right to govern itself is a beautiful thing (I find effective, accountable government structures sexy, don't you?). Different states have different populations with different needs. For example, California has been dealing with intense droughts during recent years; this creates a unique set of challenges that wouldn't be applicable in a state like Hawaii, which can get up to a hundred inches of rain per year. So it only makes sense that each state has the ability to create its own rules and budgets.

Besides, the Tenth Amendment of the U.S. Constitution is clear. It says, "The powers not delegated to the United States by the Constitution, nor prohibited by it to the States, are reserved to the States respectively, or to the people." The

Founders understood that a strong federal government could lead to a dictatorship. Thomas Jefferson once even said, "The Tenth Amendment is *the foundation* of the Constitution."[1]

Unfortunately, the federal government has made repeated attempts to squash states' rights over the years. When it comes to issues like the legalization of marijuana, immigration laws, and health care, President Obama has shown over and over that he couldn't care less about states' rights. Perhaps the best example of his disrespect for states' rights is Obamacare.

In early 2015, twenty-four state leaders spoke up in favor of their constituents who did not want their health care controlled by Washington.[2] Some of these leaders said they would not implement certain parts of the Affordable Health Care Act—others said they would reject the entire thing. A combined 117 million people live in those twenty-four states. They don't want Obamacare, yet the federal government is forcing it down their throats. It seems obvious that this is a clear violation of the Tenth Amendment.

If citizens don't want Obamacare in their state—or if they want to legalize marijuana, allow polygamous marriages, or do away with Common Core for their schools—it should be their own choice. As the Tenth Amendment, the *foundation of our Constitution*, continues to be threatened by Washington bureaucrats, it's up to us to stand up for states' rights. After all, do you really want silver-haired cronies in a land far, far away deciding what should be taught to the kids at your local school, or which roads in your town should be repaved? Of course not. People who actually live in your state have a much better sense of what the community needs—and what it does not.

Support Charity

My mom and dad have been divorced since before I can remember, and they would trade off who got to spend holidays with my brother and me. One year my mom got us on Thanksgiving and my dad got us on Christmas, the next year my dad got us on Thanksgiving and my mom got us on Christmas, and so on.

Thanksgivings with my mom were how every New England Thanksgiving should be—a huge, delicious turkey, tons of fattening, tasty sides, and lots of family and friends around. But on those Thanksgivings at my dad's house, things were a bit different. My dad didn't know how to cook, and his family lives far away. So most years we either spent the holiday at a friend's house and enjoyed their cooking, or bought turkey sandwiches and had a low-key Thanksgiving at home.

One year, though, we decided to do something a little different. My dad signed us up as volunteers to serve turkey at the local church. I was not looking forward to this, and I let my dad know it. This was the year that I was going through my Goth / Marilyn Manson phase, so the idea of wearing an ugly cafeteria cap and serving cheap turkey dinners all day to uncool people made me want to vomit. I tried telling my dad that I didn't feel well, but he forced me to join in.

We showed up at the church early with the other volunteers and set up shop. There were hundreds of tubs of turkey, cranberry sauce, and other Thanksgiving food items. Before I could blink, people started pouring in to eat the food—families, old people, young people, the works. After an hour or two, my hostile attitude started to fade away. I began talking to lots of people I never would have met otherwise, and I started to realize that there were a lot of people who struggled to make ends meet in my own community.

Finally, my family took a break from serving turkey to eat our own meal. We sat next to an older woman named Maureen. She told me the same general story I'd been hearing from folks all day: she was struggling, but so thankful to have this place to come and eat with members of the community. Maureen struggled in life; she was a widow with no children who had made her living as a grocery bagger. But that Thanksgiving, she was happy. We talked for over an hour. And that's when it hit me: Most people need to feel like they are a part of their community. They need human interaction.

My family loved our experience that Thanksgiving, so we started getting more involved with charities around our community. We even traveled to a few low-income nursing homes in the area and played our saxophones for the residents there. (Yes, my whole family plays the saxophone—supercheesy, I know.) At first, the old folks would sit there with their arms crossed, not wanting to even be in the room; but after a few songs, they'd always loosen up and start dancing.

The more I got involved in charities, the more I realized what an enormous impact they can have. And not just at the local level—there are plenty of huge organizations that have a national impact, too.

Charities are organizations of compassion. The people who found them understand the people they want to help. They do not pity them. They do not promise to sustain them indefinitely in ways that will damage the prospects of other citizens.

They are, in other words, the opposite of our welfare state, which looks like charity but, as we've seen, is not. Our welfare program helps poor people stay poor. This is not the action of a compassionate, thoughtful government. It is the action of a government that throws money at a problem and hopes to avoid the issue until next election cycle.

As we've seen, there's strong evidence that welfare does little to decrease poverty—despite spending nearly $800 billion on welfare since the early 1960s, the poverty level is only 2.5 percent lower than it was then.[3] We've basically just created an entire class of people who could not survive without the government. It's just like the dealer who gives you that first hit for free, knowing you'll be hooked for life. And if you get a job or start making money, you have to kiss your government goodies good-bye. As we established earlier, there's no incentive to become a productive member of society.

Try to imagine a compassionate drug dealer who is truly invested in the long-term well-being of his clients. An oxymoron, but no more so than many of our welfare champions.

If you want to help the underprivileged, support or get involved with private charities. They are often far more effective, accountable, and *compassionate*. Government agencies absorb about two-thirds of each dollar in "overhead costs" (translation: Most of our money goes to overpaid administrators who sit around pushing pencils). On the other hand, two-thirds of each dollar received by private charities goes directly to those who need help.[4] It's a no-brainer. (Be sure to check out the charity of your choice on Charity Navigator or other watchdog organizations that track how charities spend the monies they receive.)

Bear in mind: Private charities must prove to the public that they're worthy of a donation. If a charity isn't producing results, it will likely have a hard time fund-raising. As a result, these organizations tend to be a lot more accountable, cost-efficient, and effective than those unaccountable government programs that will get funded year after year no matter what.

But charities aren't just exceptional when it comes to welfare—they also do a notable job when it comes to disaster relief, too. I was living in New York City when Hurricane Sandy hit. The impact of the storm was devastating—many city dwellers had no electricity in their apartments for several days and the subway system flooded. The entire city effectively shut down. About three days after the storm, I got an alert on my iPhone from the Federal Emergency Management Agency (FEMA). The message warned me to stay inside "due to severe weather." I couldn't help laughing when I received that message. A warning three days into the storm is a bit late!

Apparently this small experience I had with FEMA was wholly representative of the agency's relief efforts, which were disorganized and riddled with communication errors. Staten Island and parts of New Jersey were practically ignored by the federal government immediately after the storm hit. In other parts of New Jersey and New York, residents whose homes were destroyed were living in tent cities or homes with no power for several months. Many of these folks were still struggling when severe winter weather arrived in January. And to this date many have still not been able to rebuild their homes.

No doubt, FEMA helped with the Sandy situation in some ways—the agency spent more than $60 billion in the aftermath of the hurricane.[5] But the agency clearly doesn't operate as efficiently and effectively as it could.

Meanwhile, the American Red Cross—an organization that provides emergency relief and is run by volunteers—did a phenomenal job providing relief during and after Sandy, given the resources it had. The Red Cross receives its funding from donations, as well as fees that are charged for some services. Tens of thousands of volunteers with the charity provided immediate assistance as soon as the hurricane hit. The organization spent a total of $313 million on Sandy relief (just a fraction of the funds spent by FEMA).[6] With those funds Red Cross set up more than 81,000 shelters, 103,000 health service centers, and provided 9 million meals and 6.7 million relief items to those affected by the storm.[7]

Hurricane Katrina was another egregious example of government incompetence when it comes to disaster relief. New Orleans is a city located below sea level in an area that is notorious for hurricanes—yet when Katrina hit in 2005, the government was completely unprepared to deal with the disaster. Even President Bush admitted that "all levels of government" failed to respond effectively to the hurricane.[8] Once again, private charities stepped up to help those in need.

The government wasn't just ineffective during Katrina—it actually prevented New Orleans residents from getting help in many cases. Amtrak offered to evacuate citizens before the storm hit, but the city declined its offer.[9] And at the start of Katrina, Louisiana governor Kathleen Babineaux Blanco's

Department of Homeland Security refused to give permission for private organizations to enter the city to provide relief. The Red Cross and Salvation Army were initially banned from giving victims water, food, and medicine. On the very day that Katrina hit, FEMA issued a stern press release with the title, "First Responders Urged Not to Respond to Hurricane Impact Areas." The government enforced this order—FEMA turned away several Walmart trucks full of water, and even turned away the Coast Guard trying to deliver diesel fuel. Volunteers and medical professionals waited for days, unable to give aid to those in dire need.[10]

The bottom line is that private charities are often more effective when it comes to welfare and disaster relief. In general, these organizations use their money wisely. Perhaps if taxes weren't so high, and government wasn't funneling our money into FEMA and the like, Americans would have more funds to donate to their favorite nonprofits.

America is a compassionate country. But stealing from some to give to others is not charity. So if you want to make a difference, get out there and be an advocate for one of these life-changing charity organizations.

Elect New Blood to Congress

I had a lot of shitty jobs growing up, but the prize has to go to my first one ever: I was a cleaner in a deli at a large hospital. My job was to scrub dishes, walls, counters—basically anything that needed scrubbing. And given that I was in a hospital, with tons of sick people, there was always something nasty that needed my attention.

I was only fifteen at the time and thankful to have a

paying job (most places wouldn't hire anyone under sixteen). So I worked my little butt off and didn't even mind washing dishes full of leftover lasagna and even vomit. But I quickly noticed that everyone else working at the deli had a bad attitude. They were all much older (I was the only worker there under the age of fifty), and they hated their jobs. I was also the only newbie—everyone else had been an employee there for several years at least. All day they complained, found ways to get out of working, and took as many cigarette breaks as possible. I even saw some employees stealing food at times; and they would laugh about it. Robbie, the dude with a ponytail who trained me, told me on my first day, "You'll get sick of this place real fast. Bunch of f*cking a**holes around here." Robbie practically instructed me to make it look like I was busy while not really doing anything.

Eventually, I turned sixteen and got a job that didn't include cleaning up bodily waste. A few months later, though, I went to the hospital for a checkup and thought I'd stop in at the deli to say hello to my old coworkers.

When I walked in, I didn't see anyone I recognized. Where was Robbie and his flowing hank of hair? Where was Jane, the obese woman who smelled like cigarettes and mothballs? Where was Danny, the tatted-up motorcycle dude? Where was Debbie, the woman with an eyebrow piercing, so thin she looked as though she might vanish at any moment?

They were all gone.

I was met by a new cast of characters. A cheerful woman behind the counter asked if she could help me. I looked around—noticing how clean and organized the place appeared—and inquired about what had happened to everyone who worked there a few months ago. She told me there had been a "scandal of sorts" (but didn't go into any detail), which resulted in a mass firing of employees.

I could tell that the purge had had a positive impact on the business. The entire deli was sparkling clean, and all of the employees seemed cheerful and professional. Gone were the ungrateful, lazy workers who didn't give a damn about their jobs. They had been there so long that they stopped caring and didn't have pride in their place of employment or their work.

Granted, there are lots of other issues that could have contributed to the collective bad attitude among the deli workers—maybe they weren't given good benefits, maybe the boss didn't give them as many days off as they wanted, and I can tell you from firsthand experience that the pay sucked. But bringing in fresh workers who actually appreciated a paying job clearly did wonders for the joint.

It's kind of like Congress. Many of the people we send to Capitol Hill are there far too long. They show up all fresh faced and ready to work on behalf of their constituents; but after spending a few terms in D.C., they're worn out, cranky, and couldn't care less about their voters. It's all about their own careers, and their own power.

Washington is run by people corrupted by the system, and Americans know it. A whopping 75 percent of Americans think corruption is widespread in D.C.[11] The nation's capitol has become a cesspool of egotistical, entrenched career politicians who will say and do whatever it takes to further their own careers.

Twenty-five members of Congress have been in the

House since before 1990. Maybe I'm just being skeptical, but I find it hard to believe you're really busting your hump every day to represent the good people in your home state, when "home" has been Washington, D.C., for the last thirty years. Some have been in Congress even longer than that. Charles Rangel (D, New York) had been a congressman since 1971! At least he announced his retirement last year, deciding not to run for reelection for what would have been his twenty-third term. But it's not like he's leaving behind a bunch of spring chickens.

Don Young (R, Alaska) has been in Congress since 1973. And this guy is a *real* winner—in 2007, Young was under federal investigation for possibly taking bribes from a company based in Anchorage.[12] Executives at the company even pleaded guilty to bribing Young. But in 2010, the FBI suddenly closed its investigations.[13] Umm...*hello?!* Is this not totally sketchy to anyone else? Why is this dude still in office, and why do people keep reelecting him?

State governments, on the other hand, are often more accountable than the federal government, because they don't foster a culture of career politicians. Many state legislative branches meet for as little as six weeks per year. These representatives leave their real, full-time jobs, come to the capital, take care of state business, and then return to the real world where they can see firsthand how the other half lives.

That's us. Why should Washington be any different?

It's obvious why D.C. blowhards keep seeking election for another term, and another, and another...For one thing they make an attractive annual salary of $174,000—over three times what the average American is bringing home each year. Meanwhile, the House is in session in Washington only 133 days out of the year.[14] That's 107 fewer workdays than ordinary American workers put in—workers who get two weeks of vacation and federal holidays off. Is it any wonder these bureaucrats never want to go back to their old lives outside of D.C.?

And when they do leave Congress, they know there are even more lucrative jobs awaiting them in the private sector as high-paid lobbyists for industry and other special interests.

Term limits would clean D.C. of career politicians and get some new blood in there. Fresh ideas would likely lead to more innovation, instead of just more of the same old same-old. This worked well back in the early 1990s, when twenty-one states limited the terms of their own congressmen by popular vote. But in '95, the Supreme Court put an end to that, ruling that states lacked the power to prevent experienced incumbents from running again...and again and again.[15] There's little doubt that D.C.'s entrenched bureaucrats celebrated that day.

Americans on both sides of the aisle overwhelmingly support term limits. Seventy-five percent of the U.S. population is in support of term limits for Congress.[16]

Realistically though, term limits on Congress aren't going to happen anytime soon—in its '95 ruling, the Supreme Court said that a constitutional amendment would be required to put them in place. But we can still support new ideas and fresh blood in D.C. by simply not voting for the same blowhards over and over. These a**holes care more about digging their heels in and remaining in power than doing what's right for the people they're supposed to be serving. Remember: The only reason they're allowed to be D.C.

bureaucrats because *we* continue to elect them! So let's start supporting fresh faces and rid the Capitol of the desiccated barnacles who have moved in and latched on.

Let Pragmatism Rule

If we're going to dig ourselves out of this epic hole, we're going to need a whole lot of common sense and pragmatism. The kind of change we need isn't going to happen overnight and at the highest level. That's called revolution, and if you're going to rely on it as a strategy, you may as well become a comedian, because that's nothing more than a joke.

We must be willing to work with both Democrats *and* Republicans. There are no perfect political parties or candidates. It's time to stop paying so much attention to the Rs and Ds on our ballots and start asking the real questions: Is this person serious about downsizing government? Are they interested in protecting and restoring my civil liberties? Do they have a realistic plan to rein in federal spending?

We also need to be willing to work with the same folks with whom we disagree. You may be asking, "Why is that so hard to do?" Well, we're all formed by different families, traditions, religions, and so on. Sometimes that upbringing instills in us a core belief that what our own kind practices is the one right way. That would indicate anyone doing something differently is off the correct path. But that small-mindedness is what keeps us from finding our strength in numbers. In order to work together with the people with whom we disagree, we have to prove that we have more than just our self-interest at heart.

When the *Titanic* was sinking, do you think the

passengers' political opinions mattered? Hell, no. Those people were just desperate to stay alive. They worked together getting into lifeboats and trying to stay calm. Sure, some immoral types snuck off with their own boats, and many ended up tragically freezing to death in the water, but the ones working together saved many lives. Substitute the sinking of the *Titanic* with a thousand other tragedies, and it can't be denied; when the human race comes together for self-preservation, we get it done. And how about when Americans from all walks of life banded together to win World War II? It didn't matter whom anyone had voted for; citizens of every kind came together to defeat a common enemy.

It will take forfeiting some of our own wants on behalf of everyone—on behalf of the greater good. But we can do it. We can stop lashing out at one another via online political posts. We can put aside our blue and red allegiances, and quit putting our faith in the latest flashy candidate. There's no single politician who will turn us around. But there is a middle ground just waiting for us to seize.

Be a Wolf, Not a Sheep

Being followers will lead us nowhere. It's time to start thinking for ourselves instead of believing everything that the government—or any political party—promises us.

New technology has made it possible for all of us to be aware and connected citizens; there is no longer an excuse for anyone to be uninformed about what's going on. Young Americans must harness the power of the Internet to cut new political trails with their fresh, creative energy. Most voters are sick of the status quo, and it's up to everyone to start taking this country back for the people in a bold way that supports individualism. Everyone needs to work and to work better, from the up and coming millennials, to the established baby boomers who have done so much to pave the way for whatever comes next.

We have amazing tools at our disposal to do research, fact-check, and make our voices heard. Use them. Use the Internet. Use social media. Use traditional media. Let those bumbling idiots in D.C. know how we feel and how we think—and call them out when they flip-flop or flat-out lie. Connect with voters on both sides of the aisle and teach them to follow their real interests. Speak the truth, even if your voice trembles.

George Washington once said, "Liberty, when it begins to take root, is a plant of rapid growth."[17] A freer, more prosperous America is not out of reach. Liberty is contagious; it's time to show Americans from all walks of life how good freedom feels, unimpeded by excessive government taxation, surveillance, handouts, and mandates. It's up to *us*.

But it does start with each one of us making a choice. A choice to stay informed, to speak up, to dissent, to be compassionate, and to *care* enough to do the work. It would be easier to do nothing than to do something, but if we all feel that way, then we'll all sink together.

I choose to speak.

I choose to think.

I choose to fight.

I choose compassion.

I hope you'll join me.

Notes

Chapter 1 *Don't Tell Us How to Live Our Lives*

1. http://www.huffingtonpost.com/2013/09/03/marijuana-deaths_n_3860418.html
2. http://www.denverpost.com/news/ci_25475533/denver-coroner-man-fell-death-after-eating-marijuana
3. http://www.huffingtonpost.com/2014/02/28/marijuana-deaths_n_4868209.html; http://www.drugwarfacts.org/cms/Causes_of_Death#sthash.vlYZZ5Xh.dpbs
4. http://www.washingtonpost.com/wp-dyn/content/article/2006/05/25/AR2006052501729.html
5. http://object.cato.org/sites/cato.org/files/pubs/pdf/pa157.pdf
6. http://www.cato.org/pubs/pas/pa-157.html
7. Ibid.
8. Ibid.
9. http://www.drugpolicy.org/drug-war-statistics
10. Ibid.
11. Ibid.
12. http://www.huffingtonpost.com/2014/09/22/legal-marijuana-taxes_n_5863860.html
13. https://www.colorado.gov/pacific/marijuanainfodenver/marijuana-retailers-home-growers
14. https://www.drugpolicy.org/sites/default/files/Colorado_Marijuana_Legalization_One_Year_Status_Report.pdf
15. http://www.denverpost.com/2016/02/09/colorado-marijuana-sales-skyrocket-to-more-than-996-million-in-2015/
16. http://www.huffingtonpost.com/2015/01/05/marijuana-illnesses_n_6419530.html
17. http://www.npr.org/sections/health-shots/2015/09/04/436918240/when-pets-do-pot-a-high-thats-not-so-mighty

18. http://www.politico.com/story/2015/06/ted-cruz-gay-marriage
-ruling-reaction-npr-interview-119559.html

19. http://www.businessinsider.com/scott-walker-calls-for-marriage
-amendment-to-constitution-2015-6

20. http://www.cbn.com/cbnnews/us/2015/july/oregon-christian-bakers
-wont-be-silenced/

21. http://cnsnews.com/news/article/oregon-ag-investigates-bakers
-refusal-make-wedding-cake-lesbians

22. http://www.breitbart.com/texas/2015/06/28/texas-fights-back
-against-gay-marriage-ruling/

23. Ibid.

24. http://www.cbn.com/cbnnews/us/2015/july/oregon-christian-bakers
-wont-be-silenced/

25. http://www.foxnews.com/opinion/2015/02/03/christian-bakers-face
-government-wrath-for-refusing-to-make-cake-for-gay.html

26. http://www.washingtontimes.com/news/2015/apr/25/sweet-cakes
-christian-owned-bakery-gofundme-drive-/?page=all

27. http://www.washingtonexaminer.com/sweetcakes-owner-defiant
-in-face-of-135000-fine-for-refusing-to-bake-gay-wedding
-cake-get-ready-to-take-a-stand/article/2567584

28. http://www.texasobserver.org/new-coalition-pledges-to-fight-gay
-marriage/

29. http://www.foxnews.com/opinion/2014/06/03/baker-forced-to
-make-gay-wedding-cakes-undergo-sensitivity-training-after.html

30. http://time.com/3948644/marriage-equality-wedding-cake/

31. http://www.foxnews.com/opinion/2014/06/03/baker-forced-to
-make-gay-wedding-cakes-undergo-sensitivity-training-after.html

32. http://www.foxnews.com/opinion/2015/01/07/atlanta-fire-chief-was
-fired-because-my-christian-faith.html

33. Ibid.

34. https://www.law.cornell.edu/constitution/first_amendment

35. http://www.theblaze.com/stories/2015/07/01/the-shocking
-proportion-of-americans-who-believe-that-religious-institutions-or
-clergy-should-be-forced-to-perform-gay-weddings/

36. http://www.theblaze.com/stories/2015/07/20/are-you-stupid
-gay-baker-lashes-out-at-his-fellow-gays-and-lesbians-for-bullying
-christian-bakers-who-declined-to-make-same-sex-wedding-cake/

37. http://www.ferris.edu/jimcrow/what.htm

38. Ibid.

39. http://www.slate.com/blogs/the_slatest/2015/07/18/kkk_african
    _american_group_plan_opposing_rallies_at_s_c_capitol.html
40. https://twitter.com/SteveBenjaminSC/status/621432266045136900
    ?ref_src=twsrc%5Etfw
41. http://www.mediaite.com/tv/wednesday-cable-ratings-msnbcs-al
    -sharpton-last-in-demo-at-6pm/

Chapter 2 ...*And Don't Tell Us How to Spend Our Money*

1. http://blog.credit.com/2014/05/what-happens-if-i-dont-pay-my
   -credit-card-bill-83231/
2. http://www.usdebtclock.org/
3. Ibid.
4. http://www.nbcnews.com/id/27150961/ns/business-stocks_and
   _economy/t/national-debt-clock-runs-out-numbers/
5. http://townhall.com/columnists/timphillips/2012/09/17/105
   _billion_per_day/page/full
6. http://www.snopes.com/inboxer/trivia/billions.asp
7. http://dailycaller.com/2014/04/16/obama-administration-begins
   -stealth-bailout-of-detroit-contradicting-earlier-statements/
8. http://www.washingtontimes.com/news/2015/may/20/kristin-tate
   -how-republicans-can-capture-the-mille/?page=all
9. http://dailysignal.com/2013/07/19/detroit-bankruptcy-is-no-time
   -for-federal-bailouts/
10. http://nypost.com/2013/09/27/obama-to-give-more-than
    -100m-to-broke-detroit/
11. http://www.nytimes.com/2013/09/27/us/300-million-in-detroit-aid
    -but-no-bailout.html?_r=0
12. http://www.breitbart.com/big-government/2016/08/22/puerto-ricos
    -70-billion-defaulted-debt-jumps-113-billion/; *see also* http://www
    .nationalreview.com/article/421243/puerto-ricos-debt-crisis-could
    -be-bad-news-gop-2016-kristin-tate
13. http://www.newsweek.com/2015/06/05/millennial-college
    -graduates-young-educated-jobless-335821.html
14. http://thinkprogress.org/economy/2015/05/26/3662773/
    sanders-90-percent-tax/
15. http://www.azquotes.com/quote/1136725
16. http://www.capitalpress.com/Research/20150224/group-asks
    -congress-to-reject-closure-of-idaho-sheep-station

17. http://showmethespending.com/wp-content/uploads/2014/10/wastebook2014.pdf
18. http://dailycaller.com/2015/04/14/happy-tax-day-irs-spent-millions-on-office-furniture-and-toys/
19. http://www.foxnews.com/politics/2013/06/01/newly-released-irs-video-shows-employees-dancing/
20. http://www.washingtontimes.com/news/2015/apr/14/irs-spent-millions-furniture-stuffed-animals/
21. http://www.theatlantic.com/politics/archive/2011/09/-16-for-a-muffin-a-justice-department-boondoggle/245385/
22. http://showmethespending.com/wp-content/uploads/2014/10/wastebook2014.pdf
23. Ibid.
24. http://abcnews.go.com/Politics/heres-happened-time-government-shut/story?id=26997023
25. http://www.breitbart.com/big-government/2013/10/05/list-obama-closures-for-shutdown/
26. http://www.kpopstarz.com/articles/43883/20131004/world-news-government-shutdown-medical-research-nih.htm
27. http://www.breitbart.com/big-government/2013/10/05/list-obama-closures-for-shutdown/
28. http://www.creators.com/opinion/john-stossel/ponzi-ponzi-ponzi.html
29. http://www.usnews.com/news/the-report/articles/2015/06/17/can-bernie-sanders-save-retirement-by-expanding-social-security
30. http://www.cato.org/publications/policy-analysis/still-better-deal-private-investment-vs-social-security
31. Ibid.
32. http://www.thefiscaltimes.com/Columns/2014/03/27/Obamacare-Taxpayers-Hole-15-Trillion
33. http://reason.com/archives/2015/06/12/outside-the-liberal-la-la-land-obamacare
34. https://www.healthcare.gov/fees/fee-for-not-being-covered/
35. https://about.usps.com/news/national-releases/2013/pr13_087.htm
36. http://www.breitbart.com/big-government/2014/08/01/busted-obamacare-website-cost-taxpayers-840-million-so-far/

Chapter 3 *The Department of Duh-fense*

1. http://www.cnbc.com/2014/07/31/how-dods-15-trillion-f-35-broke-the-air-force.html

2. https://www.washingtonpost.com/news/wonkblog/wp/2013/01/07/everything-chuck-hagel-needs-to-know-about-the-defense-budget-in-charts/
3. http://theweek.com/articles/570764/time-military-leave-south-korea
4. http://www.foxnews.com/politics/2013/04/17/us-reportedly-footing-more-bill-for-overseas-bases-despite-cuts-to-military/
5. https://www.washingtonpost.com/world/national-security/study-iraq-afghan-war-costs-to-top-4-trillion/2013/03/28/b82a5dce-97ed-11e2-814b-063623d80a60_story.html
6. http://www.seattletimes.com/nation-world/us-soldiers-killed-while-training-iraqis/
7. http://acqnotes.com/acqnote/acquisitions/color-of-money
8. https://www.washingtonpost.com/world/national-security/black-budget-summary-details-us-spy-networks-successes-failures-and-objectives/2013/08/29/7e57bb78-10ab-11e3-8cdd-bcdc09410972_story.html
9. http://time.com/43836/afghanistan-is-the-big-winner-in-u-s-foreign-aid/
10. http://watson.brown.edu/costsofwar/files/cow/imce/papers/2015/US%20Reconstruction%20Aid%20for%20Afghanistan.pdf
11. https://www.washingtonpost.com/world/asia_pacific/after-billions-in-us-investment-afghan-roads-are-falling-apart/2014/01/30/9bd07764-7986-11e3-b1c5-739e63e9c9a7_story.html
12. https://www.sigar.mil/pdf/spotlight/High-Risk_List.pdf
13. http://www.worldaffairsjournal.org/article/money-pit-monstrous-failure-us-aid-afghanistan
14. Ibid.
15. http://www.cnn.com/2014/08/05/world/asia/afghanistan-violence/
16. http://www.9-11commission.gov/report/911Report.pdf
17. http://www.worldaffairsjournal.org/article/money-pit-monstrous-failure-us-aid-afghanistan
18. Ibid.
19. Ibid.
20. http://www.motherjones.com/politics/2014/09/iraq-army-security-force-billions
21. http://www.nytimes.com/2006/10/24/world/americas/24iht-assess.3272521.html?_r=1&
22. http://www.motherjones.com/politics/2014/09/iraq-army-security-force-billions

23. http://www.nbcnews.com/id/38903955/ns/world_news-mideast_n
    _africa/t/us-wasted-billions-rebuilding-iraq/#.VaahLsZViko
24. http://www.paraglideonline.net/news/article_ceb515ce-20cc-11e5
    -a089-1fc5c69156e8.html
25. https://explorer.usaid.gov/
26. http://www.benefits.va.gov/COMPENSATION/resources
    _comp0113.asp
27. http://www.cnn.com/2014/06/24/us/senator-va-report/
28. http://www.cbssports.com/nfl/eye-on-football/25181085/nfl-teams
    -received-54-million-from-defense-department-in-last-4-years
29. http://www.washingtonpost.com/news/business/wp/2015/04/28/the-nfl
    -is-dropping-its-tax-exempt-status-why-that-ends-up-helping-them-out/
30. http://security.blogs.cnn.com/2013/06/21/u-s-cutting-back-on-hot
    -chow-for-troops/
31. http://www.defense.gov/home/features/2013/0213_sequestration/
32. http://www.dodbuzz.com/2012/10/01/pentagon-shuts-mrap
    -production-line/
33. http://www.bga-aeroweb.com/DoD-Vehicle-Programs.html
34. http://www.bizjournals.com/washington/blog/fedbiz_daily/2014/01/
    lawsuit-filed-over-general-dynamics.html
35. http://www.dodbuzz.com/2012/10/01/pentagon-shuts-mrap
    -production-line/
36. http://articles.latimes.com/2013/dec/27/world/la-fg
    -afghanistan-armor-20131227
37. http://www.pennlive.com/nation-world/2014/08/afghan_soldier
    _who_killed_us_g.html
38. http://www.thefiscaltimes.com/2015/06/04/Fog-War-US-Has
    -Armed-ISIS
39. http://www.bga-aeroweb.com/DoD-Vehicle-Programs.html

Chapter 4 *How Do You Spell "Educashun"?*

1. https://www.washingtonpost.com/news/wonkblog/wp/2012/09/11/
   how-much-do-chicago-teachers-make/
2. https://www.danielsongroup.org/press-item/university-of-chicago
   -researchers-believe-their-teacher-evaluation-study-could-drive
   -national-discussion/
3. http://cnsnews.com/news/article/us-department-education-79
   -chicago-8th-graders-not-proficient-reading

4. https://rankingamerica.wordpress.com/category/education/
5. https://www.illinoispolicy.org/ctu-demands-huge-raise-on-top-of-million-dollar-pensions/
6. http://www.chicagotribune.com/news/local/politics/chi-bruce-rauner-tries-to-block-fees-for-state-workers-who-dont-want-to-join-union-20150209-story.html#page=1
7. Ibid.
8. http://www.politifact.com/truth-o-meter/statements/2011/mar/15/republican-national-committee-republican/rnc-said-unions-raised-400-million-obama-2008/
9. http://thehill.com/homenews/administration/212034-teachers-unions-turn-on-obama
10. https://www.hslda.org/docs/news/2013/201309030.asp
11. http://www.nheri.org/research/research-facts-on-homeschooling.html
12. http://www.standardnewswire.com/news/201382795.html
13. http://content.time.com/time/nation/article/0,8599,1720697,00.html
14. http://nche.hslda.org/courtreport/V24N5/V24N501.asp
15. http://www.publiccharters.org/dashboard/home; *see also* https://nces.ed.gov/fastfacts/display.asp?id=30
16. http://www.nytimes.com/2015/04/07/nyregion/at-success-academy-charter-schools-polarizing-methods-and-superior-results.html?_r=0
17. Ibid.
18. Ibid.
19. http://www.uaedreform.org/wp-content/uploads/charter-funding-inequity-expands.pdf
20. http://www.nydailynews.com/new-york/education/city-secures-spaces-success-academy-charter-schools-article-1.1770041
21. http://www.usatoday.com/story/opinion/2014/04/17/illinois-charter-schools-education-teachers-column/7710697/
22. Ibid.
23. http://www.ed.gov/budget15
24. http://www.cato.org/publications/congressional-testimony/impact-federal-involvement-americas-classrooms
25. Ibid.
26. http://www.corestandards.org/about-the-standards/
27. http://www.glennbeck.com/2013/04/08/the-whole-story-on-common-core/

28. http://wjla.com/news/local/virginia-declines-to-apply-for-race-to-the-top-funding-95188
29. http://www.usnews.com/news/special-reports/a-guide-to-common-core/articles/2014/03/06/the-politics-of-common-core
30. http://www.ncee.org/2014/10/kentucky-and-the-common-core-interview-with-terry-holliday-and-felicia-smith/
31. http://dailycaller.com/2014/07/12/follow-the-money-microsofts-plan-to-cash-in-on-common-core/
32. http://www.microsoft.com/en-us/education/school-leaders/default.aspx
33. http://dailycaller.com/2014/07/12/follow-the-money-microsofts-plan-to-cash-in-on-common-core/
34. http://www.washingtonpost.com/blogs/answer-sheet/wp/2014/07/12/how-microsoft-will-make-money-from-common-core-despite-what-bill-gates-said/
35. http://www.achieve.org/our-board-directors
36. http://www.mercurynews.com/business/ci_26190113/from-archive-2004-intel-ceo-craig-barrett-not
37. http://www.cnbc.com/2015/03/11/companies-cash-in-on-common-core-despite-controversy.html
38. http://www.theatlantic.com/education/archive/2015/08/common-core-schools-parents/400559/
39. http://www.newyorker.com/news/daily-comment/louis-c-k-against-the-common-core
40. https://twitter.com/hoffmanrich/status/384806802262470656/photo/1
41. http://twitchy.com/2013/08/07/new-york-city-students-flunk-new-common-core-aligned-tests-bloomberg-cheers/
42. http://news.yahoo.com/fifty-shades-common-core-much-porn-too-much-125010622.html
43. http://dailycaller.com/2013/11/01/common-porn-another-school-district-pulls-a-raunchy-common-core-approved-book/
44. http://eaglerising.com/6047/dad-arrested-protesting-soft-core-porn-common-core-curriculum/
45. http://money.cnn.com/2012/10/18/pf/college/student-loan-debt/
46. http://www.theatlantic.com/business/archive/2012/04/53-of-recent-college-grads-are-jobless-or-underemployed-how/256237/
47. http://www.thecollegesolution.com/stunning-how-many-are-borrowing-for-college/

48. http://trends.collegeboard.org/sites/default/files/student-aid-2013
-full-report.pdf
49. http://www.forbes.com/sites/jeffreydorfman/2015/07/13/financial
-aid-helps-colleges-more-than-students/
50. http://www.fastweb.com/student-life/articles/the-15-college-dorms
-with-crazy-awesome-amenities
51. http://www.washingtonmonthly.com/magazine/septemberoctober
_2011/features/administrators_ate_my_tuition031641.php?page=all
52. http://www.mass.gov/ago/consumer-resources/consumer
-information/schools-and-education/for-profit-schools/for-profit-school
-fact-sheet.html
53. http://www.investopedia.com/articles/personal-finance/010915/cost
-studying-new-york-university-nyu.asp
54. http://www.cbsnews.com/news/janitors-clerks-and-waiters-with
-college-degrees/

Chapter 5 *Wanna Start a Business? Bahahaha!*

1. http://smallbusiness.chron.com/beauty-salon-licensing
-requirements-57829.html
2. http://www.creators.com/opinion/john-stossel/the-cancer-of
-regulation.html
3. http://www.deseretnews.com/article/865560427/Court-ruling
-Centerville-woman-has-a-right-to-braid-hair-without-a-cosmetology
-license.html?pg=all
4. http://mayflowerhistory.com/voyage/
5. http://www.history.com/topics/jamestown
6. https://capitalalliance.com/2015/07/02/our-nations-founding
-fathers-were-small-business-owners/
7. http://www.biography.com/people/sam-walton-9523270#synopsis
8. http://www.entrepreneur.com/article/197560
9. http://www.cato.org/policy-report/julyaugust-2013/why-capitalism
-awesome
10. https://reason.com/archives/2015/07/22/the-politicians-war-on-uber
11. http://www.creators.com/opinion/john-stossel/strangulation
-by-union.html
12. http://www.economist.com/node/21547789
13. http://topics.nytimes.com/top/reference/timestopics/subjects/g/
glass_steagall_act_1933/index.html

14. http://www.businessweek.com/debateroom/archives/2009/05/government_stay_out_of_the_economy.html
15. http://www.nber.org/digest/may09/w14604.html
16. http://www.heritage.org/research/reports/2014/10/regulation-killing-opportunity
17. http://www.huffingtonpost.com/entry/minimum-wage-poll_us_570ead92e4b08a2d32b8e671
18. http://www.heritage.org/research/testimony/2013/06/what-is-minimum-wage-its-history-and-effects-on-the-economy
19. http://www.bls.gov/opub/reports/cps/characteristics-of-minimum-wage-workers-2014.pdf
20. http://www.cato.org/publications/policy-analysis/negative-effects-minimum-wage-laws
21. http://www.businessinsider.com/raising-the-minimum-wage-to-15-an-hour-would-hurt-millions-of-vulnerable-people-2015-4
22. http://www.entrepreneur.com/article/230727
23. http://www.foxbusiness.com/personal-finance/2013/05/30/nanny-taxes-what-parents-need-to-know/
24. http://www.foxnews.com/opinion/2010/09/08/john-stossel-entrepreneur-government-protectionism-libertarian-new-york.html
25. http://www.wsj.com/articles/SB10001424052748703396604576088272112103698
26. http://www.businessinsider.com/killing-government-red-tape-saving-us-22-bil-2015-8
27. http://www.investorwords.com/11046/self_regulation.html

Chapter 6 *Regulation Nation*

1. http://www.usatoday.com/story/news/nation-now/2015/06/11/lemonade-stand-shut-down-texas/71064934/
2. Ibid.
3. http://www.theagitator.com/2010/11/15/city-councilman-calls-cops-on-kids-selling-cupcakes/?utm_source=feedburner&utm_medium=feed&utm_campaign=Feed%3A+radleybalko+%28The+Agitator%29
4. http://www.cato.org/research/nanny-state
5. http://www.nbcnews.com/health/health-news/new-york-require-salt-warnings-n372606
6. Ibid.
7. http://www.webmd.com/diet/salt-dont-ban-entirely

8. http://www.webmd.com/women/picture-of-the-thyroid; http://www.webmd.com/brain/picture-of-the-brain
9. http://cumberlink.com/news/local/communities/mechanicsburg/cv-elementary-school-bans-costumes-cancels-halloween-parade/article_44a39d82-319b-11e3-8698-0019bb2963f4.html
10. http://newyork.cbslocal.com/2013/09/09/proposed-think-before-you-ink-law-seeks-to-prevent-regrettable-tattoos/
11. https://reason.com/archives/2014/03/08/the-rise-and-fall-of-the-new-york-city-t
12. http://nypost.com/2013/07/18/health-nut-mayor-bloomberg-wants-nyers-to-take-the-stairs-instead-of-the-elevator/
13. http://www.becker-posner-blog.com/2012/06/controls-over-consumer-choices-becker.html
14. http://gizmodo.com/the-complete-list-of-everything-banned-by-mayor-michael-1490476691
15. http://www.nytimes.com/2014/06/27/nyregion/city-loses-final-appeal-on-limiting-sales-of-large-sodas.html?_r=1
16. http://www.areavibes.com/holland-ny/crime/
17. https://en.wikipedia.org/wiki/Oudekerksplein
18. http://nypost.com/2014/11/02/terminally-ill-woman-has-ended-her-own-life/
19. https://www.deathwithdignity.org/take-action/
20. http://content.time.com/time/nation/article/0,8599,1564465,00.html

Chapter 7 *The Problem with Free Money*

1. http://bradfordtaxinstitute.com/Free_Resources/Federal-Income-Tax-Rates.aspx
2. http://www.politifact.com/truth-o-meter/statements/2016/jul/21/donald-trump/trump-43-million-americans-food-stamps/
3. Ibid.
4. http://www.governing.com/gov-data/food-stamp-snap-benefits-enrollment-participation-totals-map.html
5. https://www.rt.com/usa/food-stamps-record-americans-119/
6. http://dailycaller.com/2015/05/10/government-study-40-percent-of-americans-on-food-stamps-are-obese/
7. http://www.fns.usda.gov/sites/default/files/pd/snapsummary.pdf
8. http://dailycaller.com/2013/06/11/taxpayers-spend-41-3-million-in-a-year-to-advertise-food-stamps-a-6-fold-increase-over-last-decade/

9. http://www.breitbart.com/big-government/2014/01/14/omnibus
   -spending-bill-continues-funding-food-stamp-ads-in-mexico-despite
   -appropriations-committee-claims-of-prohibition/
10. http://www.judicialwatch.org/press-room/press-releases/judicial
    -watch-uncovers-usda-records-sponsoring-u-s-food-stamp-program
    -for-illegal-aliens/
11. http://www.breitbart.com/big-government/2013/12/31/usda-6-2
    -billion-improperly-spent-in-2013-including-2-billion-on-food-stamp
    -overpayments/
12. http://www.foxnews.com/us/2013/10/22/craigslist-makes-turning
    -food-stamps-into-cash-snap/
13. http://dailycaller.com/2014/06/30/11-things-you-didnt-know-you
    -could-buy-with-food-stamps/
14. http://townhall.com/tipsheet/christinerousselle/2014/03/14/lingerie
    -store-in-louisiana-accepts-ebt-cards-as-payment-n1809127
15. http://nypost.com/2013/01/06/welfare-recipients-take-out-cash-at
    -strip-clubs-liquor-stores-and-x-rated-shops/
16. http://dailycaller.com/2014/06/30/11-things-you-didnt-know-you
    -could-buy-with-food-stamps/
17. http://www.bloombergview.com/articles/2013-11-13/how
    -mcdonald-s-and-wal-mart-became-welfare-queens
18. Ibid.
19. http://www.heritage.org/research/reports/2012/07/reforming
    -the-food-stamp-program
20. http://www.obpa.usda.gov/budsum/FY14budsum.pdf
21. http://www.downsizinggovernment.org/agriculture/subsidies
22. http://theweek.com/articles/461227/farm-subsidies-welfare
    -program-agribusiness
23. http://dailycaller.com/2013/02/14/confidential-expensive-usda
    -sensitivity-training-the-pilgrims-were-illegal-aliens-videos/
24. http://cnsnews.com/news/article/first-term-americans-collecting
    -disability-increased-1385418-now-1-each-13-full-time
25. http://www.forbes.com/sites/theapothecary/2013/04/08/how-americans
    -game-the-200-billion-a-year-disability-industrial-complex/
26. http://www.newsmax.com/newsfront/social-security-disability
    -depleted/2013/12/17/id/542390/
27. http://www.newsmax.com/newsfront/social-security-disability
    -depleted/2013/12/17/id/542390/
28. http://cnsnews.com/news/article/first-term-americans-collecting
    -disability-increased-1385418-now-1-each-13-full-time

29. http://www.forbes.com/sites/theapothecary/2013/04/08/how -americans-game-the-200-billion-a-year-disability-industrial-complex/
30. Ibid.
31. Ibid.
32. Ibid.
33. http://www.forbes.com/sites/theapothecary/2013/09/02/on-labor-day -2013-welfare-pays-more-than-minimum-wage-work-in-35-states/
34. Ibid.
35. http://rare.us/story/do-welfare-programs-help-or-hurt-poverty-the -answer-may-surprise-you/
36. http://cnsnews.com/news/article/terence-p-jeffrey/census-49 -americans-get-gov-t-benefits-82m-households-medicaid
37. http://www.gallup.com/poll/164444/americans-remain-divided-role -gov-play.aspx
38. http://nation.foxnews.com/homelessness/2011/12/01/homeless -lady-15-kids-somebody-needs-pay-all-my-children
39. http://nation.foxnews.com/2015/09/10/report-87-illegal-immigrant -families-welfare-72-legal-immigrants-it
40. http://www.washingtonexaminer.com/on-the-dole-report-87-illegal -immigrant-families-on-welfare-72-of-legal-immigrants-on-it/article /2571730
41. http://www.heritageresearchinstitute.org/founders.html
42. http://motls.blogspot.com/2008/10/founding-fathers-on -redistribution-of.html
43. http://press-pubs.uchicago.edu/founders/documents/v1ch16s15 .html
44. http://www.wnd.com/2001/07/9913/
45. http://econfaculty.gmu.edu/wew/articles/fee/Nov06.pdf
46. http://www.forbes.com/2009/01/19/obama-roosevelt-constitution -oped-cx_jb_0120bowyer.html
47. http://www.wmtw.com/politics/maine-sees-dramatic-drop-in -ablebodied-adults-on-food-stamps/32300444

Chapter 8 *Party! Party! Party!*

1. http://www.breitbart.com/texas/2014/05/30/log-cabin-republicans -denied-booth-at-texas-gop-convention/
2. http://www.bloomberg.com/news/articles/2016-11-09/what-this -election-taught-us-about-millennial-voters
3. http://louderwithcrowder.com/caught-top-5-hillary-clinton-lies/

4. http://www.chicagotribune.com/news/local/breaking/ct-dennis
   -hastert-guilty-plea-hearing-met-20151027-story.html
5. http://thehill.com/homenews/house/241573-ethics-panel-finds-rep
   -laura-richardson-guilty-on-seven-counts
6. http://www.redding.com/ugc/opinion-ugc/politicians-are-not-above
   -the-law-553
7. http://www.thedailybeast.com/articles/2015/08/04/hillary-clinton-s
   -mega-donors-are-also-funding-jeb-bush.html
8. http://theantimedia.org/10-ways-hillary-clinton-and-jeb-bush-are
   -basically-the-same/
9. http://www.businessinsider.com/jeb-bushs-role-on-corporate-boards
   -could-become-a-problem-in-the-2016-campaign-2015-5;http://www
   .washingtonexaminer.com/clintons-walmart-connection-fueling-lefts
   -doubts/article/2558826
10. http://www.newsmax.com/FastFeatures/Barack-Obama
    -Solyndra-Scandal-Green-Energy/2015/01/29/id/621537/
11. https://theintercept.com/2015/06/05/40-years-democratic
    -presidents-talking-much-want-get-money-politics/
12. http://reason.com/blog/2016/11/09/where-the-third-party-candi
    dates-were-st
13. http://articles.baltimoresun.com/2011-05-06/entertainment/
    bal-ron-paul-makes-case-for-drug-legalization-during-first-gop
    -debate-20110505_1_gop-debate-ron-paul-heroin
14. https://reason.com/poll/2012/01/13/ron-paul-rising-evidenc-from
    -national-po
15. https://jaretglenn.wordpress.com/2012/07/31/how-the-republican
    -party-stole-the-nomination-from-ron-paul/
16. https://en.wikiquote.org/wiki/Groupthink
17. Irving L. Janis, "Groupthink," *Psychology Today*, November 1971,
    pp. 271–79.
18. https://maloney.house.gov/sites/maloney.house.gov/files/documents/
    The%20Economic%20Impact%20of%20the%20Fashion%20
    Industry%20--%20JEC%20report%20FINAL.pdf
19. http://origins.osu.edu/article/breaking-hard-do-americas-love-affair
    -two-party-system

Chapter 9 *Our Unprecedented Opportunity for Success—or Jackassery*

1. http://www.mrc.org/media-bias-101/journalists-admitting-liberal
   -bias-part-one

2. http://www.nytimes.com/2015/06/22/business/media/brian
-williams-scandal-shows-power-of-social-media.html?_r=0

3. http://www.businessinsider.com/how-facebook-was-founded-2010-3

4. http://www.forbes.com/profile/mark-zuckerberg/

5. http://www.forbes.com/profile/jack-dorsey/

6. http://www.npr.org/2011/12/17/143897126/the-arab-spring-a-year
-of-revolution

7. http://www.wired.com/2013/04/arabspring/

8. http://www.mccormick.northwestern.edu/news/articles/2015/04/
how-facebook-sparked-a-revolution.html

9. http://www.slate.com/articles/double_x/doublex/2010/05/is_the
_tea_party_a_feminist_movement.html

10. http://arc3communications.com/the-top-ten-most-social-media
-savvy-u-s-politicians/

11. http://www.washingtonpost.com/news/politics/wp/2015/05/26/
heres-how-the-first-president-of-the-social-media-age-has
-chosen-to-connect-with-americans/

12. http://www.davemanuel.com/the-most-popular-us-politicians-by
-twitter-followers-163/

13. http://www.pewresearch.org/fact-tank/2015/05/19/more-americans
-are-using-social-media-to-connect-with-politicians/

14. http://www.pewinternet.org/2014/11/03/cell-phones-social-media
-and-campaign-2014/

15. http://www.journalism.org/2015/06/01/millennials-political-news/

16. http://mprcenter.org/blog/2013/01/how-obama-won-the-social
-media-battle-in-the-2012-presidential-campaign/

17. http://uglyrenaissancebabies.tumblr.com/

18. http://www.history.com/topics/us-presidents/kennedy-nixon-debates

19. http://www.npr.org/sections/thetwo-way/2016/09/27/495692196/
clinton-trump-showdown-is-most-watched-presidential-debate

20. http://www.motherjones.com/politics/2014/03/turkey
-facebook-youtube-twitter-blocked

Chapter 10 *What We Can Do to Fix America Now*

1. https://www.lewrockwell.com/2007/07/adam-robb/restoring-the
-tenth-amendment/

2. http://www.washingtontimes.com/news/2012/jul/4/states-rights
-war-over-obamacare/

3. http://rare.us/story/do-welfare-programs-help-or-hurt-poverty-the-answer-may-surprise-you/
4. https://mises.org/sites/default/files/21_2_1.pdf
5. http://www.nydailynews.com/new-york/hurricane-sandy/sandy-vics-60-billion-aid-article-1.1499613
6. http://www.redcross.org/support/donating-fundraising/where-your-money-goes/sandy-response
7. http://www.redcross.org/news/article/Red-Cross-Recovery-Efforts-to-Help-Sandy-Survivors
8. http://www.cato.org/publications/commentary/catastrophe-big-easy-demonstrates-big-governments-failure
9. Ibid.
10. Ibid.
11. http://www.nationalreview.com/article/424320/most-americans-support-term-limits
12. http://www.washingtonpost.com/news/the-fix/wp/2013/03/29/don-young-no-stranger-to-scandal/
13. http://www.adn.com/article/20120410/document-list-outlines-fbis-florida-investigation-young
14. http://abcnews.go.com/politics/heres-congress-works/story?id=24810354
15. http://www.nationalreview.com/article/424320/most-americans-support-term-limits
16. Ibid.
17. http://www.brainyquote.com/quotes/quotes/g/georgewash118444.html

Index

Author: Kristin Tate
Photo Credit: Chris Gillett

KRISTIN TATE is a prolific opinion writer and investigative journalist with a commitment to advancing libertarian-style policies and outlooks. She is a contributor at *The Hill* and appears regularly on Fox News, CNN, and MSNBC. In 2016, Red Alert Politics named Tate to their list of 30 of the most influential right-of-center leaders under the age of 30.